# Not
## Your Mother's®
## Weeknight
## Cooking

## Also by Beth Hensperger

*Not Your Mother's Slow Cooker Recipes for Two*

*The Gourmet Potluck*

*The Bread Lover's Bread Machine Cookbook*

*The Best Quick Breads*

*Bread for Breakfast*

*Bread Made Easy*

*The Pleasure of Whole Grain Breads*

*The Bread Bible*

*Breads of the Southwest*

*Beth's Basic Bread Book*

*Bread for All Seasons*

*Baking Bread*

*Bread*


## Also by Beth Hensperger and Julie Kaufmann

*Not Your Mother's Slow Cooker Recipes for Entertaining*

*Not Your Mother's Slow Cooker Cookbook*

*The Ultimate Rice Cooker Cookbook*

# Not Your Mother's® Weeknight Cooking

*Quick and Easy Wholesome Homemade Dinners*

## Beth Hensperger

The Harvard Common Press
Boston, Massachusetts

The Harvard Common Press
535 Albany Street
Boston, Massachusetts 02118
www.harvardcommonpress.com

Printed in the United States of America
Printed on acid-free paper

*Library of Congress Cataloging-in-Publication Data*

Hensperger, Beth.
  Not your mother's weeknight cooking : quick and easy wholesome homemade
dinners / Beth Hensperger.
    p.   cm.
ISBN-13: 978-1-55832-367-4 (hardcover : alk. paper)
ISBN-13: 978-1-55832-368-1 (pbk. : alk. paper)
  1. Suppers.  2. Quick and easy cookery.  I. Title.
TX738.H5785   2008
641.5'38—dc22                                                        2008003496

Special bulk-order discounts are available on this and other Harvard Common Press
books. Companies and organizations may purchase books for premiums or resale, or
may arrange a custom edition, by contacting the Marketing Director at the address
above.

*Book design by Ralph Fowler / rlf design*
*Cover and interior photographs by Eskite Photography*
*Food styling by Andrea Lucich; prop styling by Carol Hacker*

10 9 8 7 6 5 4 3 2 1

Not Your Mother's is a registered trademark of The Harvard Common Press.

To these loyal practitioners (and their wives & associates),
who have become kind friends, who have been so extremely
supportive, who deserve a special commendation for always
answering my questions and making sense of the
inner workings with patience and skill:

**Dr. Ken Felch and Dr. Bob Culver**

# Contents

# Not
# Your Mother's®
# Weeknight
# Cooking

# Quick, Healthy, and Delicious

Food serves a three-fold purpose, wrote nutritionist turned cookbook author Adele Davis in 1947: to bring delight to the sense of taste, smell, and sight; to produce health; and to provide the opportunity for artistic expression. It is the perennial culinary philosophy of pleasure, efficiency, and economics put into action every single day, whether we are aware of it or not.

I love good food, and I like to cook when I have the time. It doesn't have to be complicated, but it should be easy, nourishing, and comforting, reflecting my daily needs. Cooking is an evolution of sorts, changing from day to day, season to season, and year to year. Some days I don't have the time, but I still need to cook. You might rarely cook, but still have the desire to cook with more confidence at home. Dinner need not be an elaborate meal, yet there needs to be some choice involved.

Food choices are very personal; what is a delight for one may not be satisfying to another.

There are two basic methods for choosing what to make for dinner. The first is to shop and look for what appeals to you at that moment—the specials, your mood, what vegetables look the best. Then you go home and figure out what to do with them. The second way is to read a recipe and then go shop for those specific ingredients to prepare that recipe. Both of these ways of deciding what to eat are equal, but each comes from a different perspective. If you have done a big shop on the weekend, you would make your choices out of your freezer, pantry, and refrigerator, and then proceed to prep and cook.

I enjoy the inspiration of finding a new recipe, preparing my favorites on a regular basis, looking for healthy alternatives to my tried-and-true recipes, and planning wholesome meals for friends. With a busy work schedule and family responsibilities, however, I want the food I cook to fit into the available time slot. Even though there can be a great temptation after a hectic day to pick up take-out or eat in a restaurant, in essence, I want a healthy, delicious meal that is budget conscious, is easy and quick to prepare myself, and contains a minimum of processed foods.

## Quick

Quick means not only a short list of ingredients, but also a minimum amount of cooking time and techniques. Wholesome food from fresh ingredients can take slightly more time than using lots of convenience products, but the payoff in both flavor and nutrition is huge. There are many dishes that fall naturally in the quick-option category—big salads, stir-fries, quick pan sautés, eggs, and pastas.

The most time-consuming part of preparing a meal is assembling and preparing the food for the cooking process. For most recipes, you will achieve the greatest efficiency in meal prep by having the ingredients ready before you start cooking. You can prepare most recipes in this book from scratch, often with some good-quality prepackaged ingredients readily available in well-stocked supermarkets. If there are convenience products on the supermarket shelf, such as good salsa, condiments, spice blends, ready-made wonton skins and pizza crusts, canned or boxed broths, fresh bread, and fresh or frozen pasta, I will definitely use them rather than making them from scratch. If the frozen food section has some items that I can use later in the week when I don't have time to go to the supermarket for fresh, I will also make use of them.

Cooking has basic fundamentals that are consistent in all recipes, and once you get the hang of those, your speed in the kitchen will improve. That said, if there is a shortcut that will speed preparation and help me create great food when I am pressed for time, I will use it.

Remember that a large kitchen filled with every single tool under the sun is not necessary. Some of the best dishes take advantage of the simplest equipment. Keep in mind, though, that excellent-quality equipment is synonymous with respect for labor-saving tools, so buy the best you can afford. I also take advantage of the latest technology, like an immersion blender (one of my favorite tools) instead of a food mill. Equipment usually has a specific purpose, but no fancy specialized equipment is necessary to make good food (although I depend on my restaurant-style sauté pans bought at the local food warehouse). If you cook regularly, you will not have any problem with my recipes and cooking methods. After making a recipe for the first time, you can customize and adjust it to fit your taste.

If you are an inexperienced cook, success is just a few meals away; the recipes within are easier than those in most other cookbooks, since they are designed for ease of preparation and short cooking time. If you are an experienced cook, you will find new recipes that I hope will quickly become old standbys.

## Healthy

You don't need to confine yourself to "health food" to prepare healthy meals. Well-balanced eating need not be complicated or drab. With its cross-section of homey, practical foods, this book will become, I hope, a frequent tool and inspirational companion in your kitchen. Let *Not Your Mother's Weeknight Cooking* be your guide for selecting a hearty soup, salad, or entrée that suits your palate, and build your meal around it. The book does not adhere to any specific diet, nor does it limit you to certain foods. It follows an "everything in moderation" philosophy, so if you are on a low-sodium, high-protein, low-carb, kosher, or fat-free diet, you will have to make the appropriate adjustments.

Shopping is integral to the process of tasty cooking. Learning to love food shopping is a good idea; it also means taking the time to shop properly. I won't be telling you to buy outrageously expensive or hard-to-find ingredients, or that you must shop organic, but I will advise you to shop using your intelligence. For quality ingredients, first visit the supermarket, then the butcher counter and produce stand. Look for items that are value-priced for simplicity and availability, such as seasonal vegetables and meat specials. Well-stocked supermarkets offer an increasing array of restaurant-quality items beloved by chefs, such as specialty vinegars, high-quality artisan oils, certain cuts of meat, and aseptically packaged broths. Be sure to check out your local farmers' market for fresh, seasonal ingredients. Also take advantage of warehouse shopping if you can, especially for expansive selections of frozen premium items such as ready-to-cook lobster tails, shrimp, chicken breast cutlets, and stuffed pastas. By keeping a freezer, fridge, and pantry full of homey staples, you can create many interesting meals very quickly. With a bit of practice, you just might find yourself becoming more creative in the kitchen.

## Delicious

The older I get, the more I appreciate an uncomplicated dish, and the more I appreciate fine ingredients and flavorful food. If the food tastes good and makes me feel good, it is delicious.

It's no surprise that delicious food starts with shopping for quality ingredients. Often what is best is what is in season in your produce department. Quality canned and frozen foods are available year-round, of course, as are meats and poultry. Check the seasonal availability of your favorite fish and shellfish. Indulge in a new item now and then, like an Asian hoisin sauce or a different canned bean, such as borlotti, and experiment with the flavors in your cooking. I encourage you to broaden your culinary horizons by tasting new foods one by one; this is especially true of vegetables.

While my energy is focused on saving time, I also cook by mood. (Do I want soup tonight or a more filling pasta? Do I want a sassy little sauce on my sautéed hamburger? How about a big salad?) Whether you are eating a fresh baguette with some cheese, olives, and ripe tomatoes; a big bowl of 30-minute minestrone; some fluffy scrambled eggs flecked with chives and topped with a layer of smoked salmon; or a hearty beef fillet, remember to keep it simple.

"American food is anything you eat at home," quipped our culinary godfather, James Beard, decades ago. For me, contemporary American cooking means incorporating an appreciation of diverse ethnic and indigenous culinary influences (Asian, Indian, Mexican, Middle Eastern, Mediterranean, Eastern European) that have plenty of adult and kid appeal by combining old-fashioned comfort food with easy-to-find modern ingredients.

Of course, one of the most vital steps to delicious food is seasoning. Proper seasoning with salt and pepper (black or white peppercorns), and a bit of herbs and spices, can be the difference between a fabulous and a bland dinner. I always use the pep-per grinder for fresh pepper, never pre-ground. Seasoning is often done before and during the cooking process rather than just at the end. Although these recipes give specific instructions on seasonings, don't be afraid to experiment with your own favorite seasonings and methods for adding them.

The other crucial step to delicious food is not to overcook it. A dry roast pork tenderloin, mushy vegetables, or gummy pasta will most certainly affect the taste and appearance of your overall dish. But practice makes perfect, so if you do make a mistake, make a note on the recipe as a reminder for next time.

## The Fundamentals of Weeknight Cooking

Here's a quick rundown of the equipment and techniques used in this book to create great weekday meals.

### Equipment

Here is my list of minimum equipment. As you cook more and more, you will doubtless acquire other equipment that you find necessary and enjoy using.

*Cookware:* The criteria for pots (with lids) and pans depends on how many people you are cooking for. These recipes are geared for four people. You need 1- and 2-quart saucepans; a 4-quart saucepan for cooking pasta; a glass or ceramic 9 × 13-inch baking pan; two rimmed baking sheets; and one or two large frying pans, skillets, or sauté pans. A wok is optional. Although high-quality cookware is expensive, it is really worth it, because the materials transfer heat better. And these items do go on sale regularly. Please avoid aluminum cookware.

*Knives:* You need basic knives kept in good condition and properly sharpened on a regular basis. These will become your trusted companions in the kitchen. You need a 4-inch paring knife, an 8-inch chef's knife for chopping, a serrated knife for cutting bread, and a medium-size slicing knife. Store them in a knife block for safety and convenience.

*Measuring Tools:* There are three types of measuring tools that every kitchen needs: a set of metal or plastic nested dry measuring cups, 1- and 2-cup liquid measuring cups, and a set of standard measuring spoons. A scale, in both American and metric weight, is useful but not necessary.

*Other Tools:* Other important utensils include a small and medium-size whisk, a slotted spoon, metal or plastic spatulas, long-handled wooden spoons, a hand-held grater or a food processor, two sizes of cutting boards in your favorite material, a timer, an instant-read thermometer, a colander, and an immersion blender. Metal tongs, like those used in restaurants, are indispensable when pan-sautéing.

## Methods

There are two basic cooking methods used for all foods: moist heat (steaming, poaching, braising, and boiling) and dry heat (baking or roasting, broiling, grilling, deep-frying, and sautéing). Moist heat seals in flavor, and no extra fat is needed for cooking. Dry cooking uses either fat or a high temperature to seal the surface of the food. There are a few methods that are especially useful for quick weeknight cooking. Once you thoroughly understand these techniques and practice them, you will be assured of excellent-tasting food.

*Steaming:* Steaming is cooking food with the aid of steam that is created by a small amount of boiling liquid that does not come in direct contact with the food. Fish, poultry, and vegetables are best prepared with this technique. Steaming preserves nutrients and is especially beloved in low-calorie cooking. There are several types of steamers. The stacked metal, bamboo, or plastic varieties are very popular, allowing for different types of foods to cook at the same time. You can improvise a steamer with a French folding steamer rack set into a deep saucepan, which is great for vegetables, or you may use an electric steamer appliance. Steaming can also be done in the oven in a covered casserole.

*Poaching:* Poaching is submerging food in a boiling liquid, then cooking it over low heat. This is used a lot for cooking poultry, fish, and eggs. In poaching, there is a flavor exchange between the liquid and the food, so the liquid is often flavored. Take care not to overcook, or the poached food will get rubbery. Use a medium-size saucepan, either a narrow one or a wider saucepan with lower sides.

*Braising:* Braising, along with stewing, is especially used for long-cooked meat, poultry, and vegetable dishes, so I generally don't encourage it for weeknight cooking. You would need a Dutch oven or specific casserole dishes for this type of cooking.

*Boiling:* Boiling is the important method for cooking pasta, rice, and beans. The food is immersed in the boiling liquid to cook. Vegetables like broccoli rabe or green beans are often plunged briefly into boiling water, known as blanching. Hard root vegetables are often cooked by boiling. Soups are cooked by simmering (gently bubbling as opposed to vigorous boiling), which is boiling at a lower temperature. Use a deep, heavy saucepan or a small Dutch oven.

*Sautéing:* Next to roasting, sautéing is probably the most popular way to cook, since it is so simple. Food is cooked in a small amount of fat over fairly high heat for a short time. There is no loss of natural taste, since the hot fat seals the food. You can use a French sauté pan with curved sides, a cast-iron skillet, or a frying pan interchangeably, but it must be large enough to hold the food

without crowding, otherwise you must cook in batches or use a second pan. Crowding the food will result in the temperature dropping and steam forming, and the dish will not turn out as well as it could. Food must be dry before sautéing to prevent steam from forming and splattering. Searing is when the food is cooked at high heat in fat for a short time until it browns. Pan-roasting is searing the food (which is a thicker portion than used in searing), then placing it in the oven to finish cooking. Stir-frying uses a rounded-bottom pan, and the food is cooked over high heat for a short time and constantly tossed for even cooking.

*Roasting:* Roasting is usually associated with large cuts of meat, such as leg of lamb or roast turkey, but it also works nicely and quickly with small cuts. It is used for tender cuts, such as chicken breasts, turkey tenderloins, salmon and other seafood, and London broil. The food is cooked in an oven at an even temperature, either high or low; the outer portion browns and the inner portion stays moist. Lean cuts are marinated, basted, or cooked in a sauce to keep them moist and flavorful. Vegetables are especially nice roasted. You can roast and bake in metal, glass, or ceramic roasting pans. I have varying sizes from small to large, and I especially like French ceramic ware. I always use an instant-read thermometer (it is more accurate than a regular meat thermometer) when I am in doubt that a meat is properly cooked; temperatures are given in specific recipes as a guide.

*Broiling and Grilling:* Broiling and grilling are wildly popular cooking methods since they are so quick and the food tastes so good with the crisp, browned or blackened outer layer. Food is seared by very high heat and placed on a rack so as not to sit and cook in its own juices. A broiled or grilled chicken breast tastes remarkably different from a pan-sautéed one because of its smoky quality. Broiling is done under an oven broiler, and grilling is done over a gas or charcoal fire outdoors; a ridged grill pan for stovetop use is a good alternative. This method is good for small tender cuts like chops and steaks of veal, pork, lamb, and beef, as well as poultry and thick fish fillets.

*Deep-Frying:* Deep-frying is probably the most popular and tastiest way to prepare foods like French fries, vegetable fritters, and fried fish and chicken, but immersing foods completely in fat is not encouraged too often in health-oriented diets. Fried foods usually need a crunchy coating to protect them, acting as a layer between the food and the oil. Deep-frying needs a deep, heavy saucepan or a countertop electric appliance designed especially for it. Pan-frying uses only a small amount of oil and the food is not submerged.

# Supper Specials:
# Fish and Shellfish

Are you tired of the same recipe of baked salmon or pan-fried sole every time you cook? Here is a chapter for you to explore the possibilities of fabulous, yet simple, fish preparations. I looked at what was available every day at the fish counter and have given recipes for a wide variety of easy-to-find fish, attempting to match each fish with the best way to cook it and complementary flavors.

I usually choose fresh fish over frozen thawed, although shrimp of all sizes is usually only available frozen in the United States. Remember that when buying fish, it should have a glossy sheen and smell like the sea, not "fishy" or with any off odor. Fish is best prepared the day it is purchased.

Professional chefs do not rinse fish, but many home cooks are in the habit of doing so. Fish is porous and does absorb some water, but any bacteria will not be totally washed away. All bacteria will be killed in the cooking process. Fish is often marinated for a short time, letting the lovely flavors accent the flavors of the sea. Marinate fish for 15 to 30 minutes in the refrigerator and do not add salt to the marinade, as it will draw out the natural moisture.

You can choose your method of cooking salmon and other fish—pan sautéing or frying, broiling, poaching in the oven or on the stovetop, slow- or flash-roasting in the oven, grilling on a stovetop grill pan, baking in parchment or foil, or steaming. Flavors run from Asian influenced to Mediterranean, with cheese or a little pan sauce, with a cold mayonnaise sauce or salsa, and with vegetables or a grain like quinoa or rice as accompaniment. The cooking rule for fish runs true—10 minutes per inch, no matter which cooking method you use.

# Mustard-Soy Glazed Salmon with Brown Sugar and Ginger

When I asked my chiropractor, Dr. Ken Felch, for his favorite salmon recipe, he sent this gem. "I hope it fits your criterion," he said. "It is borrowed/stolen from a fishing resort in northern British Columbia on Stuart Island. It is perfectly delicious." The combination of the French mustard, lemon juice, butter, and Worcestershire sauce makes for a totally different flavor than typical Asian marinades. The layer of Dijon is thin and the sprinkling of brown sugar is light; I use my fingers and rub some brown sugar over the fish, but you can use a small sieve if you like. Serve with rice and a steamed green vegetable. ● *Serves 4*

**COOKING METHOD:** Oven
**PREP TIME:** 10 minutes
**COOK TIME:** 12 to 15 minutes

Four ¾- to 1-inch-thick center-cut salmon fillets (6 ounces each), skin on
4 teaspoons Dijon mustard
4 tablespoons fresh lemon juice
4 tablespoons Worcestershire sauce
½ cup reduced-sodium soy sauce
1½ teaspoons ground ginger
3 to 4 cloves garlic, crushed
4 teaspoons light brown sugar
2 tablespoons unsalted butter

1. Preheat the oven to 350°F.

2. Cover a shallow rimmed baking sheet with aluminum foil. Arrange the fish skin side down on the baking sheet. Spread each fillet with a thin layer of mustard.

3. In a small bowl, combine the lemon juice, Worcestershire sauce, soy sauce, ginger, and garlic. Drizzle over the fillets. Then sprinkle each with a teaspoon of the brown sugar and dot with little bits of the butter. Bake in the center of the oven for 12 to 15 minutes, until firm and opaque. Remove from the oven and let stand for 5 minutes; the fish will continue to cook as it stands. Serve immediately.

# Baked Salmon with Avocado Fruit Salsa

**T**his is from my friend and recipe tester Bobbe Torgerson. "This is my favorite," she wrote. "It is simple, fast, and delicious. I am not wild about fish, but my husband is, so I have to prepare it for him, but this one is so good that I love it myself. The salmon ends up so tender! I serve it with my own fruit or regular fresh salsa or tartar sauce." The salsa is easy as can be and can be conveniently made up to 6 hours ahead since there is some chopping involved.

● *Serves 4*

**COOKING METHOD:** Oven
**PREP TIME:** 10 minutes
**COOK TIME:** 8 to 10 minutes

AVOCADO FRUIT SALSA
1 large ripe mango or papaya, peeled and coarsely chopped
1 firm-ripe avocado, chopped
1½ tablespoons minced fresh cilantro
1 tablespoon minced green onion
1 tablespoon minced seeded jalapeño chile
1 to 2 tablespoons fresh lime juice (1 lime)

2 to 3 tablespoons olive oil
2 to 3 tablespoons unsalted butter
Four ¾- to 1-inch-thick salmon fillets (6 ounces each), skin on
Salt and freshly ground black pepper
Juice of 1 lemon

**1.** To make the salsa, combine the salsa ingredients in a small bowl, mixing lightly. Leave at room temperature, or cover and refrigerate if made a few hours before.

**2.** Preheat the oven to 425°F.

**3.** Place the oil and butter in a 9 × 13-inch baking dish and place in the oven to melt for 2 minutes. Remove from the oven, let cool for a few minutes, then stir to mix. Pat the salmon dry with paper towels. Place the salmon in the dish and turn to coat both sides. Season both sides with salt and pepper. Place in the oven and bake for 8 to 10 minutes, or until just cooked through and slightly opaque in the very center (check with the tip of a knife). Baste with the butter mixture and pour the lemon juice over the top. Serve hot with two big spoonfuls of the fruit salsa on the side of each fillet.

## •• About Salmon ••

More salmon is consumed in the United States than any other fish, thanks to its health benefits, ease of handling, and great taste. Enticingly colored, rich in flavor, and meaty in texture, salmon has become the favorite fish of American home cooks. It is not only easy to prepare, but it is also deliciously versatile and nutritious. Salmon is usually sold as fillets of various weights and thicknesses or as steaks, which are a cross-section of the whole fish. Fillets are more popular, since they have fewer bones. You can leave the skin on or off, as desired (many people love to munch on the crispy broiled skin), but the skin does keep the fish together while cooking; just slip it off after cooking. Salmon can be cooked to a variety of tastes, medium or rare, with no problem. Since it is a firm, high-fat fish, it takes to an incredibly wide variety of flavor enhancers. In addition, canned salmon is great for quiches, salmon cake patties, and salads.

At one time, all salmon was wild, from rivers and the ocean's open waters. They are carnivores and live on a diet of shrimp, squid, and small fish. Since wild salmon is so depleted and with limited availability, this fish can be quite expensive. Pacific salmon is wild; Atlantic salmon refers to the saltwater floating feedlots of farm-raised salmon. The Atlantic commercial salmon fishing industry has been extinct for over a decade, although Chile, Norway, and Scotland all fish salmon. Although farmed salmon at first seemed like a perfect solution for supplying the world year-round with plenty of its favorite fish, some environmental concerns have surfaced in the past years due to its negative impact on surrounding marine environments and wildlife. In addition, since the diet of the farmed salmon is different from that of the wild salmon, farmed salmon needs red food coloring to give it the bright red color that consumers expect.

Whether to eat wild or farm-raised salmon is certainly a personal choice. Many chefs, dieticians, nutritionists, and food industry consultants recommend eating only wild salmon. But look into the fishmonger's case and choose the fish that is the freshest smelling and best looking that day, and decide what fits your budget best.

# Salmon Teriyaki with Cabbage Salad

**I** thought I'd better not leave out of this book one of the most popular marinades for salmon, the classic Japanese teriyaki sauce. Although there are many bottled sauces on the market, this homemade sauce is so great you will use it many times, even for chicken or beef. It is originally from the Canyon Ranch spa in Arizona and is one of the easiest little flavor enhancers for salmon; you can change the proportions of garlic and ginger if you like. The surprise ingredient is frozen apple juice concentrate, which gives the sugary glaze. The salmon marinates for 30 minutes before baking in the oven, but it is infused with flavor. This is also good cold, in case you have leftovers. ◦ *Serves 4*

**COOKING METHOD:** Oven
**PREP TIME:** 20 minutes
**COOK TIME:** 10 to 15 minutes

One 2-inch piece fresh ginger, cut into little chunks
2 to 3 cloves garlic
1½ cups (one 12-ounce can) frozen unsweetened apple juice concentrate,
   thawed and undiluted
½ cup reduced-sodium soy sauce
3 tablespoons rice vinegar
½ cup finely chopped green onions (white part and some of the green)
Four ¾- to 1-inch-thick center-cut salmon fillets (6 ounces each), skin on

**CABBAGE SALAD**
½ small head green cabbage, finely shredded
3 green onions (white part and 2 inches of the green), chopped
2 tablespoons Asian sesame oil
2 tablespoons rice vinegar
1 tablespoon sesame seeds, toasted in a dry skillet

**1.** In a food processor, drop in the ginger and garlic, processing to chop. Add the undiluted apple juice concentrate, soy sauce, and rice vinegar. Stir in the green onions. Place the salmon in a 9 × 13-inch glass baking dish and pour the marinade over it. Cover with plastic wrap and refrigerate for 20 to 30 minutes.

**2.** Preheat the oven to 350°F.

**3.** Meanwhile, make the cabbage salad. Combine the cabbage, green onions, oil, and vinegar in a large bowl. Toss well and chill until ready to serve. Add the sesame seeds and toss again before serving.

**4.** Remove the salmon from the refrigerator and turn it over. Bake in the center of the oven, in the marinade, for 10 to 15 minutes, until firm and opaque. Serve immediately with a portion of cabbage salad on the side.

# Verde Salmon in Parchment with Green Olives

This recipe for green salmon is the brainchild of Joanie Walsh Culver, nutritional coach and wife of my chiropractor. She is the creator of the Verde Wellness Healthy Living Program for weight loss and disease management in Los Altos, California. Joanie provides recipes for clients on her program, and this is one of the most popular offerings, which she also makes at home for herself and guests. It has all healthy ingredients—lemon, cilantro, garlic, a pinch of cayenne, parsley, and olive oil. Joanie says to use wild salmon if you can. You may also use heavy-duty aluminum foil if you don't have parchment paper. Serve with Sweet Potato Puree with Chipotle Chile (page 106) or rice. ● *Serves 4*

**COOKING METHOD:** Oven
**PREP TIME:** 10 minutes
**COOK TIME:** About 12 minutes

2 cloves garlic
½ cup fresh flat-leaf parsley leaves
½ cup fresh cilantro leaves
½ teaspoon cayenne pepper
Juice of 2 lemons
Salt and freshly ground black pepper
½ cup olive oil
Four ¾- to 1-inch-thick salmon fillets (4 to 6 ounces each), skin on
8 green olives stuffed with pimentos, sliced
1 lemon, cut into 8 thin slices

**1.** Preheat the oven to 500°F.

**2.** Drop the garlic cloves into a food processor and finely chop. Add the parsley and cilantro; pulse to chop. Add the cayenne, lemon juice, and some salt and pepper. Then add the olive oil; process to make an almost smooth paste.

**3.** Cut four 12-inch square sheets of parchment paper. Fold each in half crosswise. Open up each piece of parchment and place a salmon fillet in the middle of the top half of the paper, skin side down. Spread one-quarter of the verde paste on top of each salmon fillet. Top each fillet with 2 sliced olives, then arrange 2 slices of lemon on top. Fold the paper over the fish. Starting on one side, fold the edges of the parchment over in 1-inch increments, crimping as you go, to securely wrap the salmon and make it airtight. Repeat with the remaining fish and parchment, and place on a clean baking sheet. (If you are not baking immediately, you can hold the packets for a few hours in the refrigerator.)

**4.** Bake on the middle rack for 12 minutes (it may take 15 minutes if the fish is thick), until the bag puffs up and turns golden brown. Remove from the oven and transfer to individual dinner plates. Using a steak knife or scissors, diners can tear open their own bag of salmon and dive in.

# Grill-Pan Balsamic Salmon

**N**atalie Haughton is a food writer at the *Los Angles Daily News* and a cookbook author. One day she mentioned her research on an article about stovetop grill pans, which are great for cooking fish. Grill pans are round, rectangular, or square, and have ridges, which give a striking pattern of scoring the food, like outdoor grills do. Grill pans have another purpose, too, which is to cause some air to circulate under the fish by lifting it up off the solid surface. The pan's ridges elevate the food so oil and fat do not touch it. Her recipe is pure simplicity and quite brilliant. The salmon is basted a few times with balsamic vinegar. Amen. Timing is important, so have the rest of your meal ready to hit the table when you make the salmon. Serve with sautéed bell peppers and steamed sliced potatoes, both of which will benefit from the balsamic juices. You can use this technique with other thick cuts of firm fish, such as halibut, sea bass, mackerel, haddock, grouper, and mahi-mahi. ● *Serves 4*

**COOKING METHOD:** Stovetop
**PREP TIME:** 5 minutes
**COOK TIME:** About 6 minutes

Four ¾- to 1-inch-thick salmon fillets or steaks
    (6 to 8 ounces each), skin on
2 tablespoons olive oil
Salt
8 tablespoons good-quality balsamic vinegar

**1.** Preheat the grill pan over medium-high to high heat for 5 to 8 minutes, or per your manufacturer's instructions if using an electric grill.

**2.** While the pan is heating, rinse and pat dry the salmon. Brush both sides of the fish with olive oil and sprinkle with a bit of salt. Do not put any oil on the grill pan or it will burn and smoke. Reduce the heat under the grill pan to medium. Position the fish on the hot pan with plenty of room in between the pieces (cook in two batches, if necessary) and cook for 3 minutes.

**3.** Splash 1 tablespoon of vinegar on each fillet with a large spoon. Carefully turn the fillets, cook for another 3 minutes, and splash on another tablespoon of vinegar on each. Cut one fillet to check for degree of doneness. Cook for an additional 15 to 30 seconds, if necessary. Remove from the pan with a spatula and place on dinner plates. Serve immediately.

# Pan-Seared Peppered Tuna with Cucumber–Pickled Ginger Salad

resh tuna is best served like no other fish—cooked almost to charred on the outside and left rare on the inside, so don't be tempted to cook it further than this point because you are squeamish about raw fish. Fully cooked tuna becomes very chewy and dry. The cooking phase goes really fast, so have the rest of your meal ready to serve and pan-sear the tuna at the last minute. You can serve the tuna with tartar sauce or even a fresh fruit salsa, but to me, tuna is best with the taste of pickled ginger, the pink strips served in Japanese restaurants alongside sashimi; it balances the richness of the fish. Serve with rice. ● *Serves 4*

**COOKING METHOD:** Stovetop
**PREP TIME:** 10 minutes
**COOK TIME:** About 4 minutes

CUCUMBER–PICKLED GINGER SALAD
1½ cups peeled, seeded, and diced cucumber
¼ cup finely chopped red or green onions
4 tablespoons thinly sliced and chopped pickled ginger
3 tablespoons finely chopped fresh cilantro
Juice of 1 lemon
Juice of 1 lime
2 tablespoons rice vinegar
Pinch of salt

2 pounds 1-inch-thick tuna steaks, rinsed and patted dry
4 tablespoons olive oil
½ teaspoon salt
2 tablespoons peppercorns (black, white, green, pink, or a combination),
    coarsely crushed
Finely grated zest of 1 lemon
Finely grated zest of 1 lime
Lime wedges for serving

**1.** For the salad, in a small bowl, stir together the cucumber, onion, ginger, cilantro, lemon and lime juices, and vinegar; toss to combine. Season with salt and set aside or refrigerate until serving.

**2.** Cut the tuna into 2-inch-thick strips. Rub the tuna strips all over with 3 tablespoons of the oil. On a plate, combine the salt, pepper, and lemon and lime zests; press each side of the fish into the mixture to coat, shaking off any extra.

**3.** Brush a large skillet over high heat with the remaining 1 tablespoon oil. Place the strips of tuna in the very hot pan and cook for 30 to 40 seconds on each side (you have 4 sides on each piece), turning with tongs. The exterior will be well cooked, even browned, and the interior rare. Immediately remove from the skillet to divide the strips equally among dinner plates. Serve at once with a small heap of cucumber salad on the side and plenty of lime wedges.

# Sake Swordfish with Asian Greens

**S**wordfish is a very firm, flavorful fish, and it is an occasional treat. This is a healthy preparation that works equally well with fresh halibut or sea bass. The greens used are available in Asian markets and the produce section of large supermarkets. Certainly you can substitute other greens, but try to find these if you can. The combination is dynamite. Serve with jasmine rice or buckwheat noodles. ● *Serves 4*

**COOKING METHOD:** Oven and stovetop
**PREP TIME:** 15 to 30 minutes
**COOK TIME:** 12 to 15 minutes

¼ cup reduced-sodium soy sauce

¼ cup sake

2 tablespoons dry sherry

2 tablespoons grated fresh ginger

2 cloves garlic, crushed

2 teaspoons light or dark brown sugar

½ teaspoon hot chili oil

Four 6- to 8-ounce swordfish steaks (about 1½ pounds total)

2 to 3 tablespoons olive oil or peanut oil

¾ pound baby bok choy, washed and sliced diagonally

1 cup shelled, blanched edamame (fresh or frozen)

8 ounces Chinese broccoli

8 ounces baby spinach (4 generous handfuls)

⅓ cup chicken broth

Pinch of salt

Toasted sesame seeds and chopped green onion for garnish

Lemon wedges

1. Combine the soy sauce, sake, sherry, ginger, garlic, brown sugar, and chili oil in a small bowl. Place the swordfish in a glass dish and pour the marinade over it. Let stand for 15 to 30 minutes in the refrigerator. Preheat the oven to 450°F.

2. Remove the fish from the marinade and place on a rack in a roasting pan. Bake for 12 to 15 minutes (12 minutes per inch), until opaque and firm (touch with your finger; swordfish does not flake).

3. While the swordfish is cooking, add the olive oil to a large skillet over medium-high heat. Add the bok choy, edamame, and broccoli; stir-fry for a minute or two. Add the spinach and stir-fry for another minute. Add the broth and bring to a boil, stirring constantly. Season with salt and a few more drops of hot chili oil.

4. Place the vegetables and broth in the center of large shallow bowls and top with the swordfish. Garnish with the sesame seeds and green onions and serve immediately with the lemon wedges.

## ·· Oven Poaching ··

One of the most fabulous ways to cook thick fish such as halibut, salmon, cod, sea bass, and swordfish is oven poaching in a foil package. The fish poaches beautifully in a combination of wine and its own juices. Preheat the oven to 450°F. Cut as many pieces of 10 × 12-inch aluminum foil as you have pieces of fish. Sprinkle your fish steaks or fillets with salt, pepper, and any herb or seasoning blend you like. Spread out a piece of foil with the short edge facing you. Brush the bottom half of the foil with some oil. Place the fish on the oiled section and sprinkle each piece with a teaspoon or two of dry white wine. Make a rectangular package by folding over the top section of foil and double folding the three edges to enclose the fish. Place on a baking sheet and bake for 10 minutes. Serve immediately with lemon wedges or your favorite sauce.

# Pan-Roasted Halibut with Chipotle-Lime Butter

T he mild flavor and firm flesh of halibut make it a perennial favorite in the kitchen. It takes to almost every manner of cooking technique and flavor enhancer, and is available fresh year-round. This recipe comes from my home chef brother-in-law, Don Rohacek, who not only cooks like a wild man, but also skis, plays tournament poker and golf, hits all the local Little League and soccer games, and manages a credit union conglomerate by day. "This recipe is done in 15 minutes," he explained. "The chipotle butter is remarkable. Not only does it flavor the fish, but it also glazes it at the same time while in the oven." Serve with a fresh baguette and a big green salad with tomatoes. ● *Serves 4*

**COOKING METHOD:** Stovetop and oven
**PREP TIME:** 10 minutes
**COOK TIME:** About 10 minutes

CHIPOTLE-LIME BUTTER
2 small cloves garlic
Strips of zest from 1 lime
2 small chipotle chiles in adobo sauce, seeded
2 tablespoons fresh cilantro leaves
½ cup (1 stick) unsalted butter, softened
2 tablespoons fresh lime juice
2 teaspoons honey
1 teaspoon salt

4 halibut fillets (6 to 8 ounces each, about 2 pounds total),
    cut in half down the middle to make 2 chunks from each
Salt and freshly ground black or white pepper
4 tablespoons olive oil

**1.** Preheat the oven to 400°F.

**2.** In a food processor, drop in the garlic and lime zest; pulse to chop. Add the chiles and cilantro; pulse to chop. Add the butter, lime juice, honey, and salt; pulse to combine. Scrape down the sides. Do not overprocess; the butter should be fluffy. Remove with a spatula and place in a small bowl. Set aside.

**3.** Sprinkle both sides of the halibut with salt and pepper. In a large ovenproof sauté pan, heat the oil over high heat until very hot. Turn the heat down to medium-high and swirl the oil to coat the entire bottom of the pan. Arrange the fillets in the pan. Sear for 2 to 3 minutes, not touching the fillets, until lightly browned. Turn over. Divide the chipotle-lime butter among the 4 fillets and spread over the top surface of the fish.

**4.** Bake for 7 minutes, or until the fish loses its translucency and flakes when pressed with the back of a spoon. Transfer 2 pieces to each dinner plate and serve immediately.

# Baked Halibut Parmesan

I used to make this for catering dinner parties all the time. It was a great hit. It uses the convenient technique of slathering the lily-white flesh of halibut with a savory coating to keep it moist and complement the delicate sweet flavor. Halibut can be prepared in many of the same ways as salmon, especially wrapped in prosciutto or in parchment, coated with a hoisin glaze or teriyaki marinade, or pan-sautéed with tartar sauce. Serve with Lemon Rice (page 167) and steamed asparagus or snow peas. ● *Serves 4*

**COOKING METHOD:** Oven
**PREP TIME:** 5 minutes
**COOK TIME:** 20 to 25 minutes

4 halibut steaks (about 2 pounds total)
Salt and freshly ground white pepper
½ cup sour cream
¼ cup mayonnaise
⅓ cup grated Parmesan cheese
1 tablespoon dry white wine
Pinch of dried dillweed
2 tablespoons unsalted butter, melted
Paprika for sprinkling
1 lemon, cut into 8 wedges, for serving

**1.** Preheat the oven to 375°F.

**2.** Line a 9 × 13-inch baking dish with parchment paper and spray it with nonstick cooking spray. Place the steaks in a single layer and season lightly with salt and pepper.

**3.** In a small bowl, whisk to combine the sour cream, mayonnaise, Parmesan, wine, dillweed, and butter. Cover the fish evenly with a thick coating of the sauce and sprinkle with a light dusting of paprika. Bake for 20 to 25 minutes, or until the fish loses its translucency and flakes with a fork. Serve with the lemon wedges.

# •• Fabulous Fish Tacos ••

I have found that no matter what the glaze or cooking method, leftover cold fish, or even freshly cooked, makes a fabulous fish taco for dinner. The homemade mayonnaise is really special and whips up in a few minutes (if you are pressed for time, add 3 tablespoons lime juice and the zest of 1 lime to ¾ cup prepared mayonnaise). This recipe is made with pasteurized egg product for safety. Serve with a side of refried beans. ❍ **Serves 4**

**PREP TIME:** 20 minutes

**LIME MAYONNAISE**
¼ cup pasteurized liquid egg product
   (such as Egg Beaters)
1 clove garlic
2 tablespoons fresh lime juice
1 teaspoon grated lime zest
1½ teaspoons Dijon mustard
¼ teaspoons salt
Pinch of chili powder
1 cup olive oil or combination of half
   olive oil and half vegetable oil

8 fresh corn tortillas
1 pound cooked warm or cold salmon, halibut,
   cod, tuna, or sea bass, crumbled
½ red onion, thinly sliced
2 jarred whole roasted red peppers or whole
   roasted green chiles, rinsed, patted dry,
   and cut into strips
3 cups packaged coleslaw mix
⅓ cup fresh cilantro leaves
1 avocado, cut into thin slices
⅔ cup crumbled queso fresco
Juice of 1 lime
Salt

1. To make the lime mayonnaise, in a food processor or in the mixing beaker with an immersion blender, combine the egg product, garlic, lime juice and zest, mustard, salt, and chili powder. Process until the mixture begins to thicken, 15 to 20 seconds. Immediately begin to add the oil in a slow, steady stream. Continue processing, with an up and down motion if using the immersion blender, for another 30 seconds, until thick and creamy. Do not overmix or the mayonnaise can break. Refrigerate, covered, until ready to serve.

2. Wrap the stack of tortillas in moistened paper towels and microwave for 2 minutes, until steamy.

3. To assemble the tacos, place 2 tortillas on each plate and spread with 2 or 3 tablespoons of lime mayonnaise. Layer in the following order, dividing the ingredients equally among the 8 tacos: crumbled fish, red onion, pepper strips, coleslaw mix, cilantro, avocado slices, and crumbled cheese. Sprinkle with some lime juice and salt. Serve immediately.

# Pan-Seared Sea Bass with Mashed Purple Potatoes and Green Yogurt Sauce

For a while sea bass meant Chilean sea bass, and there was lots of it around. It was available long enough to get dedicated fish eaters hooked on its exquisite flavor. Unfortunately, Chilean sea bass is now heavily overfished, and you should not eat it. But in its place is the striped bass, a farm-raised fish that is a cross between wild and freshwater species, with the same creamy white, firm flesh, mild flavor, and healthy fat content that makes it so versatile. Purple potatoes are a low-starch variety, like white or red new potatoes, with a lovely delicate potato flavor. Serve with any seasonal steamed vegetable. ○ *Serves 4*

**COOKING METHOD:** Stovetop and oven
**PREP TIME:** 20 minutes
**COOK TIME:** About 30 minutes

**MASHED PURPLE POTATOES**
1½ to 2 pounds purple potatoes, peeled
Salt
¾ cup milk or half-and-half
¼ cup unsalted butter, at room temperature

**GREEN YOGURT SAUCE**
5 leaves arugula or a handful of watercress
3 sprigs fresh cilantro (stems okay)
Leaves from 2 sprigs fresh flat-leaf parsley
4 chives (about 1 tablespoon chopped)
3 green onions
1 cup thick plain yogurt or Greek yogurt, or half yogurt and
    half mayonnaise if your yogurt is thin
1 tablespoon fresh lemon juice
Salt and freshly ground white pepper

4 sea bass fillets (6 to 8 ounces each), skin removed
Salt and freshly ground black or white pepper
4 tablespoons grapeseed oil

**1.** To make the potatoes, place the potatoes in a saucepan and cover with cold water and a pinch of salt. Bring to a boil and simmer until tender, about 20 minutes. Drain well and put through a potato ricer or food mill, or use a hand masher, and return to the saucepan. Bring the milk to a boil. Meanwhile, with a wooden spoon or an electric mixer on low speed, beat in the butter, then the milk and salt until the potatoes are fluffy. Cover and keep warm.

**2.** To make the yogurt sauce, place all of the greens in a food processor or blender and pulse until finely chopped. Add the yogurt and lemon juice; process until smooth. Season with salt and pepper. Transfer to a covered container and refrigerate until serving.

**3.** Preheat the oven to 400°F.

**4.** Season the sea bass with salt and pepper on both sides. Heat a large ovenproof skillet over medium-high heat. Add the grapeseed oil and heat just until it begins to smoke. Carefully place the fillets, skin side up, in the pan. Sear on one side, no more than 1 minute, until golden brown and crispy. Remove from the heat, turn the fillets over with a metal spatula, and place the skillet in the center of the oven. Bake for about 7 minutes, until opaque in the center and the fish flakes easily when probed with a fork.

**5.** To serve, place a mound of the purple potatoes on each plate. Set the sea bass to the side, then place a spoonful of the green sauce over the fish. Serve immediately.

# Snapper Veracruz

**S**napper prepared in the style of Veracruz is one of the culinary highlights of traveling in Mexico. Fillets are quickly braised in a characteristic Mexican-style tomato sauce, and the resulting fish is moist and flavorful. The first step of sprinkling the fish with lime juice and salt is a basic technique. You can make the tangy sauce (it is not spicy) ahead and keep in the freezer for quick access; there is no canned product that compares with the homemade version of this sauce. In Mexico this would be served with steamed white long-grain rice and green peas, or a sautéed mélange of local vegetables, including sliced chayote.

○ *Serves 4*

**COOKING METHOD:** Stovetop
**PREP TIME:** 15 minutes
**COOK TIME:** About 50 minutes

2 tablespoons olive oil

1 medium-size red onion, chopped

2 cloves garlic, chopped

One 4-ounce can chopped roasted green chiles, drained

One 14½-ounce can plum tomatoes, undrained

One 8-ounce can tomato sauce

2 tablespoons tomato paste

1 teaspoon sugar

1 teaspoon cider vinegar

½ teaspoon crumbled dried oregano or 1 teaspoon chopped fresh

Salt and freshly ground black pepper

Juice of 2 limes

4 red snapper fillets (1½ to 2 pounds total), patted dry

2 to 3 canned jalapeño chiles, drained and cut into strips

⅔ cup sliced or chopped pitted black olives (I use California canned)

2 tablespoons nonpareil capers, rinsed

**1.** In a medium-size saucepan, heat the oil and add the onion; sauté over medium-high heat for 3 to 4 minutes, until they are translucent. Add the garlic and chiles; cook for 1 minute. Add the tomatoes, tomato sauce, tomato paste, sugar, vinegar, and oregano. Season lightly with salt and pepper. Simmer, uncovered, over medium heat for 20 minutes. Use immediately or refrigerate or freeze for later use.

**2.** Heat the sauce in a large skillet. Squeeze lime juice over the fillets and sprinkle with some salt. Slip the fillets into the sauce, cover, and bring to a low simmer over medium heat. Cook for 15 to 20 minutes over medium-low heat, until the thickest part of the fish is white and flakes when tested with a fork. Carefully remove the cooked fillets with a slotted spatula to a plate and cover with aluminum foil to keep warm.

**3.** Bring the sauce to a boil; boil for about 3 minutes to reduce slightly. Portion the fillets onto individual plates and ladle plenty of sauce over each. Garnish with jalapeño strips, olives, and capers. Serve immediately.

# Red Snapper with Jack Cheese

T his recipe is so fast and efficient, you will make it often. The fillets are first cooked with some chopped vegetables, then finished off with a bit of cheese, which is unique for fish. I keep a can of olive oil cooking spray in the pantry just for dishes like this. Serve with plain white or brown rice and a green salad with grapefruit segments, dressed with a chive vinaigrette. ○ *Serves 4*

**COOKING METHOD:** Microwave
**PREP TIME:** 10 minutes
**COOK TIME:** 12 minutes

2 tablespoons olive oil
4 red snapper fillets (1¼ to 1½ pounds total), patted dry
Salt and freshly ground black pepper
1 medium-size to large shallot, minced
1 plum tomato, seeded and minced
¼ cup minced green bell pepper
2 ounces fresh white mushrooms, chopped
4 slices or 1 cup shredded Monterey Jack cheese

**1.** Grease a 10-inch square microwave-proof baking dish with 1 tablespoon of the olive oil. Season the fillets lightly on both sides with salt and pepper and place in the pan, side by side. Sprinkle the shallot, tomato, pepper, and mushrooms over the fillets. Drizzle with the remaining 1 tablespoon olive oil. Cover with a piece of parchment paper or microwave-safe plastic wrap. Cook on High for 9 minutes, or until the fish is just cooked through and flakes when tested with a fork.

**2.** Remove the cover and lay or sprinkle the cheese over each fillet. Return to the microwave and cook for 1 to 2 minutes, until the cheese is melted. Serve immediately.

# Pan-Fried Trout with
# Hot Garlic Pecan Sauce

T his is another winner from my cache of Louise Fiszer recipes from her now-just-a-memory cooking school, Louise's Pantry, in Menlo Park, California. Louise is not only a practical home cook, but an inventive one as well. Buy farm-raised trout with clear eyes and skin that has an iridescent sheen. If you have a fisherman in the family, just keep the pan ready and waiting. Remember not to remove the head, as it is beautiful on the plate and the cheeks are considered a delicacy. The fishmonger can bone and butterfly the trout, or you can easily do it yourself after cooking. You can also use catfish or salmon in this recipe. Serve with Fragrant Coconut Rice (page 165) and steamed mixed vegetables. ○ *Serves 4*

**COOKING METHOD:** Stovetop
**PREP TIME:** 10 minutes
**COOK TIME:** About 20 minutes

HOT GARLIC PECAN SAUCE

3 tablespoons unsalted butter

½ cup finely chopped pecans

1 small jalapeño chile, seeded, deveined, and chopped

2 cloves garlic, minced

¼ teaspoon fennel seed, crushed

4 ounces fresh white mushrooms, chopped

½ cup chicken broth

2 tablespoons fresh lemon juice

Salt and freshly ground black or white pepper

4 whole trout (8 to 12 ounces each), boned, rinsed inside and out, and patted dry

Salt and freshly ground black or white pepper

4 to 6 tablespoons cornstarch

2 tablespoons olive oil

2 tablespoons unsalted butter

4 tablespoons fresh flat-leaf parsley or cilantro, chopped

**1.** To make the pecan sauce, in a medium-size skillet over medium heat, melt the butter and add the pecans. Stir until the pecans are lightly toasted, about 3 minutes. Add the jalapeño, garlic, fennel, and mushrooms; cook for 2 to 3 minutes. Add the broth and bring to a boil. Reduce to a simmer and cook for 5 minutes. Add the lemon juice and salt and pepper. Set aside to keep warm while cooking the trout.

**2.** Sprinkle the trout with salt and pepper on both sides and inside the cavity, then rub with the cornstarch on both sides. Work in batches or use two sauté pans (in both cases, use half the butter and oil for each batch or each pan). In a large skillet over medium-high heat, heat the oil and butter until very hot. Pan-fry the trout, turning once, about 2 minutes per side, adjusting the heat so the trout is always sizzling in the pan, until the trout is golden and begins to flake when prodded with a fork. Immediately remove to dinner plates and pour spoonfuls of the hot pecan sauce over the fish. Sprinkle with parsley and serve at once.

# Herb-Coated Tilapia

**A**ll of a sudden, out of nowhere, there is a lot of a tilapia available at the fish counter, and it is inexpensive. That's because it is now farm-raised in the United States. Tilapia goes well with assertive flavors such as roasted peppers, pimento, tomatoes, olives, curry, chili, salsa, dried Mediterranean herbs, and garlic. Here is a basic preparation I learned from a woman who was next to me at the fish counter buying fresh tilapia; it involves cooking the fillets in olive oil and a coating of herbs. Tilapia cooks in a flash, so have your accompaniments ready to serve as you put it in the pan. Serve with black olive bread or steamed new potatoes and broccoli. ◦ *Serves 4*

**COOKING METHOD:** Stovetop
**PREP TIME:** 10 minutes
**COOK TIME:** 4 to 5 minutes per batch

CREAMY DIJON SAUCE
½ cup mayonnaise
½ cup plain yogurt
Grated zest and juice of 1 lemon
2 tablespoons Dijon mustard
2 tablespoons chopped fresh dill

1 lemon
¾ cup chopped fresh mixed herbs, such as parsley, chives, thyme,
    marjoram, and cilantro, or ¼ cup dried mixed Italian herbs or
    herb blend for seafood
4 tilapia fillets (4 to 6 ounces each)
Salt and freshly ground black or white pepper
2 to 3 tablespoons olive oil

**1.** To make the Dijon sauce, in a small bowl, stir together all the ingredients until evenly combined. Cover and refrigerate until serving. The sauce keeps for 1 to 2 weeks refrigerated.

**2.** Grate the zest of the lemon and cut the lemon into quarters and set aside. Mix the zest and the herbs on a plate. Season the tilapia fillets on both sides with salt and pepper. Lay the fillets in the herbs and turn to coat both sides.

**3.** Heat the olive oil in a large nonstick skillet over medium heat. Place the fillets in the pan, cooking in two batches, if necessary. Cook for about 2 minutes per side, turning once, until the fish is firm and the flesh is opaque. Remove from the pan with a spatula and place on dinner plates. Serve immediately with a dollop of the cold sauce on the side and a lemon quarter.

# Sole Dijon

T his is adapted from a community cookbook called *Can't Believe It's Kosher*, compiled by the Milwaukee Congregation Beth Israel Sisterhood. Fillet of sole is laid on top of a bed of vegetables and seasoned with a lovely lemon and Dijon mustard sauce, then baked. It is one of my favorite ways to prepare sole and is convenient and easy. ○ *Serves 4*

**COOKING METHOD:** Oven
**PREP TIME:** 10 minutes
**COOK TIME:** 45 to 50 minutes

8 white new potatoes or Yukon Gold potatoes, sliced ¼ inch thick
2 green bell peppers, sliced ¼ inch thick
1 large white onion, sliced ¼ inch thick and then cut into half-moons
¼ cup (½ stick) unsalted butter
1 cup mayonnaise (reduced-fat okay)
2 tablespoons fresh lemon juice
2 tablespoons Dijon mustard
4 sole fillets (about 2 pounds total)
Paprika for sprinkling
1 lemon, cut into 8 wedges, for serving

**1.** Preheat the oven to 400°F (375°F if using a Pyrex dish). Line two 9 × 13-inch baking dishes with parchment paper and spray them with nonstick cooking spray.

**2.** Divide the vegetables between the two pans, placing the potatoes in the first layer, then the green peppers and onion on top. Dot with the butter. Bake in the center of the oven for 30 minutes.

**3.** In a small bowl, combine the mayonnaise, lemon juice, and mustard.

**4.** Remove the pan from the oven. Arrange the sole in a single layer over the hot vegetables. Spread the mayonnaise mixture evenly over the sole and sprinkle with paprika. Bake for 14 to 18 minutes, or until the fish loses its translucency and flakes easily with a fork. Use a large spatula to portion the fish and vegetables onto dinner plates. Serve with lemon wedges.

# Sole with Lemon Caper Butter Sauce

his is the classic piccata stovetop preparation, and it is very fast. When you see a recipe that says "piccata," you are tipped off to the Italian style of finishing the cooking with butter, capers, and lemon. Sole fillets are notoriously varied in size. You want 6 to 7 ounces per person, whether that is one large fillet or two smaller ones. Be prepared to sauté this in two batches, or have two pans going at one time. Serve with steamed vegetables cut shoestring style and breadsticks.

o *Serves 4*

**COOKING METHOD:** Stovetop
**PREP TIME:** 5 minutes
**COOK TIME:** 5 to 10 minutes

¾ cup all-purpose flour or whole wheat pastry flour
Salt and freshly ground black or white pepper
4 sole fillets (6 to 7 ounces each)
6 tablespoons unsalted butter or olive oil, or more as needed if cooking in 2 batches
⅓ cup fresh lemon juice (2 to 3 lemons)
⅓ cup dry white wine, such as Sauvignon Blanc
2 tablespoons capers, rinsed

1. Place the flour on a dinner plate and season with salt and pepper. Dredge each fillet in the flour and shake off the extra.

2. Heat a large nonstick skillet over medium-high heat with 3 tablespoons of the butter. When the butter is bubbly, sauté 2 of the fillets for 2 to 3 minutes, until they begin to brown around the edges. Turn once and cook the other side for 1 minute. Remove from the pan with a spatula and place on a platter; keep warm. Sauté the last 2 fillets, adding a little more butter to the pan if needed, and remove to the platter.

3. Add the lemon juice, wine, and capers to the hot pan. Turn up the heat to high and bring to a boil. Turn off the heat and immediately add the remaining 3 table-spoons of butter, swirling the pan or stirring until the butter is melted and forms a smooth sauce. Pour over the sole and serve immediately.

# Coquilles St. Jacques au Naturel

W hen the food world was just turned on to Julia Child, it seemed like all recipe titles were suddenly in French. Well, here is one recipe from the good old days, originally created by Simone Beck, Julia's food writing partner in France and known as Simca to the French culinary world. It is a recipe I used to make all the time for catered luncheons, as it is fast and easy. Scallops have a perennial appeal because they combine the qualities of sweet meatiness with a melt-in-your-mouth texture. Simca would make bread crumbs from stale home-made bread, but you can use packaged dry bread crumbs just as well. Serve with a mix of sautéed green beans and julienned red or yellow bell peppers. **o** *Serves 4*

**COOKING METHOD:** Oven
**PREP TIME:** 15 minutes
**COOK TIME:** About 20 minutes

1½ pounds bay or sea scallops, rinsed and patted dry
Salt and freshly ground black or white pepper
5 tablespoons unsalted butter
4 small or 2 large shallots, minced
½ cup dry bread crumbs
2 tablespoons chopped fresh flat-leaf parsley

1. Preheat the oven to 375°F.

2. Bay scallops can stay whole. If you use sea scallops instead of the small bay scallops, cut in half or thirds. Butter 4 individual gratin dishes or 4-inch ceramic ramekins and divide the scallops equally among them. Season lightly with salt and pepper.

3. In a small skillet, melt the butter over medium heat. Sauté the shallots until soft, about 4 minutes. Spoon the shallots and butter over the scallops. Sprinkle each with about 2 tablespoons of the bread crumbs. Arrange the dishes or ramekins on a baking sheet and set in the center of the oven. Bake for 12 to 15 minutes, until tender when pierced with the tip of a knife. Place each dish on an individual dinner plate, sprinkle with the parsley, and serve immediately.

# Jumbo Shrimp and Polenta

**I** was thrilled when I learned how to make the fastest, creamiest polenta. The secret is the oversized tubes of prepared polenta that I usually just slice and pan-fry in olive oil. In this recipe, you cook the polenta in milk until it is the consistency of your morning cereal and then serve with those impressive-looking jumbo shrimp, quickly sautéed. Accompanied by a green salad, this is a really filling and satisfying meal. ● *Serves 4*

**COOKING METHOD:** Stovetop
**PREP TIME:** 10 minutes
**COOK TIME:** About 15 minutes

POLENTA

One 17-ounce tube ready-made plain polenta, chopped into chunks
1 cup whole milk
3 tablespoons unsalted butter
Salt

2 tablespoons olive oil
12 jumbo shrimp (10/15 count), peeled and deveined
Salt and freshly ground black pepper
⅓ cup dry white wine or vermouth
2 tablespoons cold unsalted butter, cut into pieces
3 tablespoons chopped fresh flat-leaf parsley

**1.** To make the polenta, in a medium-size deep saucepan over medium heat, combine the polenta and milk. Heat slowly. Whisk to dissolve the chunks; they will dissolve into a creamy cereal-like mush. Stir in the butter and season with salt. Adjust the consistency with more hot milk, if necessary, but I like this pretty thick. Set aside and keep warm while cooking the shrimp.

**2.** Heat the oil in a large skillet over high heat. Add the shrimp and sauté, stirring constantly, until firm and pink, about 3 minutes. Season lightly with salt and pepper, then add the wine. Bring to a boil quickly and let reduce for 1 minute. Add the butter, swirling to combine it, then add the parsley.

**3.** Portion the hot polenta into the center of dinner plates and arrange 3 shrimp for each serving around it. Serve immediately.

# Shrimp Provençal

T his is a dazzling little dinner made in about 30 minutes, and when I was catering, it was the most popular fast entrée in my repertoire. I even typed up the recipe and carried it with me, I had so many requests for it. I have also made this with monkfish in place of the shrimp, which was also luscious, but monkfish is now only occasionally available. Serve with green salad, a crusty French baguette, and a steamed veggie like artichokes. No cheese, please—cheese is not traditionally used with fish dishes. ● *Serves 4*

**COOKING METHOD:** Stovetop
**PREP TIME:** 15 minutes
**COOK TIME:** About 30 minutes

⅓ **cup olive oil**
**1 medium-size yellow onion, chopped**
**2 medium-size shallots, chopped**
**2 cloves garlic, minced**
**15 leaves fresh basil, chopped**
**1 teaspoon crushed dried thyme**
**Two 28-ounce cans Italian plum tomatoes, drained and chopped**
⅔ **cup white wine**
**Salt and freshly ground black pepper**
**1 pound fresh spinach fettuccine**
**1 pound large shrimp (23/30 count), peeled and deveined**

**1.** Bring a large pot of salted water to a boil.

**2.** Heat the oil in a large, deep skillet over medium to medium-high heat. Add the onion and shallots; sauté until just soft, 5 to 7 minutes. Add the garlic and sauté for 30 seconds. Add the basil, thyme, tomatoes, and wine; simmer uncovered for 15 minutes. Season with salt and pepper.

**3.** Meanwhile, cook the pasta according to package directions.

**4.** Add the shrimp to the hot tomato sauce and cook for 2 to 3 minutes, until pink, stirring a few times. Drain the pasta and divide among 4 shallow plates. Ladle the shrimp and sauce over the pasta. Serve immediately.

# Scampi

**W**hile we associate the word *scampi* with all large shrimp, it is the Italian word for the specific tail portion of certain small Mediterranean lobsterettes. Scampi is the plural, meaning a nice portion of *scampo*, the word for a singular prawn. There is no substitute for the dry sherry; it is integral to the success of this dish. Also, don't skip the bit of parsley at the end just because it looks like a small amount. Every ingredient adds to the final dish. Serve with fluffy steamed rice and a green salad. ● *Serves 4*

**COOKING METHOD:** Stovetop
**PREP TIME:** 10 minutes
**COOK TIME:** About 5 minutes

¼ cup olive oil
¼ cup (½ stick) unsalted butter
2 cloves garlic, crushed
1 pound large shrimp (23/30 count), peeled and deveined
3 tablespoons seasoned dry bread crumbs (I use Progresso)
⅛ teaspoon freshly ground black pepper
½ cup dry sherry
Juice of 2 lemons
1 tablespoon minced fresh flat-leaf parsley
Salt

Heat the oil and butter in a large skillet over medium to medium-high heat. Add the garlic and cook for no more than 30 seconds. Do not brown or burn. Add the shrimp, bread crumbs, and pepper; simmer for 1 minute. Add the sherry, lemon juice, and parsley; simmer for 1 to 2 minutes to thicken. Season with salt and serve immediately.

# Baked Crab Cakes with Caper-Dill Sauce and Red Pepper Coulis

C rab cakes, once down-home food in seaport towns, are the darling of the restaurant scene these days. They are so very easy to whip together, especially if you keep cans of premium crabmeat on your shelf, although fresh is always lovely. These crab cakes are baked instead of fried, which makes for a less messy preparation, so if you like that fried crust, you can sear them in a hot sauté pan for a minute on both sides before placing in the oven. Keep a few jars of roasted red peppers in your cupboard as well. You can whip up this delicious, colorful sauce in minutes in the food processor. You can prepare both sauces ahead if you wish, making this recipe really easy to put together. These cakes are also good made with half crab and half salmon, especially if you are using canned. Serve with Celery Root Salad on the side (page 45), which tastes great with seafood.

*○ Serves 4*

**COOKING METHOD:** Oven
**PREP TIME:** 25 minutes
**COOK TIME:** About 25 minutes

1 pound fresh or canned lump crabmeat
2 cups dry bread crumbs
⅔ cup minced celery
½ cup minced red onion
¼ cup minced fresh flat-leaf parsley
Salt and freshly ground black or white pepper
1 tablespoon Dijon mustard
1½ teaspoons Worcestershire sauce
1 teaspoon hot sauce, such as Tabasco
1 egg
1 egg yolk

**CAPER-DILL SAUCE**

1½ cups mayonnaise

⅓ cup chopped rinsed capers

¼ cup chopped green onions (white part and some of the green)

3 tablespoons chopped fresh flat-leaf parsley

3 tablespoons fresh lemon juice

2 tablespoons chopped fresh dill

Few splashes hot sauce, such as Tabasco

**RED PEPPER COULIS**

One 15- or 16-ounce jar roasted red peppers, drained

Pinch of dried thyme or ½ teaspoon fresh thyme leaves

3 to 4 tablespoons olive oil

3 to 4 tablespoons chicken or vegetable broth

Freshly ground black pepper

**1.** Preheat the oven to 375°F. Line a baking sheet with parchment paper.

**2.** In a medium-size bowl, combine the crab, 1 cup of the bread crumbs, the celery, red onion, and parsley. Sprinkle with salt and pepper. Add the mustard, Worcestershire sauce, hot sauce, and eggs; stir to combine and evenly moisten. Shape the mixture by ¼ cupfuls into small rounds, then slightly flatten to make eight 1-inch-thick patties. Place the remaining 1 cup of bread crumbs on a plate and press each patty into the bread crumbs to lightly coat; tap off any extra. Place on the baking sheet, with space in between each patty. Spray with some olive oil cooking spray. Place in the center of the oven and bake for 25 minutes, until firm.

**3.** To make the caper-dill sauce, in a small bowl, stir together the sauce ingredients until evenly combined. Cover and refrigerate until ready to serve if you are not making the crab cakes immediately.

**4.** To make the red pepper coulis, place the peppers and thyme in a food processor and pulse until a puree is formed. Pulse in the olive oil and broth until it reaches the desired sauce consistency. Pour into a covered container and stir in some black pepper. Refrigerate until ready to serve. Heat over low heat on the stovetop or in the microwave before serving.

**5.** To serve, place 2 crab cakes on each dinner plate next to a bit of Celery Root Salad. Top each cake with some caper-dill sauce and spoon some coulis around the cakes. Serve immediately.

# Celery Root Salad

Celery root is probably one of the ugliest vegetables. It comes from a special celery plant cultivated just for its oversized root. It is crisp and crunchy with a distinctive pungent flavor that is described as a cross between celery and parsley. This rendition of *céleri rémoulade*, a classic bistro salad, is a real treat with crab cakes.

○ *Makes about 3 cups*

1 large celery root (1 to 1½ pounds), peeled and cut into thin strips
　(can be shredded in a food processor or on a mandoline)
¾ cup mayonnaise
3 to 4 tablespoons buttermilk or plain yogurt
4 tablespoons whole-grain mustard
1 tablespoon fresh lemon juice
Pinch of salt and freshly ground black pepper

Put the celery root in a medium-size bowl (if not making immediately, add water and lemon juice to prevent discoloration). In a small bowl, stir together the mayonnaise, buttermilk, mustard, lemon juice, salt, and pepper. Stir into the celery root with a rubber spatula and fold to evenly coat. Cover and refrigerate until serving.

# *Supper Specials:*
# Poultry

Poultry is the ultimate weeknight supper. But how can you jazz up the old standbys and not add a lot of time in the process? Enter the boneless chicken breast and the turkey breast cutlet, which cook exceptionally fast and are extremely versatile. The secret is seasoning and accompaniments, plus the fact that good poultry can be very, very simple and still taste great. So, except for a few exceptions that I've included in this chapter, leave the whole birds and bone-in

parts for weekend cooking. Of course, always remember that organizing your ingredients and equipment is essential to fast cooking.

The family of quick-cooking poultry includes boneless chicken half-breasts, pounded breasts (called cutlets or paillards), chicken tenders (the little tenderloin strips on the side of the breast), boneless thighs, drumsticks, and turkey tenderloins and cutlets (sliced from the breast). Please don't confuse regular boneless chicken breasts with cutlets. Cutlets are pounded to an even thickness, ¼ to ½ inch, no more. I also include here frozen boneless duck breast, known in France as *magret*; there is a recipe for preparing it in the salad chapter (page 244). All poultry can be served simply or embellished with rich-tasting sauces of all types.

Poultry is easily checked for doneness either visually or by using an instant-read thermometer. To check for doneness visually, press on the chicken with a fork. You want it to feel firm and springy. When pierced, the juices will run clear. An

instant-read thermometer inserted into the thickest part should register 160°F for breasts and 175°F for thighs. With thin pieces, a quick flash in the pan will cook it thoroughly with no fuss. Never leave any raw or rare portions in cooked poultry like you might with beef. Refrigerate leftover cooked poultry and use it within 2 to 3 days, or else place it in plastic freezer bags and freeze.

Here are a few pointers on buying poultry. I never buy a package that has any accumulated liquid. That tells me that it has sat too long on the shelf. As soon as I return from shopping, I refrigerate poultry. The sell-by date indicates 7 days after the bird was processed and is the cutoff date for sale. Refrigerated, the bird will still be good after that date. If you have any doubt, ask the butcher how fresh the bird is and when it should be cooked by. Freeze poultry for 9 to 10 months maximum. Use all unfrozen poultry within 2 to 3 days of purchase. If I cannot use it within 2 days, I freeze it. Thaw poultry in the refrigerator in its original wrapping with a plate underneath in case of dripping. Refrigerate cooked poultry within 2 hours of cooking, never letting it come to room temperature first before refrigerating.

Many cooks have a cutting board just for poultry. I recommend a plastic one that can be easily washed in hot soapy water or sterilized in the dishwasher after each use. Because uncooked poultry may carry potential harmful organisms or bacteria, take care when handling it. Thoroughly wash the poultry and dry it before preparing your meal. Wash your hands, work surfaces, and utensils with hot soapy water before and after handling raw poultry.

You will note that there are many chicken recipes in the following collection in which you can substitute turkey, if you prefer. I made sure to use a number of techniques, so you'll see pounded paillards and breast slices; plain boneless breasts cooked in the oven or on the stovetop; thighs cut into pieces, some roasted with the bone in; a stir-fry; a butterflied whole bird; a chili; and roasted tenderloin of turkey. You have your choice, along with a bevy of flavor combinations.

# Paillards of Chicken with Sautéed Cherry Tomatoes

I used to make this chicken with just butter and bread crumbs, but it was always dramatically swimming in butter at the end of cooking. So over the years I evolved to making more of a coating and ending up with less pan fat. This is so darn tasty you won't believe it, and the combination with the hot little tomatoes is perfect culinary symmetry. Sorry to make you count the tomatoes, but really it is more practical than calling for a measurement in cups. Serve with rice or plain fettuccine, and break out the Chardonnay. ○ *Serves 4*

**COOKING METHOD:** Stovetop
**PREP TIME:** 15 minutes
**COOK TIME:** About 15 minutes

4 boneless, skinless chicken breast halves (about 1½ pounds), pounded thin
Juice of 1 lemon
¼ cup all-purpose flour or oat flour (made by grinding quick-cooking or
    old-fashioned oats in a blender or food processor) mixed with a pinch of
    thyme, salt, and freshly ground black or white pepper, for dredging
1 large egg, beaten
¾ cup fresh white bread crumbs, made in the food processor
2 tablespoons olive oil or grapeseed oil

**SAUTÉED CHERRY TOMATOES**
24 cherry tomatoes
2 tablespoons unsalted butter
2 tablespoons minced fresh basil, chives, flat-leaf parsley, or dill
Salt and freshly ground black or white pepper

**1.** Sprinkle the chicken with the lemon juice. Place the flour on a plate. Place the egg in a shallow bowl and the bread crumbs on a plate. In a large skillet over medium-high heat, add the olive oil. Dredge the breasts on both sides in the flour, then the egg, then the bread crumbs; place in the hot pan. Sauté the chicken until crispy golden brown, 4 to 5 minutes on each side. Remove the chicken to a platter and cover with aluminum foil to keep warm.

**2.** To make the tomatoes, either wipe out the skillet or use another clean pan. Prick each cherry tomato with the tip of a sharp knife to prevent the skin from bursting. Melt the butter over medium-high heat and add the tomatoes, tossing frequently until hot, about 1 minute. Toss with the basil and season to taste with salt and pepper. Remove the chicken to individual plates and divide the hot tomatoes among the plates. Serve immediately.

# Chicken Piccata

O nce you know how to make a tangy piccata, you will never be without it and will just possibly serve it once a week. This is where you perfect your technique of pounding the breast with a flat mallet (never use the uneven side or it will decimate the meat). Slip each breast into a quart-size zipper-top plastic bag and pound with the smooth side of a meat mallet or the bottom of a small, heavy saucepan. You are looking to get it about ¼ inch thick. Serve with brown rice or mashed potatoes and steamed green beans. This makes excellent leftovers for the next day.  ●  *Serves 4*

**COOKING METHOD:** Stovetop
**PREP TIME:** 5 minutes
**COOK TIME:** About 15 minutes

4 boneless, skinless chicken breast halves (about 1½ pounds),
    pounded thin (see above) or butterflied to open like a
    book if thick enough
Salt and freshly ground white pepper
½ cup all-purpose flour or oat flour (made by grinding
    quick-cooking or old-fashioned oats in a blender or
    food processor), for dredging
¼ cup (½ stick) unsalted butter
2 tablespoons extra virgin olive oil
1 medium-size shallot, minced
½ cup dry white wine or low-sodium chicken broth
⅓ cup fresh lemon juice (2 to 3 lemons)
2 tablespoons chopped drained capers, or more to your taste
2 tablespoons chopped fresh flat-leaf parsley

**1.** Sprinkle the chicken on both sides with salt and pepper. Place the flour on a plate and dredge the breasts on both sides.

**2.** In a large skillet over medium-high heat, melt the butter and add the olive oil. Sauté the chicken until golden brown, 2 to 3 minutes on each side. Remove the chicken to a platter and cover with aluminum foil to keep warm.

**3.** Add the shallot and cook until translucent, 1 minute, stirring constantly. Add the wine, lemon juice, and capers. Bring to a low boil and stir for a few minutes to reduce and thicken slightly. Return the breasts to the skillet and partially cover. Spoon the sauce mixture over the top of the chicken as you lift the lid every few minutes. Simmer until the chicken is cooked through, 5 to 10 minutes depending on the thickness of the breast, but be careful not to overcook.

**4.** Add the parsley to the sauce. Remove the chicken to individual plates and divide the sauce among the portions. Serve immediately.

# Mozzarella Chicken Breasts

T his is a superbly simple recipe from Paula Lambert (*The Cheese Lover's Cookbook and Guide*, Simon & Schuster, 2000), owner of the Mozzarella Company in Texas. Paula came to the San Francisco Professional Food Society in the 1980s to give a tasting and lecture on her then-fledgling company, maker of fresh, high-quality Italian-style cheese, which was unique at the time. We tasted all sorts of fresh mozzarella not then available domestically—plain fresh mozzarella, bocconcini (little balls), capriella (goat's milk mozzarella), and smoked mozzarella—gobbling our way through the tasty bites, swearing to never eat another morsel of packaged skim-milk mozzarella. I've added a dash more wine to this recipe for more sauce and I vary the herb seasonally. You may use turkey breast cutlets here as well. Serve with Steamed New Potatoes with White Wine (page 105) and a green salad with red wine vinaigrette. ○ *Serves 4*

**COOKING METHOD:** Stovetop
**PREP TIME:** 10 minutes
**COOK TIME:** About 20 minutes

4 boneless, skinless chicken breast halves (about 1½ pounds)

Salt and freshly ground black pepper

3 tablespoons unsalted butter

1 clove garlic

¾ cup dry white wine

8 ounces fresh mozzarella cheese, cut into 8 slices

4 sprigs fresh tarragon, marjoram, or basil

**1.** Season the chicken with salt and pepper. In a large skillet over medium heat, melt the butter. Add the chicken breasts and the whole clove of garlic. Sauté the chicken until golden brown on both sides and almost cooked through, 3 to 5 minutes on each side. Remove the chicken to a platter and cover with aluminum foil to keep warm.

**2.** Add the wine to the hot pan, stirring for a few minutes to reduce it a bit. Bring to a low boil to evaporate the liquid by about half its volume, 1 to 2 minutes. Return the chicken to the skillet and cook for 1 minute in the liquid.

**3.** Place 2 slices of mozzarella, then a sprig of herb, on each breast. Discard the garlic. Cover and remove from the heat. Let stand for 5 minutes to melt the cheese. Remove the chicken to individual dinner plates and spoon some pan sauce over each one. Serve immediately.

# Baked Chicken with Parmesan Herb Crust

**C**hicken baked with a crispy, crunchy coating is a weekly favorite fast meal. You can crush the saltines with a rolling pin or in a food processor, whichever is more convenient. If you have panko, crispy Japanese bread crumbs, on hand, you can substitute them for the cracker crumbs, or you can use buttery Ritz crackers or Waverly Wafers. I have a friend who supplies me with a stash of her own dried herbs, which I use liberally, but if you use store-bought, make sure they have not been on the shelf for more than 12 months for the best flavor. Serve with Saffron Rice with Green Onions (page 167) or roasted small red potatoes (put them in the oven at the same time as the chicken) and steamed broccoli. ● *Serves 4*

**COOKING METHOD:** Oven
**PREP TIME:** 15 minutes
**COOK TIME:** 30 to 40 minutes

1 cup oyster crackers or plain or whole wheat saltines (with saltless tops, if possible)
¼ cup grated Parmesan cheese
2 tablespoons minced fresh flat-leaf parsley
½ teaspoon crumbled dried basil
½ teaspoon crumbled dried marjoram
½ teaspoon paprika
Pinch of salt and a few grinds of black pepper
½ cup buttermilk
4 large boneless, skinless chicken breast halves (about 1½ pounds)
1 tablespoon olive oil

1. Preheat the oven to 400°F.

2. Place the crackers in a gallon-size zipper-top plastic bag and crush with your hands or a rolling pin. Add the Parmesan, parsley, basil, marjoram, paprika, and salt and pepper; shake to combine.

3. Place the buttermilk in a shallow bowl. Brush the chicken with the olive oil, then dip in the buttermilk. Place in the plastic bag and shake to evenly coat.

4. Place in an earthenware baking dish and bake for 30 to 40 minutes, until tender and the juices run clear when pierced with a knife. Serve hot.

# Hungarian Paprika Chicken

**B**eing of Hungarian descent, I adore the little family of dishes that are prepared with a paprika and sour cream sauce. Hungarians love *paprikás* so much that they consider it an essential dish for every cook to know how to make. Paprika is considered "the poor man's pepper," and it is comfort food for me. If you're used to using it only as a colorful garnish, this dish will be a revelation. Here I mix both mild and hot paprika, but if you can find *félédes*, the sweet-hot blend, buy it immediately. Serve with rice, egg noodles, or traditional spaetzle dumplings. ○ *Serves 4*

**COOKING METHOD:** Stovetop
**PREP TIME:** 10 minutes
**COOK TIME:** About 35 minutes

2 tablespoons olive oil
1 large yellow onion, chopped
4 boneless, skinless chicken thighs (about 1½ pounds), trimmed and cut
   into 3-inch-square chunks and seasoned with salt and pepper
1 large red, yellow, or green bell pepper, chopped
3 fresh or canned plum tomatoes, chopped
1 teaspoon hot Hungarian paprika
1 teaspoon sweet Hungarian paprika
2 teaspoons cornstarch
8 ounces sour cream (regular or reduced-fat)
Pinch of salt and a few grinds of black pepper

**1.** Heat the oil in a large skillet over medium-high heat. Add the onion and cook for 3 to 4 minutes, until softened. Add the chicken, cover, and cook for about 5 minutes; do not brown it or it will be tough. Add the bell pepper, tomatoes, and paprika. Reduce the heat to low and simmer, covered, for 15 to 20 minutes.

**2.** In a small bowl, stir the cornstarch into the sour cream. Add to the pan and cook, uncovered, for 5 to 10 minutes, until the sauce is hot and thickened. Season with salt and pepper and serve immediately.

# Lemon Chicken with Mint

**T**his is one of those remarkable dishes that looks sooooo simple and turns out really delicious, and the individual ingredients add up to a whole lot more in flavor than expected. This recipe originally came from Anna Beck, whose family owned Tassajara Hot Springs in Big Sur, California, before the Zen monks took it over as a retreat site and made it famous for vegetarian fare. This was the first savory dish in which I ever used mint. Serve with couscous and a steamed green vegetable of your choice.  ○ *Serves 4*

**COOKING METHOD:** Stovetop and oven
**PREP TIME:** 15 minutes
**COOK TIME:** 40 to 45 minutes

4 bone-in chicken breasts, skinned, or 8 bone-in chicken thighs,
    skinned, or a combination
Zest and juice of 1 lemon
⅓ cup all-purpose flour
1½ teaspoons salt
½ teaspoon freshly ground black pepper
½ teaspoon paprika
4 tablespoons olive oil
2 tablespoons light brown sugar
1 lemon, sliced
1 cup chicken broth
Two 4-inch sprigs fresh mint

**1.** Preheat the oven to 375°F. Spray a 10 × 14-inch ceramic baking dish with non-stick cooking spray.

**2.** Drizzle the chicken with the lemon juice. Place the flour, salt, pepper, and paprika in a gallon-size zipper-top plastic bag. Add the pieces of chicken to the bag and toss to lightly coat with flour.

**3.** In a 12-inch skillet over medium-high heat, heat the oil. Add the chicken pieces, a few at a time, and sear until golden brown on both sides, about 10 minutes. As the chicken browns, arrange it in a single layer in the baking dish. Sprinkle the chicken with the lemon zest and brown sugar. Place a slice of lemon on each piece, then pour the broth over the chicken. Place the mint sprigs on top.

**4.** Place in the center of the oven and bake for 40 to 45 minutes, uncovered, until the juices run clear when pierced with the tip of a knife. Discard the mint and serve hot.

# Butterflied Roast Chicken and Creamer Potatoes with Herbes de Provence

**T**here is some beauty in roasting a whole chicken, and it is an easy meal for four. But roasting the intact chicken takes way over an hour. Enter the wonderful world of high-heat cooking and butterflying, or spatchcocking. In a wink you have brown-crusted, juicy roast chicken. Here the bird is simply rubbed with oil or butter, but you can tuck a compound butter under the skin if you like. *Herbes de Provence* is a unique dried herb blend (primarily rosemary, thyme, lavender, savory, and fennel) that originated in the south of France. Serve this with your favorite green vegetable or roasted red peppers. ● *Serves 4*

**COOKING METHOD:** Oven
**PREP TIME:** 15 minutes
**COOK TIME:** About 40 minutes, depending on the size of the chicken

One 2½- to 4-pound chicken
1 lemon, cut in half
Olive oil or unsalted butter, softened
Salt and freshly ground black pepper

CREAMER POTATOES
1 pound small red potatoes, left whole
2 to 3 tablespoons olive oil
2 tablespoons *herbes de Provence*
Few pinches of fine sea salt

**1.** Preheat the oven to 450°F. Line a 12 × 18-inch shallow roasting pan or half-sheet roasting pan with aluminum foil.

**2.** Set the bird so the legs are face down and you are looking at the back (it will look like it is upside down). With kitchen shears, cut on either side of the backbone and remove it (discard, save for stock, or roast with the chicken). Turn over and press down to crack the breastbone and flatten; this will butterfly the bird. Rinse and pat dry. Squeeze the lemon over the bird. Place it skin side up on the pan. Rub the skin with the olive oil and season with salt and pepper. Place in the hot oven and roast for 40 minutes, until the skin is crisp and an instant-read thermometer reads 160°F in the breast and 180°F in the thigh.

**3.** After putting the chicken in the oven, prepare the potatoes. On a half-sheet baking pan or in a large shallow gratin dish, toss the potatoes with the oil to coat. Sprinkle with the *herbes de Provence* and salt. Roast alongside the chicken, uncovered, until browned, about 30 minutes, turning over with a metal spatula once during the roasting for even browning.

**4.** Remove the chicken from the oven and let stand for 10 minutes before carving. Serve with the crisp potatoes.

**Note:** While classic *herbes de Provence* is imported, many domestic specialty herb companies mix their own blend. You can get freshly mixed *herbes de Provence* from Penzeys Spices (800-741-7787, www.penzeys.com).

# Coq au Vin in Dijon Yogurt Sauce and Frisée Salad with Roasted Mushrooms

T his recipe is a fancy French name for chicken cooked in wine, but that is where the similarity ends. Many cultures, including modern French home cooks, use yogurt instead of cream, and frankly I like it better, since yogurt is an excellent tenderizer. Use the thickest plain yogurt you can find; Greek-style yogurt is excellent. French country salads are distinctly earthy and often use different greens than American salads do. Frisée, also called curly French endive, is bitter and holds up well to the additions of bacon and mushrooms. You can make the salad while the chicken is cooking. *Bon appétit!* ○ *Serves 4*

**COOKING METHOD:** Oven
**PREP TIME:** 20 minutes
**COOK TIME:** 45 to 50 minutes

4 bone-in chicken breast halves, skinned
½ cup dry white wine
Pinch of salt and a few grinds of black pepper
1 cup thick plain yogurt
¼ cup Dijon mustard
1 tablespoon chopped fresh tarragon or thyme leaves

FRISÉE SALAD WITH ROASTED MUSHROOMS
½ pound thick-sliced smoked bacon, coarsely chopped
2 shallots, minced
½ teaspoon Dijon mustard
2 tablespoons balsamic vinegar
4 tablespoons extra virgin olive oil
Salt and freshly ground black pepper
1 pound small fresh mushrooms of your choice, such as
   white or brown, stems trimmed
1 large head frisée (curly French endive)

1. Preheat the oven to 350°F.

2. Arrange the chicken in an earthenware baking dish. Pour the wine over the chicken and sprinkle with the salt and pepper. In a small bowl, whisk together the yogurt, mustard, and tarragon; spoon the sauce over the chicken. Cover with aluminum foil and bake for 30 minutes.

3. Remove the foil and bake, uncovered, another 15 to 20 minutes, until the chicken is tender and the juices run clear when pierced with a knife.

4. Meanwhile, make the salad. Cook the bacon over medium heat in a large skillet until crisp. Drain on paper towels. Reserve 2 tablespoons of the fat in a small bowl. Add the shallots. Whisk in the mustard, vinegar, and olive oil. Season lightly with salt and pepper.

5. Place the mushrooms on a baking sheet and brush with some of the vinaigrette. Tear the frisée into bite-size pieces and place in a serving bowl. Add the bacon and set aside.

6. When the chicken is done, remove and cover with foil; set the oven to broil. Place the mushrooms under the broiler for about 3 minutes on each side, turning once, until golden. Add the hot mushrooms to the salad and toss with the remaining vinaigrette. Serve immediately.

# Spicy Chicken with Cilantro and Mushrooms

**T**his recipe, from Mexican cooking expert Marge Poore, uses a steamer basket and is the epitome of good, low-fat cooking. It is composed of spicy chicken bits and mushrooms in a gently spicy sauce. It makes a terrific topping for hot steamed long-grain white or brown rice. The ingredients are wrapped loosely in aluminum foil to catch all the delicious juices. Serve with a simple grated cabbage and carrot salad.  ○ *Serves 4*

**COOKING METHOD:** Stovetop
**PREP TIME:** 20 minutes
**COOK TIME:** 25 minutes

4 boneless, skinless chicken thighs (about 1½ pounds),
    trimmed and cut into ½-inch pieces
2 large cloves garlic, minced
1 tablespoon minced fresh ginger
½ teaspoon red pepper flakes
2 tablespoons olive oil
1½ cups water
8 medium-size fresh white mushrooms, coarsely chopped
4 green onions, sliced into ½-inch-long pieces
3 tablespoons light soy sauce
1 tablespoon rice vinegar
½ cup lightly packed chopped fresh cilantro leaves

**1.** In a medium-size bowl, toss together the chicken, garlic, ginger, red pepper flakes, and olive oil. Cover and marinate in the refrigerator for 15 minutes. Pour the water into a saucepan or the water reservoir of an electric steamer. Position the steaming basket over the water.

**2.** Cut a $12 \times 16$-inch piece of aluminum foil and place the foil in the steaming basket with the excess edges turned up. Make a layer of the mushrooms and green onions in the foil, spreading them gently over the surface. Arrange the marinated chicken over the mushrooms and green onions. Fold the foil edges over to cover (it's okay if a little steam drips in while cooking). Cover and cook for 25 minutes.

**3.** Using potholders, carefully remove the lid and open the foil to make sure the chicken is no longer pink inside. If necessary, replace the lid, cover, and cook for a few more minutes. Carefully lift the foil so as not to lose any of the juices and transfer the chicken to a serving bowl. Stir to separate the pieces. Add the soy sauce, vinegar, chopped cilantro, and juices to the hot chicken. Stir well to combine. Serve immediately.

# White Chicken Chili

For such a short cooking time (which keeps the chicken tender), this is a killer batch of chili. It has the added flavor dimensions of tomatillos and roasted green chiles, as well as delicious white kidney beans, also known as cannellini beans. You can make this chili from your pantry if you are stocked up. It is a mild chili, so it has wide appeal for all ages. Warm tortillas or a fresh baguette taste fantastic with this, as does a crunchy green salad. ● *Serves 4*

**COOKING METHOD:** Stovetop
**PREP TIME:** 15 minutes
**COOK TIME:** About 35 minutes

1 tablespoon olive oil

1 pound boneless, skinless chicken breast halves, cut into bite-size pieces

2 large shallots, chopped

2 cloves garlic, minced

One 14½-ounce can diced tomatoes, undrained

One 14½-ounce can chicken broth

One 11-ounce can tomatillos, drained and chopped

One 4½-ounce can roasted chopped green chiles, undrained

½ teaspoon dried oregano or marjoram

½ teaspoon ground coriander

¼ teaspoon ground cumin

Two 15-ounce cans cannellini beans, rinsed and drained

3 tablespoons fresh lime juice (2 limes)

Salt and freshly ground black or white pepper

1 to 2 cups (8 ounces to 1 pound) shredded mild or sharp cheddar cheese,
    or combination of cheddar and Monterey Jack

Lime wedges (optional)

**1.** Place a large, deep saucepan over medium-high heat and add the oil. Add the chicken pieces and sauté for 3 minutes, until tender and no longer pink on the outside. Remove the chicken from the pan with a slotted spoon to a plate and cover with aluminum foil; set aside.

**2.** Add the shallots to the pan and sauté for 2 minutes, or until tender. Add the garlic and cook for 30 seconds. Add the tomatoes and their juices, broth, the tomatillos, the green chiles and their juices, oregano, coriander, and cumin. Bring to a boil, then reduce the heat, cover, and simmer for 20 minutes.

**3.** Add the chicken and beans. Cook for 10 minutes, or until heated thoroughly. Stir in the lime juice and season with salt and pepper. Ladle into bowls and top with the cheese. Serve with lime wedges, if desired.

# Mexican Chicken with
# Beer Glaze and Sweet Potato Fries

I was always looking for a substitute for packaged taco seasoning, since it has a lovely flavor but is so high in sodium that it makes me cringe. Jacquie McMahan came to my rescue with this home spice blend. She invented this for making chicken to use for tacos, but really my batch never got that far. The chicken is just too good eaten plain out of the pan, and the aroma while it is cooking is positively euphoric. If you don't want to make your own sweet potato fries, you can find them fresh from the produce section or frozen in many markets these days. ● *Serves 4*

**COOKING METHOD:** Stovetop
**PREP TIME:** 25 minutes
**COOK TIME:** About 35 minutes

1 teaspoon ground cumin

1 teaspoon dried crushed thyme

½ teaspoon garlic powder

½ teaspoon onion powder

¼ teaspoon cayenne pepper, chili powder, or ground chipotle chile

½ teaspoon salt

1 tablespoon all-purpose flour

4 boneless, skinless chicken breast halves (about 1½ pounds), cut into 1-inch strips

2 tablespoons olive oil

2 tablespoons unsalted butter

1 clove garlic, crushed

½ to 1 jalapeño chile, stemmed, seeded, and minced

½ to ¾ cup light-colored beer

SWEET POTATO FRIES

1 pound sweet potatoes, peeled and cut into 2- to 3-inch wedges or long thick strips

1 to 2 tablespoons olive oil

¼ teaspoon salt

**1.** In a bowl, combine the cumin, thyme, garlic and onion powders, cayenne, salt, and flour. Rub the chicken on both sides with the spice blend and place in a pan or on a plate; set aside for 10 to 20 minutes at room temperature.

**2.** Preheat the oven to 450°F. Lay the sweet potatoes on a large aluminum foil–covered baking sheet, toss with the oil, and sprinkle with the salt. Bake until golden brown and tender, 15 to 20 minutes.

**3.** Meanwhile, heat the oil and butter in a large skillet over medium heat. Add half of the chicken and sauté until golden; remove to a clean plate. Sauté the rest of the chicken, adding a bit more oil if necessary. Use paper towels to soak up any extra fat in the pan. Return the chicken to the pan, then add the garlic, jalapeño, and beer. Cover and reduce the heat to low. Cook for about 15 minutes, checking every 5 minutes, pushing and turning the chicken in the broth to coat all the pieces. You will end up with a glazed effect.

**4.** Serve the chicken immediately with the hot sweet potato fries.

# Chicken Fingers with
# Orange-Miso Dipping Sauce

**B**ags of chicken tenders, the little strip of tenderloin that is attached to the chicken breast, are easy to find in the frozen food section. They are incredibly delicious and here are cooked with a classic crumb coating for some wholesome, homemade fast food. They are served with one of my favorite Asian sauces. Miso is a fermented soybean paste and is available in Asian markets, well-stocked supermarkets, and natural foods stores. Serve with baked regular or sweet potato fries and coleslaw. ❍ *Serves 4*

**COOKING METHOD:** Stovetop
**PREP TIME:** 15 minutes
**COOK TIME:** 15 minutes

ORANGE-MISO DIPPING SAUCE
1½ tablespoons yellow miso
3 tablespoons thawed frozen orange juice concentrate
1½ cups mayonnaise or soy-based mayonnaise
2 to 3 teaspoons toasted sesame oil
2 teaspoons grated fresh ginger
Grated zest of ½ orange

½ cup all-purpose flour
2 eggs
¼ teaspoon chili powder
¾ cup panko bread crumbs
1½ pounds chicken tenders
Pinch of salt and few grinds of black pepper
¼ cup canola or peanut oil

**1.** To make the dipping sauce, place the miso and juice concentrate in a small bowl. Use a fork to mash the miso into the juice. If it does not dissolve readily, place in the microwave for a minute to warm the juice slightly. Do not boil. Set aside to cool, if necessary. When cool, add the mayonnaise, oil, ginger, and zest; stir to combine. Refrigerate until ready to serve.

**2.** Place the flour in a gallon-size zipper-top plastic bag. Place the eggs and chili powder in a shallow bowl and beat well. Place the panko bread crumbs on a large plate.

**3.** Place the tenders in the plastic bag and shake to evenly coat, then dip in the egg, letting any extra drip off. Coat both sides with the panko crumbs, then sprinkle with some salt and pepper.

**4.** Heat 2 tablespoons of the oil in a large skillet over medium-high heat. Add half of the chicken and cook for 3 minutes, then turn and cook for another 3 to 5 minutes, until the juices run clear when pierced with a knife. Remove, set on a clean plate, and cover with aluminum foil. Repeat with the remaining oil and chicken. Serve immediately with the sauce on the side for dipping.

# Oven-Fried Drumsticks
# with IOU Pasta

**W**hile this does take a bit longer, it is still one of my favorite weeknight suppers. You want to seek out panko, crispy Japanese bread crumbs, and keep them on your pantry shelf; you can substitute fresh bread crumbs if you like. Panko is a secret weapon for making crisp outer coatings, because they are coarser and drier than regular bread crumbs. You can remove the chicken skin if you wish. You might want to make extra drumsticks, since they are great cold for lunch or a picnic. The IOU pasta is from my friend Oscar Mariscal, who was the chef at Saint Michael's Alley restaurant in the 1970s and '80s. It was a recipe from his mother, who used to say "Oh! IOU the sauce" as it was dished out. ○ *Serves 4*

**COOKING METHOD:** Oven and stovetop
**PREP TIME:** 20 minutes
**COOK TIME:** 50 to 60 minutes

½ cup (1 stick) unsalted butter
1¾ cups panko bread crumbs
16 chicken drumsticks (about 4 pounds), skinned if desired
Salt and a few grinds of black or white pepper

**IOU PASTA**
12 ounces spaghetti or linguine
2 tablespoons olive oil
2 cloves garlic, minced
⅓ red bell pepper, finely chopped
6 to 8 ounces zucchini, cut into 4-inch strips, or ½ head broccoli, cut into florets
5 green onions (white part and 2 inches of the green), chopped
⅓ teaspoon dried dillweed
2 tablespoons chopped fresh flat-leaf parsley
2 tablespoons fresh lemon juice
2 tablespoons dry white wine
½ cup grated Parmesan cheese

1. Preheat the oven to 350°F. Line a large baking sheet with parchment paper.

2. Melt the butter in a shallow bowl in the microwave or on the stovetop in a small saucepan. Place the panko on a plate. Dip each drumstick into the butter, then into the panko, rolling to coat the entire surface. Place in a single layer on the baking sheet and season with salt and pepper. Bake for 50 to 60 minutes, until browned and the juices run clear when pierced with a knife.

3. While the legs are roasting, make the pasta. Bring a large pot of salted water to a boil. Cook the pasta according to the package directions. Drain in a colander.

4. Meanwhile, heat the olive oil in a large skillet over medium-high heat. Add the garlic, bell pepper, and zucchini and cook, stirring frequently, until tender. Do not overcook. Add the pasta to the skillet and gently toss with the vegetables; add the green onions, dillweed, parsley, lemon juice, and white wine. Gently toss and boil the liquid until it evaporates a bit, 1 minute.

5. Divide the pasta among 4 dinner plates and sprinkle with the Parmesan. Pile the plate with 4 drumsticks and serve immediately.

# Sicilian Chicken Livers with Tiny Herb Pasta

**T**his is a lovely old-fashioned recipe from the late Vincent Schiavelli, who had the same literary agent as me; it appeared in his *Papa Andrea's Sicilian Table* (Citadel Press, 1993). Marsala wine gives a lovely counterpoint flavor to the richness of the livers, which are sold ready to use. Use a small pasta shape, such as *semi di melone*, tiny shells, or miniature bows, for the herbed pasta, or you can sreve this with steamed rice instead.  ❍ *Serves 4*

**COOKING METHOD:** Stovetop
**PREP TIME:** 15 minutes
**COOK TIME:** About 15 minutes

2 tablespoons unsalted butter
2 tablespoons olive oil
2 medium-size white onions, sliced and cut into half-moons
1 pound fresh chicken livers
¾ cup dry Marsala
Salt and freshly ground black pepper

TINY HERB PASTA
12 ounces tiny pasta (see above)
2 tablespoons unsalted butter
1½ tablespoons olive oil
Freshly ground black pepper
2 to 3 tablespoons mixed chopped fresh flat-leaf parsley and chives

**1.** Bring a pot of lightly salted water to a rapid boil for the pasta.

**2.** In a heavy skillet, melt the 2 tablespoons butter with the 2 tablespoons olive oil over medium heat. Add the onions and cook until golden, about 8 minutes. Turn up the heat to high and add the chicken livers. Cook for 5 minutes, stirring constantly to prevent sticking. Carefully pour in the Marsala and bring to a boil. Season with salt and pepper. Cook for a few minutes to thicken the sauce.

**3.** While the chicken livers cook, cook the pasta according to the package directions. Drain and pour into a serving bowl. Immediately add the butter, oil, a few grinds of pepper, and the herbs, tossing to coat. Portion onto individual plates and add the chicken livers and onions. Serve immediately.

Don't pass up a jar of marinara sauce, premade pie crust, frozen vegetables, or condensed soup as a savory aid to making your dish. (After all, sometimes our mothers did have the right ideas!) Often, making everything from scratch is just not possible, and many commercial products are now of a very high quality. Here are updated versions of three of my favorites.

# Chicken Divan Casserole

Of course you are thinking that casseroles take too long on a weeknight. Well, here is one of the tastiest versions of the delightful chicken Divan and most certainly the fastest I've ever come across. It originally came off the label of a can of Campbell's Cream of Chicken soup, and it is a winner. Nothing is precooked; all you do is chop the broccoli and layer the ingredients. Don't be tempted to add more cheese; it is supposed to be a whisper of flavor. Be sure to pound the chicken breasts a bit or else the dish will take longer to cook. Serve with peeled sweet potato chunks doused with some olive oil and roasted in the oven at the same time as the casserole. ○ Serves 4

**COOKING METHOD:** Oven
**PREP TIME:** 15 minutes
**COOK TIME:** 30 to 40 minutes

1 head broccoli, chopped (4 cups florets)
4 boneless, skinless chicken breast halves (about 1½ pounds), pounded to ½ inch thick
One 10¾-ounce can condensed cream of chicken soup
¼ cup milk
¼ cup dry white wine
½ cup shredded mild or sharp cheddar cheese
¼ cup plain fine dry bread crumbs
¼ cup grated Parmesan cheese
1 tablespoon unsalted butter

**1.** Preheat the oven to 350°F. Spray a deep 2-quart casserole dish with nonstick cooking spray.

**2.** Arrange the broccoli in an even layer over the bottom of the dish. Place the chicken breasts on top of the broccoli in a single layer. In a small bowl, whisk together the soup, milk, and wine; pour over the chicken and broccoli. Sprinkle with the cheddar cheese and dust with the bread crumbs, then the Parmesan. Dot the top with butter.

**3.** Bake for 30 to 40 minutes, uncovered, until the broccoli is tender and the chicken juices run clear when pierced with the tip of a knife. Use an oversized spoon to serve.

## Easiest Chicken Parm

This is the fastest and easiest recipe I know for the lovely Italian-American staple dinner dish, which I adapted from an advertisement for Prego Italian tomato sauce. You can pound the breasts slightly to flatten them more if you wish. Keep jars of your favorite marinara sauce in the pantry, some type of Italian melting cheese (I love provolone) and Parmesan in the fridge, and you are good to go. Serve with pasta, and please don't forget some fresh crusty bread to scoop up the delicious sauce.  ◉ Serves 4

**COOKING METHOD:** Stovetop
**PREP TIME:** 10 minutes
**COOK TIME:** 30 minutes

1½ tablespoons olive oil
4 boneless, skinless chicken breast halves (about 1½ pounds)
¼ cup grated Parmesan cheese, plus 3 tablespoons for sprinkling
1½ cups marinara sauce of your choice
Four ¼-inch-thick slices provolone, Italian fontina, scamorza, or whole-milk mozzarella cheese

**1.** Heat the oil in a 12-inch heavy skillet over medium-high heat. Add the chicken and cook for 10 minutes, until nicely browned; turn once to brown both sides.

**2.** Stir the ¼ cup of Parmesan cheese into the marinara sauce and add to the skillet. Cover and reduce the heat to a medium simmer. Cook for 10 to 15 minutes, until the chicken is cooked through (cut with a knife to check) and no pink is left.

**3.** Lay a slice of cheese over each breast and sprinkle with a bit more Parmesan. Cover and let stand for 5 minutes to melt the cheese. Serve immediately with some sauce spooned around the chicken.

## Classic Chicken Pot Pie

You will appreciate the convenience in this recipe from food writer Rick Rodgers, developed while he was writing a chicken book for Williams-Sonoma. It is easy enough for a weeknight dinner, as it uses frozen mixed vegetables and store-bought ready-to-roll-out pie crust, which are tremendous timesavers. "The secret of great pot pie is chicken thighs, as they stay juicy," says Rick, "whereas chicken breast can easily get overcooked and tough. I use the same formula with leftover turkey meat (consider a store-bought rotisserie turkey breast), allowing about 3 cups of cubed meat. I do sauté it briefly just to warm it up in the butter, then proceed with the flour and other ingredients to make the sauce." You need only a green salad to go with this one-dish meal.  ○ **Serves 4**

**COOKING METHOD:** Stovetop and oven
**PREP TIME:** 25 minutes
**COOK TIME:** About 50 minutes

2 tablespoons unsalted butter
4 boneless, skinless chicken thighs (about 1¼ pounds), trimmed and cut into ½-inch chunks
2 tablespoons chopped shallots
¼ cup all-purpose flour
1½ cups chicken broth
½ cup dry white wine
½ cup half-and-half
1 tablespoon chopped fresh flat-leaf parsley
One 1-pound bag thawed frozen vegetable medley (use your favorite blend, such as carrots, corn, green beans, and peas)
Salt and freshly ground black pepper
One 1-pound package roll-out refrigerated pie crust
1 egg yolk mixed with 1 teaspoon water, for glaze

**1.** Preheat the oven to 400°F with the rack in the center position. Grease a 9-inch deep-dish Pyrex or ceramic pie plate.

**2.** In a large skillet, melt the butter over medium-high heat. Add the chicken and cook uncovered, turning once, until browned on both sides, about 8 minutes. Add the shallots and cook until softened, about 2 minutes. Sprinkle with the flour and stir to coat well. Stir in the broth, wine, half-and-half, and parsley and bring to a simmer. Cover and reduce the heat to low. Simmer for 10 minutes. Stir in the thawed vegetables. Season with salt and pepper and pour into the pie plate.

**3.** Roll out the pie crust to a 10-inch diameter and brush the egg glaze in a 1-inch-wide border around the outside of the crust. Place the crust, egg side down, over the filling and press the crust onto the sides of the dish to seal; it is okay if it is a bit uneven. Brush the top of the crust lightly with the egg glaze. Cut a few slits in the crust with the tip of a knife. Place the pan on a baking sheet to catch drips.

**4.** Bake until the crust is golden brown, about 30 minutes. Serve immediately, portioning the filling and some crust with an oversized spoon while hot.

# Turkey or Chicken Marsala with Olive Couscous

I adore Marsala, which is a fortified wine made in the same manner as sherry, named after the Sicilian seaport of the same name. I use dry Marsala in cooking and wouldn't go a week without serving a Marsala dish of some type. Serve with seasonal steamed mixed vegetables. If you like, you can serve this with fettucine or rice instead of the couscous.  ○ *Serves 4*

**COOKING METHOD:** Stovetop
**PREP TIME:** 20 minutes
**COOK TIME:** About 20 minutes

4 large turkey breast cutlets or boneless, skinless chicken breast halves
  (about 1½ pounds), pounded thin
Salt and freshly ground black pepper
½ cup all-purpose flour or oat flour (made by grinding quick-cooking
  or old-fashioned oats in a blender or food processor), for dredging
3 tablespoons unsalted butter
3 tablespoons olive oil
8 ounces fresh white mushrooms, sliced
1 cup dry Marsala
Juice of 1 lemon
8 ounces frozen artichoke hearts, thawed and halved

COUSCOUS
1⅓ cups couscous
3 tablespoons olive oil
2 cups water, vegetable broth, or chicken broth
Juice of 1 lemon
8 pitted black olives, quartered

**1.** Season the turkey with salt and pepper. Place the flour on a flat plate and lightly dredge the breasts on both sides.

**2.** In a large skillet over medium-high heat, melt 1 tablespoon of the butter. Sauté the turkey in two batches, adding another tablespoon of the butter for the second batch, until golden brown and a bit crispy, 2 to 3 minutes, turning once. Remove the meat to a platter and cover with aluminum foil to keep warm.

**3.** Add the remaining 1 tablespoon butter and the olive oil to the skillet and sauté the mushrooms until soft. Pour the Marsala and lemon juice into the skillet. Bring to a low boil and stir for a few minutes to evaporate the alcohol, dissolve the brown bits on the bottom of the pan, and thicken slightly.

**4.** Return the breasts to the skillet and add the artichoke hearts; partially cover. Simmer until hot, about 5 minutes, depending on the thickness of the breast, but be careful not to overcook.

**5.** To make the couscous, place the couscous in a heatproof bowl, add the oil, and toss with a fork to coat the grains. Add the water and stir; let the couscous sit for 5 to 8 minutes to absorb the water. Cover with plastic wrap or a microwave-proof lid and microwave on High for 5 minutes, until hot and steamy. Squeeze a bit of lemon juice over the top, add the olives, and fluff with a fork.

**6.** Place a breast on each dinner plate. Spoon the sauce over the top and serve with the couscous.

# Turkey Cutlets with Cherry Sauce and Saffron Mashed Potatoes

I am just mad for this sauce. Talk about easy! I am always looking for ways to use hot pepper jelly as more than just a glaze or as a spread over cream cheese on crackers. Here canned cherries, a nice pantry staple, are heated with the jalapeño jelly and served as a sauce over the simple sautéed turkey cutlet. A nice green salad rounds out the meal. ● *Serves 4*

**COOKING METHOD:** Stovetop
**PREP TIME:** 20 minutes
**COOK TIME:** About 25 minutes

SAFFRON MASHED POTATOES

2 pounds russet potatoes, peeled and cut into chunks

Pinch of saffron threads

2 tablespoons boiling water

½ cup half-and-half or whole milk

4 tablespoons extra virgin olive oil

Salt

CHERRY SAUCE

One 15-ounce can pitted dark sweet cherries, drained

¾ cup hot jalapeño jelly

4 large turkey breast cutlets (about 1½ pounds)

Salt and freshly ground black pepper

½ cup all-purpose flour or oat flour (made by grinding quick-cooking or old-fashioned oats in a blender or food processor), for dredging

3 tablespoons unsalted butter

**1.** To make the mashed potatoes, place the potatoes in a medium-size saucepan and cover with cold water. Bring to a boil, then reduce to a simmer and cook until tender, about 20 minutes. Meanwhile, place the saffron in a small bowl with the boiling water; set aside for 10 minutes. Heat the half-and-half to a simmer in a small saucepan or in the microwave. Drain the potatoes and return them to the pan. Add the saffron water, hot cream, and olive oil. Mash with a fork or potato masher until chunky. Season with salt.

**2.** To make the sauce, combine the cherries and jelly in a small saucepan or microwave-proof bowl. Bring to a boil to melt the jelly. Stir to coat the cherries. Set aside and keep warm.

**3.** Season the turkey cutlets with salt and pepper. Place the flour on a flat plate and lightly dredge the breasts on both sides. In a large skillet over medium-high heat, melt the butter. Sauté the turkey, in batches if necessary, until golden brown and a bit crispy, 2 to 3 minutes per side, turning once.

**4.** Portion a mound of potatoes and a turkey cutlet on individual dinner plates; spoon the sauce over the turkey. Serve immediately.

# Roast Turkey Tenderloin with Citrus Wine Sauce

R oasted tenderloins are so magnificent! They are small enough to cook quickly in the oven, yet are as full of flavor as the big bird itself. I give you a classic French sauce that is based on *beurre blanc* but is lower in fat, and that frankly tastes good on everything but ice cream. You can use regular store-bought lemons or Meyer lemons, which are rather sweet, if you can get them. I keep extra Meyer lemon juice in the freezer in an ice cube tray, and just pull out cubes when I need them. But if pressed for time, you can skip the sauce and serve the turkey with some good-quality store-bought chutney. Either way, serve with steamed broccoli or cauliflower. ○ *Serves 4*

**COOKING METHOD:** Oven and stovetop
**PREP TIME:** 35 minutes
**COOK TIME:** About 30 minutes

⅓ cup dry white wine
1 small clove garlic, crushed
Pinch of fresh or dried thyme leaves
¼ teaspoon salt
¼ teaspoon freshly ground black or white pepper
Few shakes of hot sauce, such as Tabasco or Pickapeppa
1 bay leaf
1½ pounds turkey tenderloins

**SAUCE**
1½ cups chicken broth
1½ cups dry white wine
1 tablespoon Dijon mustard
9 tablespoons cold unsalted butter, cut into pieces
Juice of 1 lemon

**1.** In a gallon-size zipper-top plastic bag, combine the wine, garlic, thyme, salt, pepper, hot sauce, and bay leaf. Add the tenderloins; seal the bag and roll them around to coat; refrigerate for 30 minutes.

**2.** Preheat the oven to 350°F.

**3.** Place the tenderloins side by side with some space between them in a 10 × 15-inch ceramic or metal roasting pan sprayed with nonstick cooking spray. Drizzle with the marinade. Roast the tenderloins for 25 to 30 minutes, or until the turkey is no longer pink in the center and reaches 160° to 165°F on an instant-read thermometer.

**4.** While the turkey is cooking, make the sauce. Place the broth and wine in a medium-size saucepan over medium-high heat and bring to a boil. Reduce to 1 cup. Whisk in the mustard, then the butter pieces until melted. Add the lemon juice and stir to combine. Set aside, covered, and keep warm.

**5.** Transfer the tenderloins to a cutting board and tent with foil to keep warm. Let stand for 5 minutes before carving. Slice the turkey and serve with the sauce.

# ·· Steamed Seasonal Vegetables ··

Many of my main-dish offerings go well with simple vegetables steamed in a modicum of water and maybe served with some salt and pepper, a bit of unsalted butter, Parmesan cheese, or a drizzle of olive oil. Steaming in the microwave or on the stovetop is the best technique for the weeknight cook. A combination of two or three different seasonal vegetables tastes the best. Chop or slice them into similar sizes for even cooking. ⊙ Serves 4

| SPRING AND SUMMER VEGETABLES | FALL AND WINTER VEGETABLES |
|---|---|
| Red, green, or yellow bell peppers, sliced | Rutabagas, diced |
| Zucchini, pattypan, or yellow crookneck summer squash, sliced | Parsnips, diced |
| | Fennel, sliced |
| Mushrooms, quartered | Kale, chopped |
| Asparagus | Carrots, sliced |
| Celery, sliced | Cauliflower florets |
| Leeks, coarsely chopped | Broccoli florets |
| Shallots or green onions (white and some of the green part), coarsely chopped | Onion wedges |
| | Whole white, red, or gold pearl onions |
| Snow peas, sugar snap peas, or English garden peas | Winter squash, peeled and diced |
| | Frozen mixed petite peas and artichoke hearts |
| Fresh corn sliced off the cob | Edamame |
| Baby bok choy | Zucchini, sliced |
| Broccolini florets | Canned hearts of palm |

If making in the microwave, use a 1-quart glass bowl or microwave-proof dish. Add the vegetables and 2 tablespoons water. Cover, leaving a small space for steam to escape, with microwave-proof plastic wrap, a paper plate, a piece of parchment paper, or a microwave-safe lid. Microwave for about 5 minutes, depending on your microwave, until crisp-tender. (Winter root vegetables will take approximately twice as long as summer vegetables.) Drain off the water and serve hot.

To cook on the stovetop, pour enough water into a deep saucepan to come up about 1 inch. Set a steamer basket in the pot, cover, and bring to a boil over high heat. Place the vegetables in the basket, cover, and steam summer vegetables for 5 minutes and harder winter vegetables for 10 minutes, or until crisp-tender. Remove the steamer from the pot with a potholder and serve immediately.

# Supper Specials:
# Meat

Whether beef, veal, pork, or lamb, meat is the potent flavor that satisfies. Lean cuts in individual portions, along with beef and pork tenderloin and rack of lamb, are the best bets for weeknight dinners. And, of course, there is all manner of ground meat for burgers.

When buying meat, shop at a market you trust, ask questions, and take the advice of butchers. There is a wide array of beef steaks from which to choose, and they are popular because they cook so quickly and are very tender. Beef is categorized by grade, which means the higher the grade, the more marbling. Choose from the top three: Prime (from steers), Choice, and Select. Ground beef, sausages, and other processed meats can come from the lower grades.

The best cuts for weeknight cooking are the tender cuts from the less frequently used muscles at the rear of the animal, including the rib and loin. This translates into such everyday terms as the rib-eye (also known as the Delmonico or market steak), which has a bit of a fatty patch but is known for being so flavorful; the boneless top loin (also known as New York strip, strip steak, or sirloin strip steak); the most tender tenderloin slice (a filet mignon or fillet steak); the top sirloin (also known as the shell sirloin), which is less tender than the other steaks but very popular and economical; the Porterhouse and T-bone, which have a strip of New York steak and a little piece of fillet; the flank steak; and the hard-to-find restaurant favorite, flat-iron steak or blade steak. Steaks are easily pan seared, but times vary due to thickness, size, and shape.

Veal comes from a calf less than three months old, and many people avoid this meat because of that, as well as because of the conditions under which the animals are raised. But veal remains a restaurant favorite for its lovely delicate flavor and tenderness, and there are now farms that raise veal under humane conditions; look for meat labeled "Free-Farmed." Veal is not graded, so buy a favorite brand.

For pork weeknight cooking, there are bone-in center-cut and rib chops, boneless pork loin chops, and pork tenderloin (see page 115). Pork is known for being low-fat now, since pigs are bred to have less than half the fat they did just 30 years ago. It is pale pink and graded by the amount of fat, such as USDA 1, which is the leanest. Loosen any tight packaging while storing in the refrigerator. Smoked and cured pork, such as bacon, can be stored in the coldest part of the refrigerator for 2 weeks, or up to the freshness date stamped on the package.

For delicate and tender lamb, there are small loin chops and the rib chops cut into portions off the rack. The most common grade is Choice. I prefer American lamb as opposed to imported lamb, due to its milder flavor.

While supermarkets and gourmet butcher shops carry a wide variety of meats, there is a new movement in the meat industry to provide artisan meats. This means small farms; humanely treated, antibiotic-free animals that are not fed meat byproducts; and old-fashioned hand-butchering methods that assure the top quality many gourmets crave. Many people who have shunned meat eating in protest for decades are now coming back to enjoy the artisan meat revolution.

All meats are perishable and should be handled and stored properly to avoid spoilage and food-borne illness. After purchase, refrigerate for up to 2 days before cooking. To maintain quality in the freezer, rewrap the meat tightly in heavy-duty freezer wrap or a resealable plastic freezer bag to prevent freezer burn. Freeze for up to 3 to 4 months on average. Thaw frozen meat in the refrigerator overnight. Leave it in the freezer wrap and put it on a plate to keep juices from dripping onto other foods. It will take 3 to 5 hours per pound to thaw meat in the refrigerator. When cooking, use a meat thermometer to make sure the meat is cooked to the desired doneness. Refrigerate leftovers promptly after serving and store no longer than 4 days.

# Rib-Eyes with Red Wine Pan Sauce

**R**ed wine pan sauce can make even a simple hamburger really special. But here it is paired with a rib-eye, which is basically a standing rib roast cut into individual portions and deboned. It is tender and tasty, though not as lean as a trimmed fillet. You can use this all-purpose sauce on any manner of beef steak. Even with a large skillet, plan on cooking the steaks in two shifts, since only two will fit in the pan at one time. Serve with simple steamed green beans, broccoli, or asparagus. ○ *Serves 4*

**COOKING METHOD:** Stovetop
**PREP TIME:** 10 minutes
**COOK TIME:** About 15 minutes

Four 7- to 8-ounce rib-eye steaks
Salt and freshly ground black pepper
1 tablespoon olive oil
¼ cup (½ stick) unsalted butter
2 tablespoons finely chopped shallots
¾ cup dry red wine, such as Cabernet or Zinfandel
1 cup beef or chicken broth
1 tablespoon balsamic vinegar
2 teaspoons Dijon mustard

**1.** Pat the steak dry with paper towels and sprinkle with salt and pepper. In a large skillet or sauté pan over medium-high heat, add the olive oil. Add the steaks to the hot pan and cook for 3 minutes per side for medium-rare, 4 minutes for medium, and 5 minutes for well done. Remove from the pan to a platter and cover with aluminum foil to keep warm.

**2.** Pour off any fat from the pan. Reduce the heat to medium and add 2 tablespoons of the butter. Add the shallots and cook until softened but not brown, 1 to 2 minutes. Add the wine and cook for 30 seconds. Add the broth, vinegar, and mustard and bring to a full rolling boil over high heat, stirring to dissolve the brown particles that cling to the pan. Continue to cook until the liquid is reduced by half and thickened, 3 to 4 minutes. Remove from the heat.

**3.** Cut the remaining 2 tablespoons butter into small pieces; toss into the pan and whisk until dissolved. Place the steaks on dinner plates and top each with about 3 tablespoons of the red wine sauce. Serve immediately.

## ·· What a Meat Mallet Is and How to Use It ··

Many boneless cuts of meat and poultry need to be pounded into a thin piece of even thickness to cook quickly. To achieve the perfect cutlet, it cannot be too thin, or it will dry out before it is browned, or too thick, because the interior will not cook by the time the cutlet is browned. The pounding makes the meat tender, too, breaking down the natural connective tissue.

For pork, use the loin and cut across the grain. Whole chicken breasts are cut in half, and turkey is cut from the tenderloin (turkey cutlet slices are easily found in meat cases). Cut into ½-inch-thick slices. Even if you think you don't need to pound, the cutlets need to be about ¼ inch thick, and to get an even slice with just the knife is quite difficult.

When getting ready to pound, place the meat piece in a gallon-size zipper-top plastic bag for the best shaping and no cleanup. The freezer plastic bags are best, as they can hold up to the pounding action without tearing. Then choose your mallet. The most common type is metal or wood that has a flat side and a waffle-like side and a long handle for leverage. There is a small heavy mallet especially for veal that has a large flat side and a short handle that you work with your hand in a fist. No mallet? Use a heavy saucepan bottom or a full wine bottle wrapped in plastic wrap.

The technique is simple and fast. Pound gently with the flat side of your mallet, not the waffled side, which is used strictly for tenderizing. Strike a few times until the meat is even, and you will have your perfect cutlet.

# Pan-Seared Sirloin Shell Steak with Food Processor Béarnaise Sauce

**W**ith the aid of a trusty food processor, béarnaise sauce is just moments away. Use a fabulous red wine vinegar, such as a Merlot vinegar; you will notice the difference. The delightful boneless sirloin shell steak is very tender, despite coming from the top of the hip (top butt), and with a quick flash in the pan, it is ready for dinner. Top sirloin steaks can run large, about 1 pound per steak; if that is what you buy, plan on one steak for two people, and then slice it against the grain on the bias like flank steak. Often sirloin shell steaks are precut into 8- to 10-ounce individual square steaks with no fat except some light marbling. If you like, substitute a New York (boneless top sirloin) or a Porterhouse (with bone). Make the sauce first, as the sautéing goes fast. Serve with sautéed mixed peppers and zucchini and Steamed New Potatoes with White Wine (page 105). ● *Serves 4*

**COOKING METHOD:** Stovetop
**PREP TIME:** 20 minutes
**COOK TIME:** About 15 minutes

FOOD PROCESSOR BÉARNAISE SAUCE
2 large shallots, minced
½ cup top-quality red wine vinegar
3 egg yolks
¾ cup (1½ sticks) unsalted butter, melted and hot
1 tablespoon minced fresh tarragon leaves
1 tablespoon fresh lemon juice
Salt and freshly ground black or white pepper

Four 8- to 10-ounce boneless sirloin shell steaks
Salt and freshly ground black pepper
2 tablespoons grapeseed or vegetable oil

**1.** To make the sauce, combine the shallots and vinegar in a saucepan. Bring to a boil and let boil until reduced by half, about 5 minutes. Pour into a food processor. (You can strain the vinegar into the food processor, or just dump it in with the shallots.) Cool for 5 minutes. Add the egg yolks and pulse to combine. With the machine running, slowly drizzle in the hot butter; the sauce will naturally thicken. Pour into a small saucepan, stir in the tarragon and lemon juice, and season with salt and pepper. Set over very low heat to keep warm.

**2.** Pat the steaks dry with paper towels and sprinkle with salt and pepper. In a large skillet or sauté pan over medium-high heat, add the oil. Add the steaks to the hot pan and cook for 3 minutes on each side for medium-rare, 4 minutes for medium, and 5 minutes for well done. Remove from the pan to a platter, cover with aluminum foil, and let sit for 10 minutes before slicing against the grain into ¼-inch-thick slices.

**3.** Place the slices of steak on dinner plates and top each portion with about 3 tablespoons of the béarnaise. Serve immediately.

# Fillet of Beef with Mushroom Stroganoff Sauce

Usually thin strips of beef cooked in a roux-based sauce enriched with sour cream, stroganoff gets a facelift here to cater to quicker cooking methods and lighter palates. Sometimes I see packages of fillet tail ends, and I grab them for this dish (they are great to stash in the freezer). Note the cooking method for the fillets. Plain pan sautéing overcooks the surface and leaves the center uncooked, so I've used the secret method of professionals: both the stovetop and the oven. Serve with hot cooked rice or kasha and a steamed green vegetable on the side. ○ *Serves 4*

**COOKING METHOD:** Stovetop and broiler
**PREP TIME:** 20 minutes
**COOK TIME:** About 30 minutes

Four 8-ounce beef tenderloin steaks (tail ends okay)
Salt and freshly ground black pepper
1 tablespoon olive oil
7 tablespoons unsalted butter
2 medium-size yellow onions, cut in half and sliced into half-moons
1 tablespoon sweet paprika
12 ounces fresh white mushrooms, thinly sliced
8 ounces fresh wild mushrooms of your choice, thinly sliced or quartered if small
¾ cup beef broth
1 teaspoon lemon zest
½ cup sour cream (regular or reduced-fat)

**1.** Preheat the oven to 350°F. Line a large rimmed baking sheet with parchment paper.

**2.** Season the steaks with salt and pepper. In a large skillet, heat the oil over medium-high heat. This can also be done on a ridged grill pan. Add the steaks, leaving some room in between them. Cook for 3 to 4 minutes, then turn over with tongs and cook for 3 minutes on the second side, until browned. Transfer to the baking sheet and roast in the oven for 15 to 20 minutes (for medium-rare).

**3.** While the steaks are cooking, make the sauce. In the same skillet, melt 3 tablespoons of the butter over medium heat. Add the onions and cook until tender, soft, and translucent, about 10 minutes. Sprinkle with the paprika and cook a few minutes longer to heat the spice. Remove the onions to a plate and add the remaining 4 tablespoons butter to the skillet. Raise the heat to high and add the mushrooms; they will give off their liquid and shrink a lot as they cook. Let the liquid evaporate a bit. Add the cooked onions, broth, and zest. Bring to a low boil and cook for 5 minutes. Reduce to the lowest heat and stir in the sour cream; simmer until hot, 2 minutes.

**4.** Transfer each steak to a dinner plate and spoon the stroganoff sauce over them. Serve immediately.

**Note:** If you are using tail ends, place two tails together with opposite ends touching, to make a solid and even section of meat for most efficient cooking.

# Roasted London Broil and Succotash

**T**here are just not enough recipes out there for London broil, that big slab of lean top round. It is homey enough for a weeknight supper, but fancy enough to be served at your family wedding. It cooks in less than 20 minutes with high heat. London broil is sliced and served like roast beef. While Dijon mustard is what we all seem to have in the refrigerator door, any sharp or sweet artisan mustard will do. Succotash, the humble, lip-smackingly good vegetable combination of corn, lima beans, and peppers, is a great side dish. ● *Serves 4*

**COOKING METHOD:** Stovetop and oven
**PREP TIME:** 20 minutes
**COOK TIME:** 30 to 40 minutes

SUCCOTASH
1 tablespoon olive oil
1 small white boiling onion, minced (2 to 3 tablespoons)
½ red bell pepper, minced
Salt and freshly ground black pepper
¼ teaspoon ground ginger
One 10-ounce package frozen baby white corn, thawed
One10-ounce package frozen lima beans (not baby limas), thawed
1 cup water
1 tablespoon butter (optional)

Salt and freshly ground black pepper
One 1- to 1½-pound top-round London broil, trimmed
3 tablespoons Dijon mustard
1½ teaspoons tequila
1 shallot, minced
1 cup panko bread crumbs
Olive oil cooking spray

**1.** To make the succotash, heat the olive oil in a medium-size saucepan over medium heat. Cook the onion and pepper until soft. Season liberally with salt and pepper and sprinkle in the ginger. Add the corn, lima beans, and water. Bring to a low boil, then cover and lower the heat to a simmer. Cook for 8 to 10 minutes, until the beans and corn are tender. Remove the lid, stir, and cook for a few more minutes to let all the water evaporate. Cover and set aside on a warm burner until ready to serve. If you are naughty, plop a hunk of butter in the pan.

**2.** Preheat the oven to 450°F and adjust the oven rack to the top position. Line a metal roasting pan with aluminum foil and fit it with a wire rack.

**3.** Rub salt and pepper into both sides of the London broil. Combine the mustard, tequila, and shallot in a small bowl. With a small metal spatula, coat the meat.

**4.** Place the panko on a flat plate and place the London broil on the crumbs; press the meat into the crumbs and the crumbs all over the meat so they stick to the mustard glaze. Place the meat on the rack and spray all over with olive oil cooking spray (this moistens the crumbs a little).

**5.** Roast for 18 to 26 minutes (16 to 18 minutes per pound), until the crumb coating is golden; the temperature will be 130°F on an instant-read thermometer for medium-rare (or cook to the desired doneness). Remove from the oven and transfer to a carving board. Let rest for 10 minutes, then carve into ½-inch-thick strips. Serve immediately with the hot succotash.

# Roasted Beef Tenderloin with Cannellini Beans

**B**eef tenderloin, aka filet mignon, comes in a long strip and is best roasted just like a regular roast beef. But unlike other cuts, it roasts very quickly. Here is a fast, elegant, and delicious weeknight dinner, with a simple side of white beans, parsley, and olive oil. The beans can be pureed if you want to have a different texture dimension. Serve with a fresh baguette and a green salad. ● *Serves 4*

**COOKING METHOD:** Oven and microwave
**PREP TIME:** 15 minutes
**COOK TIME:** About 30 minutes

One 3- to 3½-pound trimmed and tied center-cut beef tenderloin roast
1½ tablespoons olive oil
½ teaspoon crumbled dried thyme or mixed Italian herbs
Salt and freshly ground black pepper
Two 15-ounce cans cannellini beans, rinsed and drained
About ⅓ cup extra virgin olive oil
Zest of 1 lemon
2 to 3 tablespoons minced fresh flat-leaf parsley

1. Preheat the oven to 425°F.

2. Place the roast in a shallow roasting pan, rub the roast with the olive oil, then season it all over with the thyme, salt, and pepper. Place in the oven and roast for 30 minutes, until an instant-read thermometer reads 120°F for rare, or to the desired degree of doneness. Remove the meat to a cutting board and cover with aluminum foil. Let stand for 10 minutes. (The meat will continue to cook and the temperature will rise approximately 10 more degrees, making it medium-rare.)

3. While the roast is sitting, heat the beans in the microwave. Remove and toss with enough olive oil to evenly moisten them. Toss with the lemon zest and parsley.

4. Cut the tenderloin into ½-inch-thick slices and arrange on individual dinner plates. Spoon some beans on the side and serve immediately.

## •• When Is My Steak Done? ••

When you get the "touch" of how meat feels while cooking, you won't have to cut into the steak anymore. Check the doneness by pressing the meat with your fingers. When it is resilient on the outside but feels softer as you press a little deeper, it is still rare. This is how professional chefs do it, since a steak is too thin for a thermometer probe. With a little practice you can do it, too.

| Steak (1½ inches thick) | Timing Per Side (medium-high heat) | Touch Test |
| --- | --- | --- |
| Rare | 2 to 3 minutes | Very soft |
| Medium-rare | 3 to 4 minutes | Soft |
| Medium | 4 to 4½ minutes | Springy |
| Medium-well | 4 to 5 minutes | Firm |
| Well | 5 to 6 minutes | Very firm |

# Salisbury Steak and
# Garlic Mashed Potatoes

**S**alisbury steak was one of the first TV dinners ever. I remember we thought it quite a treat on the nights my parents were going out for dinner, since my mother was an accomplished home cook and we didn't often have prepared commercial food. It is a preparation that has become overlooked because it is very old-fashioned, but it's still a tasty dinner, and kids adore it. Yes, this recipe calls for a can of condensed soup, one of the few in this book. I have tried different sauces from scratch, but this one tastes the best and is certainly as easy as can be. The secret to the best garlic mashed potatoes? Cook the garlic with the potatoes. Do not add raw garlic to the cooked potatoes or the flavor will be too strong. ● *Serves 4*

**COOKING METHOD:** Oven and stovetop
**PREP TIME:** 20 minutes
**COOK TIME:** 40 minutes

1½ pounds ground beef chuck
1 egg, beaten
½ cup plain dry bread crumbs
¼ cup minced onion or shallots
½ teaspoon salt, or to your taste
Dash of ground allspice
One 10¾-ounce can condensed Golden Mushroom soup
⅓ cup water
Freshly ground black pepper

**GARLIC MASHED POTATOES**
4 large russet potatoes (1¾ to 2 pounds), peeled and cut into chunks
4 to 6 large cloves garlic
1½ teaspoons salt
½ cup milk
¼ cup (½ stick) unsalted butter

**1.** Preheat the oven to 350°F.

**2.** In a small bowl, combine the meat, egg, bread crumbs, onion, salt, allspice, and ¼ cup of the condensed soup with a fork or your hands. Shape into 4 oval patties, each 1 inch thick. Arrange in a single layer in a shallow roasting pan. Place in the oven and bake for 30 minutes; spoon off the fat or soak it up with paper towels.

**3.** While the meat is cooking, make the potatoes. In a medium-size saucepan, cover the potatoes with cold water. Add the garlic cloves and salt and bring to a boil over high heat. Turn the heat down to medium and simmer the potatoes until tender when pierced with the tip of a knife, 15 to 20 minutes; do not overcook or the potatoes will get watery. Immediately drain the potatoes and return them to the pot.

**4.** Heat the milk and butter in the microwave. Mash the potatoes with a potato masher, adding the milk and butter slowly to get the right consistency. You can use a handheld electric mixer in place of the hand masher, but do not use a food processor or immersion blender. Cover and set aside.

**5.** In a small bowl, whisk together the remaining soup, the water, and some pepper. Pour over the patties in the roasting pan. Return to the oven and cook an additional 10 minutes.

**6.** Place a patty on each plate and a big scoop of potatoes alongside. Spoon the sauce over the patties (and potatoes, if desired) and serve immediately.

# Flank Steak Broccoli Beef

**F**lank steak is a relatively low-fat cut of beef, as well as very flavorful, and when prepared in a quick sauté with fresh broccoli, you can understand why it is one of the most beloved of Chinese home-cooked dishes. This recipe comes from one of the unsung heroes of southern Bay Area cooking teachers, Lily Chinn, who, after teaching for 25 years, self-published her class recipes and has gone on to become a bit of a local phenomenon. You will see why; this is simple and sensible, and the flavors of the ingredients really stand out. You may think you need a wok to prepare stir-fries, but a heavy skillet will do just fine. Serve with plain steamed rice. ● *Serves 4*

**COOKING METHOD:** Stovetop
**PREP TIME:** 15 minutes
**COOK TIME:** About 12 minutes

1¼ pounds flank steak, sliced diagonally across
    the grain into ½-inch-thick slices
1 tablespoon cornstarch
1 tablespoon low-sodium soy sauce
1 clove garlic, crushed
3 to 4 slices fresh ginger, minced
5 tablespoons vegetable, grapeseed, or peanut oil
4 cups chopped broccoli, tops cut into 1-inch florets and stems cut
    into thin 1-inch-long pieces
Salt
3 to 4 tablespoons water

GRAVY
1 tablespoon cornstarch
1 tablespoon low-sodium soy sauce
1 to 2 tablespoons oyster sauce
½ cup water

**1.** In a bowl, combine the steak with the cornstarch, soy sauce, garlic, and ginger. Set aside.

**2.** In a large heavy skillet or wok, heat 3 tablespoons of the oil over high heat. Add the broccoli and season with some salt; sauté for 1 minute. Add the water, and cover and steam until barely tender, 3 to 4 minutes, lowering the heat to prevent scorching. Remove the broccoli from the pan to a bowl.

**3.** Readjust the heat to high and add 1 tablespoon of the remaining oil to the skillet. Add half the steak mixture to the hot skillet (so as not to crowd), and sauté until browned on the outside and pink on the inside, 1 to 2 minutes only. Remove to the bowl with the broccoli. Add the remaining 1 tablespoon oil and sauté the remaining beef. Set aside.

**4.** In a small bowl, make the gravy by whisking together the cornstarch, soy sauce, oyster sauce, and water; pour into the skillet and stir, letting the gravy bubble up. Return the first batch of beef and the broccoli to the pan with the beef, cooking and tossing until hot and blended. Serve immediately.

# Oven-Barbecued Beef Ribs with Veggie Packets

This is a knockout meal-in-one favorite with young diners, especially those who love to eat with their fingers. Pork ribs take hours to come to tenderness, but not so with beef ribs. While the prep time is about 15 minutes, this meal will take about 50 minutes in the oven. You can brush the ribs with my simple stir-together barbecue sauce or your favorite bottled barbecue sauce. Consider serving cornbread on the side. ● *Serves 4*

**COOKING METHOD:** Oven
**PREP TIME:** 15 to 20 minutes
**COOK TIME:** About 50 minutes

MAPLE BARBECUE SAUCE

1 cup ketchup

¼ cup firmly packed light brown sugar

3 tablespoons maple syrup

2 tablespoons tomato paste

2 tablespoons Dijon mustard

Few splashes of Tabasco sauce

1 teaspoon chili powder

1 teaspoon ground cinnamon

1 tablespoon red wine vinegar

4 to 4½ pounds beef ribs

VEGGIE PACKETS

2 ears fresh corn, husked and halved

½ bunch broccoli, broken into florets (about 2 cups)

1 red or yellow bell pepper, quartered, quarters cut into 6 slices each

4 medium-size red potatoes, thinly sliced

½ cup (1 stick) unsalted butter

Salt and freshly ground black pepper

1. Preheat the oven to 400°F. Place the oven racks in the upper- and lower-third positions.

2. To make the barbecue sauce, combine all the ingredients in a deep plastic or glass container and stir until well blended. Use at once or cover and refrigerate for up to 2 weeks.

3. Line a large baking sheet with aluminum foil and arrange the ribs on the pan. Brush with a thick coating of the barbecue sauce.

4. To make the veggie packets, tear off 8 pieces of aluminum foil 12 to 16 inches in length. Using a double thickness of foil for each packet, arrange a piece of corn, some broccoli, red pepper pieces, and potato slices on top in the center. Dot each with 2 teaspoons of butter and season with salt and pepper. Fold up the packets and pinch the ends to seal. Place on a baking sheet on the lower rack of the oven. Place the ribs on the upper rack. Bake for 40 to 50 minutes, until the ribs are tender and browned.

5. Open a veggie packet and pierce the potatoes and corn with the tip of a knife to see if they are tender. Place some ribs and a veggie packet on individual dinner plates, letting diners open the veggie packets themselves.

# Horseradish Meatloaf

**A** large meatloaf can take over an hour to cook, but the individual meat-loaves in this recipe take only half an hour. The best bread crumbs are made with fresh bread, ground in the food processor, then oven-dried at 300°F for 8 to 10 minutes. Serve with Smashed Potatoes with Green Onions and Sour Cream (right) or egg noodles and corn or steamed carrots. ● *Serves 6*

**COOKING METHOD:** Oven
**PREP TIME:** 15 minutes
**COOK TIME:** 30 to 35 minutes

1 tablespoon olive oil
¾ cup minced white onion
¼ cup finely chopped green bell pepper
2 large eggs
2½ pounds ground beef chuck
2 cups toasted coarse fresh bread crumbs (see above)
2½ tablespoons bottled creamed horseradish
⅓ cup milk or low-sodium chicken broth
¾ cup ketchup
1 teaspoon Dijon mustard
1 teaspoon salt

**1.** Preheat the oven to 400°F. Line a rimmed baking sheet with parchment paper.

**2.** In a medium-size sauté pan, heat the oil. Add the onion and bell pepper and cook over medium heat until the onions are translucent but not browned, about 5 minutes. Remove from the heat and cool slightly.

**3.** In a large mixing bowl, beat the eggs with a fork. Add the meat and mix with your hands until well blended. Add the bread crumbs; mix well. Add the onion mixture, horseradish, milk, ¼ cup of the ketchup, the mustard, and salt; mix lightly with a fork. Don't mash too hard or the meatloaf will be too dense.

**4.** Divide the mixture into 6 portions and shape each into a small, fat oval loaf. Place on the baking sheet with at least 2 inches in between each loaf and spread the tops with the remaining ½ cup ketchup. Bake for 30 to 35 minutes, until cooked through and the internal temperature is 155° to 160°F. Serve hot.

Potatoes go with meat (and everything else for that matter, even pasta in some regions of Italy). It's one of the laws of culinary attraction. Here are a few excellent potato side dishes, all a bit novel, to serve with your steaks and chops.

## Smashed Potatoes with Green Onions and Sour Cream

Really these are known as my little sister's outrageously good, chunky, smashed potatoes. While mashed potatoes are smooth and creamy, smashed potatoes are mashed with a fork and left chunky and uneven in texture, which surprisingly gives an entirely different taste. It is important not to peel the potatoes; you want the bits of skin in these. I am saying this serves four, but it has been known to feed only two potato cravers.  **○ Serves 4**

**8 large red or Yukon Gold potatoes (about 2 pounds), halved**
**1 teaspoon salt, plus more for seasoning**
**2 tablespoons unsalted butter**
**½ to ¾ cup sour cream (regular or fat-free)**
**6 green onions (white part and some of the green), chopped**
**Freshly ground black or white pepper**

**1.** Place the potatoes in a medium-size saucepan and add water to cover by 2 inches. Bring to a boil and add the 1 teaspoon salt. Cover and cook over medium heat for 10 to 15 minutes, until tender when pierced with the tip of a knife. Drain, then return to the hot saucepan.

**2.** Add the butter and sour cream. Mash coarsely with a fork or potato masher; remember, these are supposed to be chunky. Add the green onions and mix gently to distribute throughout the potatoes. Season with salt and pepper and serve immediately.

## Steamed New Potatoes with White Wine

When I was learning how to make potato salad many years ago, I found out the secret is to pour wine or wine vinegar over the hot potatoes and let them stand before proceeding. Well, one day the potato salad did not get made, and the potatoes got eaten as is. Delicious! You can top them with chopped chives, crumbled blue cheese, or crumbled bacon, if you like. ● **Serves 4**

**2 pounds new red or white potatoes, such as Yukon Gold or fingerling,**
   **left whole if small or cut into quarters if large**
**¼ cup dry white wine**
**2 tablespoons olive oil**
**Salt and freshly ground black pepper**

**1.** Place the potatoes in a steamer over boiling water, cover, and cook over medium heat until tender, 15 to 20 minutes, depending on the size of the potatoes. Transfer the potatoes to a bowl.

**2.** Pour the wine and oil over the potatoes, and season with salt and pepper. Stir gently with a rubber spatula. Let stand on the counter to come to warm room temperature while you prepare the rest of the meal.

## Sweet Potato Puree with Chipotle Chile

This comes from Deane Bussiere, a chef at the Dominican Hospital in Santa Cruz, California. I became fascinated with Deane after reading an article about his switching the hospital patients' food to nutritious and organic foods, using the same budget that once provided more processed commercially prepared foods such as instant mashed potatoes. Not stopping there, he also donated a portion of the hospital grounds to be used as an organic vegetable garden for local schoolkids to learn how to grow their own food while supplying the hospital kitchen at the same time. ● **Serves 4**

**2½ pounds sweet potatoes, peeled and cut into large chunks**
**2 tablespoons unsalted butter**
**½ cup canned coconut milk**
**2 tablespoons sour cream (regular or fat-free)**
**2 small canned chipotle chiles in adobo sauce**
**1 teaspoon salt, or to taste**

**1.** Place the potatoes in a medium-size saucepan and add water to cover by 2 inches. Simmer the sweet potatoes until very soft, about 20 minutes depending on the size of the pieces. Drain and let cool a bit so that the excess moisture can evaporate.

**2.** Add the butter and allow it to melt over the sweet potatoes. Heat the coconut milk in a small pan until just below the boiling point; there will be small bubbles around the edges.

**3.** In a food processor, puree the sour cream, chipotles and adobo, and salt. Add the sweet potatoes to the processor, pulse to begin mashing, then pour in the hot coconut milk while pulsing. You may need a little more coconut milk, which can be added cold, to get the right consistency of thick, smooth mashed potatoes. Be careful not to overprocess; you want these smooth and fluffy, not pasty. (You can use an electric mixer to make chunkier mashed potatoes than the food processor, but you must puree the chipotles first.)

## Ultimate Warm Potato Salad with Quinoa and Peas

My girlfriend was cooking for a mountain retreat center some years back. Rave reviews came in about her quinoa-potato salad, which at the time seemed like an adventurous combination to me. Well, of course quinoa and potatoes both grow in the same high altitudes and are natural and complementary foods to each other. This is a mayonnaise-free salad. Served warm, it is excellent with all types of meat, especially pork tenderloin.

**◉ Serves 4**

½ cup olive oil, plus more as needed
1 pound russet potatoes, cut into ½-inch dice
1 medium-size yellow onion, finely chopped
1½ teaspoons curry powder (hot or mild)
1½ cups vegetable broth
¾ cup quinoa, rinsed a few times and drained
¼ teaspoon salt
Freshly ground black pepper
1 cup frozen petite peas, thawed

**1.** In a deep 12-inch skillet over medium-high heat, warm the ½ cup oil. Sauté the potatoes and onion until the onions are translucent, about 8 minutes. Add the curry powder and cook for 1 to 2 minutes, stirring to coat the potatoes. Add the broth and bring to a boil. Stir in the quinoa, salt, and pepper; return to a boil. Stir, cover, and reduce the heat to low; simmer for 15 minutes.

**2.** Turn off the heat, then stir in the peas. Let stand, covered, for 5 minutes. Mix gently to fluff. Serve warm.

# Veal Chops with Balsamic Vinegar Sauce and Quick Caesar Salad

**I** got this recipe from a 1986 *House Beautiful* magazine article called "Easy Does It" and have used it for catering private dinners. Twenty years ago a veal loin chop, which looks like a baby T-bone, was quite the extravagance; nowadays it is a standard in the butcher counter case. This sauce is great with other types of pan-sautéed beef steaks as well. **o** *Serves 4*

**COOKING METHOD:** Stovetop
**PREP TIME:** 20 minutes
**COOK TIME:** 15 to 20 minutes

Olive oil cooking spray
4 veal loin chops, about 1 inch thick

QUICK CAESAR SALAD
2 cloves garlic, crushed
Salt and freshly ground black pepper
Juice of 1 lemon
¼ cup olive oil
2 anchovy fillets (optional), chopped
2 to 3 heads romaine hearts, torn into pieces
⅓ cup grated Parmesan cheese

BALSAMIC SAUCE
3 medium-size shallots, minced
¼ cup balsamic vinegar
2 tablespoons dry red wine
2 tablespoons water
2 tablespoons hot sauce, such as Pickapeppa
2 tablespoons unsalted butter
2 tablespoons sour cream
1½ tablespoons Dijon mustard

**1.** Spray a large skillet with the olive oil cooking spray and heat over medium heat. Add the chops and cook for 7 to 10 minutes per side, until nicely browned, turning once. The interior juices should run clear, but the insides should still be pink.

**2.** Meanwhile, make the salad. In the bottom of a medium-size bowl, mash the garlic with the salt and pepper. Whisk in the lemon juice and oil. Add the anchovies, if using. Add the lettuce to the bowl and toss to coat. Sprinkle with the Parmesan and toss again. Set aside.

**3.** Remove the chops from the skillet and place on a plate; cover with aluminum foil to keep warm while making the sauce.

**4.** To make the sauce, add the shallots, vinegar, wine, and water to the skillet; bring to a boil to deglaze the pan, 2 minutes. Reduce the heat to low and whisk in the hot sauce, butter, sour cream, and mustard. Mix in any juices that have collected on the plate from the chops. Place the chops on individual plates and spoon the sauce over them. Serve immediately with the Caesar salad.

# Veal Scallops with Mushrooms and Madeira

S callops of veal, also known as scaloppini, are thin slices of meat taken from the leg or loin sections. "Scaloppini" immediately tells the cook that the meat will be prepared with the technique of dredging first in flour, then pan sautéing. Madeira is a wine that came into being by accident. As kegs of red wine were being transported by masted ship, in the presence of warm circulating air, the oxidized wine was transformed into the Madeira we enjoy today. It is a fabulous wine for cooking, as it is rich and tangy and makes superior sauces. Serve this dish with rice or egg noodles, and place the scaloppini on a bed of sautéed Swiss chard or spinach. ○ *Serves 4*

**COOKING METHOD:** Stovetop
**PREP TIME:** 5 minutes
**COOK TIME:** About 10 minutes

1 to 1½ pounds veal scallops
½ to ¾ cup all-purpose flour
Salt and freshly ground black pepper
2 tablespoons olive oil
6 tablespoons unsalted butter
10 ounces fresh white or small shiitake mushrooms, sliced
¾ cup Madeira
2 tablespoons fresh lemon juice

**1.** Place the veal on a flat surface between two pieces of waxed paper or plastic wrap, and pound lightly with a flat mallet to ¼ inch thick. Blend the flour with some salt and pepper on a flat plate; dredge the meat pieces on both sides.

**2.** Divide the oil and 4 tablespoons of the butter between two large skillets over medium-high heat (if using one skillet, divide the oil and butter and cook in two batches). When the fat is sizzling, add the meat in a single layer and sauté rapidly, no more than 30 seconds to 1 minute per side; the meat will be lightly browned. Transfer the meat to a warm platter and cover with aluminum foil.

**3.** Add the remaining 2 tablespoons butter to the pan and, when melted, add the mushrooms. Sauté over medium-high heat until their liquid is evaporated, stirring a few times. Add the wine and lemon juice. Let the wine come to a rapid boil, dissolving the meat residue in the pan; reduce a bit until thickened, 1 to 2 minutes. Season with salt and pepper. Portion the veal scallops onto individual plates and pour over the sauce. Serve immediately.

# Lemon Veal with Green Beans

his could really be called veal scaloppini with lemon sauce à la Marcella Hazan. I wonder whether Ms. Hazan ever makes a bad-tasting meal. From the proof of the dishes made from her books, I doubt it, for they all turn out fantastic. So here is my rendering of pounded veal pieces in the most simple lemon sauce ever. I make a dash more sauce to suit my tastes. It is another dish that cooks so fast, you need to have the rest of your meal ready and waiting. Serve with Lemon Rice (page 167). ● *Serves 4*

**COOKING METHOD:** Stovetop
**PREP TIME:** 10 minutes
**COOK TIME:** About 10 minutes

1 to 1½ pounds veal scallops
½ cup all-purpose flour
Salt and freshly ground black pepper
12 ounces baby green beans (haricots verts), ends trimmed
2 tablespoons olive oil
5 tablespoons unsalted butter
4 tablespoons fresh lemon juice
2 tablespoons chopped fresh flat-leaf parsley
1 lemon, cut into 8 slices

**1.** Place the veal on a flat surface between two pieces of waxed paper or plastic wrap, and pound lightly with a flat mallet to ¼ inch thick. Blend the flour with some salt and pepper on a flat plate; dredge the meat pieces on both sides.

**2.** Steam the green beans in a steamer basket over boiling water for 5 minutes. Remove from the heat and set aside.

**3.** Heat the oil and 4 tablespoons of the butter in a large skillet over medium-high heat. When the pan is sizzling, add the meat in a single layer and sauté rapidly, no more than 30 seconds to 1 minute per side; the meat will be lightly browned. With tongs, transfer the meat to a warm platter and cover with aluminum foil. Work in two batches, if necessary.

**4.** Remove the empty skillet from the heat and immediately add the lemon juice. Replace over medium heat and when hot, add the remaining 1 tablespoon butter; swirl the pan to melt the butter. Add the meat back to the skillet and warm briefly.

**5.** Sprinkle the parsley over the top and distribute 2 lemon slices for each portion. Serve immediately with the green beans on the side.

# Glazed Ham Steak

I gaze longingly at the Cryo-wrapped, conveniently sized slice of ham steak in the supermarket. I wonder how best to serve it, since it would taste wonderful with mashed or roasted potatoes, sauerkraut, a pile of hot spinach, or steamed mixed vegetables. Rye or pumpernickel bread with butter would be really good, too. ○ *Serves 4*

**COOKING METHOD:** Stovetop
**PREP TIME:** 5 minutes
**COOK TIME:** About 15 minutes

Two 12-ounce ham slices
½ cup apricot jam
½ cup low-sodium chicken broth
4 teaspoons Dijon mustard
1 tablespoon white balsamic vinegar or cider vinegar

**1.** Coat a large skillet with nonstick cooking spray and heat the pan over medium-high heat. Add one ham slice to the pan and cook for 3 minutes on each side, turning once, to brown each side. Remove from the pan to a plate and cover with aluminum foil. Brown the second ham slice; transfer to the plate.

**2.** Add the jam, broth, mustard, and vinegar to the hot pan and immediately start stirring with a whisk. Cook for 2 minutes, until bubbly and smooth. Cut the ham slices in half, place one half on each plate, and drizzle with the pan sauce. Serve immediately.

Pork tenderloin is the filet mignon of the pig and has become somewhat of a phenomenon in the kitchen, since it is so low in fat and cooks quickly. The tenderloin strip is a small muscle shaped like a little boneless log that comes off the much larger loin section and is cooked in one piece, like a roast. It cooks rapidly at high heat, so it makes a fantastic weeknight meal. The high heat also retains the natural moisture. Use an instant-read thermometer when cooking tenderloins to assure the proper temperature, then let stand for 5 minutes to reabsorb the juices.

Pork tenderloins are mild flavored on their own, so they take nicely to both dry rubs and sugar-based glazes, such as orange marmalade and chipotles in adobo, smoky-hot molasses barbecue sauce (page 116), plum jam with some red wine vinegar and a dash of Dijon mustard, hoisin-ginger glaze, or pomegranate molasses. For dry rubs, consider using your favorite Jamaican jerk spice combo, smoked paprika, or *herbes de Provence* mixed with salt and pepper. Well, you get the picture.

I call for 1¼- to 1½-pound tenderloins in the following recipe and its three variations, which will feed 4 people in one sitting. If your tenderloin runs smaller, like ¾ pound, get two. Leftovers make great sandwiches.

Pork tenderloins can also be cubed for stir-fries, cut into ½-inch strips for fajitas or tacos, or sliced and pounded for more sophisticated scallops.

## Mustard Honey–Glazed Pork Tenderloin Roast

Roast some rosemary potatoes and some cauliflower florets right alongside this dish.

○ Serves 4

**COOKING METHOD:** Oven
**PREP TIME:** 10 minutes
**COOK TIME:** 20 to 35 minutes

1¼ to 1½ pounds pork tenderloin
2 small cloves garlic, slivered
1 teaspoon salt
3 tablespoons honey (warmed in the microwave until liquid, if necessary)
3 tablespoons Dijon or whole-grain mustard

1. Preheat the oven to 450°F with the oven rack positioned in the middle.

**2.** Place the tenderloin on a rimmed baking sheet lined with aluminum foil. Make ¼-inch slits on the sides of the roast and insert the garlic slivers. Sprinkle the roast with salt and rub in. Mix the honey and the mustard in a small bowl, then spread over the tenderloin.

**3.** Roast the tenderloin for 20 to 35 minutes (18 to 20 minutes per pound), until an instant-read thermometer reads 160°F. Let stand for 5 minutes, then remove from the pan and place on a cutting board. Carve just like a long baguette, in crosswise medallion-like ¼- to 1-inch-thick slices (you can get 12 slices from one roast).

**VARIATIONS**

## Smoky-Hot Molasses BBQ Sauce–Glazed Pork Tenderloin Roast

Try this with baked beans or sweet potatoes and corn or coleslaw.

**2 cloves garlic**
**¼ to ½ of a 7-ounce can chipotle chiles in adobo sauce, to your taste**
**One 12-ounce bottle of your favorite store-bought barbecue sauce**
**2 tablespoons molasses**
**1¼ to 1½ pounds pork tenderloin**

Toss the garlic in a food processor and pulse to finely chop. Add the chiles and process to puree. Add the barbecue sauce and molasses and pulse to combine; it is ready to use. Spread or brush the sauce thickly all over the tenderloin and roast as directed above. Leftover sauce can be stored in the refrigerator for up to 2 weeks.

## Southwest-Style Chili and Herb–Rubbed Pork Tenderloin Roast

Accompany this roast with white or brown rice and sautéed cherry tomatoes.

**2 tablespoons chili powder**
**1 tablespoon kosher salt**
**2 teaspoons garlic powder**
**1½ teaspoons ground cumin**
**1 teaspoon dried basil**
**1 teaspoon dried marjoram**

½ teaspoon freshly ground black or white pepper
½ teaspoon cayenne pepper
1¼ to 1½ pounds pork tenderloin
Olive oil cooking spray
Fresh cilantro
Lime wedges

Place the chili powder, salt, garlic powder, cumin, basil, marjoram, pepper, and cayenne on a plate and mix until well combined. Roll the tenderloin in the rub to coat all sides, lightly spray with olive oil cooking spray, and roast as directed above. Garnish with cilantro and lime wedges.

## Blackberry-Glazed Pork Tenderloin Roast

This goes well with rice pilaf and a green salad. Leftovers make great sandwiches on 12-grain bread.

⅔ cup blackberry preserves
2 tablespoons cider vinegar
2 tablespoons Worcestershire sauce
1 tablespoon Asian chili-garlic sauce
1¼ to 1½ pounds pork tenderloin
2 small cloves garlic, slivered

Combine the preserves, vinegar, Worcestershire sauce, and chili-garlic sauce in a heatproof bowl or small saucepan; heat in the microwave or on the stovetop to melt the preserves. Make ¼-inch slits on the sides of the roast and insert the garlic slivers. Spread or brush the sauce thickly all over the tenderloin and roast as directed above.

# Scallops of Pork with Raisins and Sherry Vinegar

**V**inegars of all sorts go incredibly well with the flavor of pork. The tart sour nature balances the inherent sweetness of pork. And, oh, sherry vinegar, the smooth, richly flavored vinegar from Portugal! I often use a combination of golden raisins and dried tart cherries instead of just raisins. This is best served with rice, which will soak up the sauce nicely. ❍ *Serves 4*

**COOKING METHOD:** Stovetop
**PREP TIME:** 10 minutes
**COOK TIME:** About 30 minutes

½ cup dark and golden raisins
1 cup low-sodium chicken broth
1½ pounds pork tenderloins
⅔ cup all-purpose flour
½ cup (1 stick) unsalted butter
½ cup sherry vinegar, plus 1 tablespoon to taste
½ teaspoon salt
Freshly ground black or white pepper

Salmon Teriyaki with Cabbage Salad (page 14)

Opposite: **Oven-Fried Drumsticks with IOU Pasta** (page 72)
Above: **Green Chile Tortilla Pie** (page 224)

Above: **Turkey Marsala with Olive Couscous** (page 78)
Opposite: **Escarole Sausage Soup** (page 201)

Opposite: **Flank Steak Broccoli Beef** (page 100)

Above: **Double Tomato Baby Lentil Salad with Olives** (page 232)

Above: **Ravioli with Mushrooms and Sweet Peas** (page 157)
Opposite: **Coq au Vin in Dijon Yogurt Sauce and Frisée Salad with Roasted Mushrooms** (page 62)

Opposite: **Mint and Lemon–Crusted Rack of Lamb with Mascarpone Creamed Spinach** (page 126)
Above: **Sweet Potato Turkey Hash** (page 210)

Above: **Tuna Burgers with Wasabi Mayo** (page 284)
Opposite: **Oriental Pork and Asparagus Salad** (page 246)

Opposite: **Oven-Barbecued Beef Ribs with Veggie Packets** (page 102)
Above: **Ratatouille Tortilla Pizzas** (page 288)

Suppertime Fried Rice with Tofu and Vegetables (page 170)

**1.** Place the raisins in a heatproof bowl with the broth; microwave for 5 minutes, or until boiling. Let stand to plump and soften the raisins while preparing the pork.

**2.** Starting at the larger end, cut 6 even slices, about ½ to ¾ inch thick, from each tenderloin. Reserve the tapered ends for another use (I freeze them for fajitas). Place the pieces of pork between two pieces of plastic wrap and pound with a smooth meat mallet or the bottom of a small saucepan to form flattened rounds. Place the flour on a plate and dredge the scallops to coat them lightly.

**3.** In a large skillet, melt 2 tablespoons of the butter over medium heat. Add a single layer of pork scallops and cook for 4 minutes. Turn and cook the second side for about 4 minutes. Remove the scallops from the pan to a plate and cover with aluminum foil. Cook the remaining scallops in batches until all are cooked, using 2 tablespoons butter for each batch. It will probably take 3 batches (you will have 2 tablespoons of butter remaining).

**4.** Add the ½ cup vinegar to the hot skillet and raise the heat to high. Boil, scraping up all the browned bits off the bottom of the pan, for 5 minutes. The vinegar will thicken. Add the raisins and their broth to the pan and bring to a boil. Return the scallops to the pan. Season with salt and pepper. Cover and simmer over medium heat for 5 minutes. Whisk in the remaining 2 tablespoons butter until melted and taste, adding a tablespoon more vinegar if you like. Remove the scallops to individual dinner plates and spoon over the sauce. Serve immediately.

# Pan-Roasted Pork Chops with Homemade Applesauce

**P**ork chops take nicely to sprinkling with dry spices, searing in a pan, and then finishing in the oven for a juicy, flavorful chop. Here they are spiked with a Caribbean flavor called jerk, which is strong with allspice and hot pepper (I use red pepper flakes in place of the traditional Scotch bonnet), but you can use a Mexican or Greek herb combination just as well. These are so fast, you should start the applesauce first. Serve with Smashed Potatoes with Green Onions and Sour Cream (page 105) or just simple microwave-cooked sweet potatoes. ○ *Serves 4*

**COOKING METHOD:** Stovetop and oven
**PREP TIME:** 15 minutes
**COOK TIME:** About 10 minutes

CARIBBEAN RUB
1 teaspoon garlic powder
1 teaspoon onion powder
1 teaspoon ground apple pie spice blend
½ teaspoon chili powder
¼ teaspoon red pepper flakes

4 pork rib chops (about 1½ pounds)
1 tablespoon vegetable or grapeseed oil

1. Preheat the oven to 400°F.

2. To make the rub, in a small bowl, combine the rub ingredients. Lightly sprinkle and pat into both sides of the chops.

3. Heat the oil in a large ovenproof skillet over medium-high heat. Add the rib chops and sear for 2 minutes. Turn the chops and place the skillet in the oven. Bake for 6 to 8 minutes, until no longer pink in the center. Serve immediately with homemade applesauce (recipe follows) on the side.

# Homemade Applesauce

Homemade applesauce is better than any in a jar. It is fantastic with pork. If you have some pears, apricots, rhubarb, or even prunes, just toss them in with the apples. If you want to jazz it up, stir in some chopped walnuts or sunflower seeds right before serving. ○ *Makes about 2½ cups*

4 to 5 large tart apples, peeled, cored, and cut into chunks
¼ cup water
1 to 2 tablespoons unsalted butter
1 tablespoon cider vinegar
½ teaspoon ground cinnamon, apple pie spice blend, or Chinese 5-spice powder

**1.** Place the apples in a medium-size saucepan with the water. Bring to a boil, then reduce to a simmer, partially covered. Cook until tender, 15 to 20 minutes.

**2.** Add the butter (it will naturally melt). Stir to mash the apples to make a chunky sauce, or use an immersion blender to make a smooth sauce. Stir in the vinegar and cinnamon. You may serve this hot, at room temperature, or chilled.

# Dijon Pork Chops with Red Cabbage

Adapted from *Prevention* magazine and a perfect fall dinner, this is one of the classic preparations for pork, with hot mustard, apples, cider vinegar, and cabbage. Cabbage is always considered one of the world's proletarian vegetables, inexpensive and easy to find. It is part of a large family of cruciferous vegetables that includes broccoli, cauliflower, Brussels sprouts, and leafy kale, all of which are good with pork. A French endearment for a child, *mon petit chou*, translates to "my dear little cabbage." I serve this with cranberry sauce and steamed green beans or broccoli. ○ *Serves 4*

**COOKING METHOD:** Stovetop
**PREP TIME:** 20 minutes
**COOK TIME:** 35 to 45 minutes

Four 4- to 5-ounce center-cut pork chops, trimmed

4 teaspoons Dijon mustard

½ head red cabbage (about 1 pound), cored and shredded

2 tart apples, peeled, cored, and coarsely grated

1 tablespoon maple syrup

Pinch of salt

2 tablespoons olive oil

1 tablespoon grated fresh ginger

¼ teaspoon ground cinnamon

1 tablespoon cider vinegar

Freshly ground black pepper

**1.** Brush both sides of the chops with the mustard; set aside. In a bowl, toss the cabbage with the apples, maple syrup, and salt.

**2.** Heat 1 tablespoon of the oil in a large skillet over medium-high heat. Add the ginger and cinnamon and stir for a few seconds to warm them. Add the cabbage, stir, then reduce the heat to medium-low. Cover and cook until tender, 20 to 30 minutes.

**3.** Heat another large skillet over medium-high heat, and add the remaining tablespoon of oil. Arrange the pork chops in the skillet in a single layer. Cook for about 10 minutes, turning once, until no longer pink in the center.

**4.** Add the vinegar to the cabbage and cook until evaporated, about 5 minutes. Season with salt and pepper. Divide the cabbage among 4 plates and place a chop on top of each.

# Lamb Curry with Apples and Apricots

This is a recipe to use with leftover roast lamb. It contains as much fruit as it does meat. It is also a versatile recipe, as the lamb may be substituted with cooked shrimp, strips of roast chicken, or even cooked lentils for a vegetarian version. Curries demand a sprinkling of condiments, such as chopped fresh parsley or cilantro, raw or roasted chopped cashews, raisins, flaked unsweetened coconut, and/or simply a dab of nice chutney. When I was served this for the first time, it was topped with roasted soy nuts, yogurt, and a homemade chutney from green tomatoes, which made it special and memorable. Serve with plain or saffron rice and fresh sliced cucumbers in yogurt. ● *Serves 4*

**COOKING METHOD:** Stovetop
**PREP TIME:** 20 minutes
**COOK TIME:** About 25 minutes

4 tablespoons olive oil
1 leek, rinsed well and white part sliced
1 medium-size yellow onion, chopped
1 clove garlic, minced
2 stalks celery, sliced
1 tablespoon curry powder
½ teaspoon ground ginger
½ teaspoon ground cumin
¼ teaspoon ground coriander
1 tablespoon all-purpose flour
¾ cup chopped dried apricots
One 14½-ounce can chicken broth
½ cup dry white wine
1 large green apple, chopped (skin on or peeled, as desired)
1 to 1½ cups cubed cooked lamb (6 ounces)
Salt

**1.** In a large skillet, warm the oil over medium-high heat. Sauté the leek, onion, garlic, and celery for 3 minutes, until limp. Add the curry powder and cook for 1 minute, stirring constantly. Add the remaining spices and the flour. Stir briefly to distribute evenly and then add the apricots, broth, and wine. Bring to a boil and immediately reduce the heat. Simmer, uncovered, until the sauce is reduced by one-quarter, 10 to 15 minutes.

**2.** Add the apple and lamb; cook for another 5 minutes. Turn off the heat, cover the pan, and let stand for 15 minutes before serving. Season with salt and serve.

# Mint and Lemon–Crusted Rack of Lamb with Mascarpone Creamed Spinach

R ack of lamb may be an extravagance, but it is also one of the easiest lamb dishes to prepare. You will look like a master chef serving it. Topping the rack with a crust is a classic preparation. While you can get fancy with nuts and herbs, I keep it simple with mustard, lemon, mint, and parsley. Serve with the mascarpone spinach, made conveniently with frozen spinach, a great flavor combination with the lamb. If you are a lover of creamed spinach, consider doubling the recipe for larger portions or leftovers. ○ *Serves 4*

**COOKING METHOD:** Oven
**PREP TIME:** 20 minutes
**COOK TIME:** 20 to 25 minutes

2 racks of lamb (about 1½ pounds each)
Salt and freshly ground black pepper
2 tablespoons Dijon mustard
Zest of 1 large lemon, cut off in long strips
3 tablespoons dry bread crumbs
1 tablespoon chopped fresh flat-leaf parsley
1 tablespoon chopped fresh mint
1 tablespoon unsalted butter, melted

**MASCARPONE CREAMED SPINACH**
1 tablespoon unsalted butter
1 small shallot, minced
One 10-ounce box frozen chopped spinach, thawed and
    squeezed dry (reserve ¼ cup of the liquid)
¼ to ⅓ cup mascarpone cheese
Salt

**1.** Preheat the oven to 400°F.

**2.** Pat the lamb racks dry with paper towels and season with salt and pepper. Place in a shallow roasting pan, meat side up. Spread the mustard on the lamb.

**3.** In a food processor, combine the lemon zest, bread crumbs, parsley, and mint. Process until the zest and herbs are ground. This will smell very fresh. Place in a small bowl and toss with the melted butter. Firmly press the herb mixture onto the racks, over the mustard. Immediately place in the oven and roast for 20 minutes for rare, 25 minutes for medium.

**4.** To make the spinach, melt the butter in a medium-size skillet over low heat. Add the shallot and cook until translucent, 3 minutes. Add the spinach and reserved water; cook until hot and most of the water has evaporated, 5 minutes. Stir in the mascarpone and cook for a few minutes, until hot. Season with salt. Serve immediately or keep warm until ready to serve.

**5.** Remove the lamb from the oven, cover, and let stand for 5 to 10 minutes before slicing.

# Pan-Sautéed Lamb Chops
# with Blackberry Sauce

**B**lackberries are fabulous with lamb, and this sauce is completed in minutes. Stash a few baskets in the freezer during berry season or buy a bag of unsweetened frozen berries; both are great. The sauce is the simplest style of reduction, which is a fancy cooking term for letting it boil and evaporate. Serve with rice pilaf and sautéed baby broccoli. **◦** *Serves 4*

**COOKING METHOD:** Stovetop
**PREP TIME:** 15 minutes
**COOK TIME:** About 20 minutes

8 small, thick loin lamb chops (about 2 pounds)
Freshly ground black or multicolored pepper

**BLACKBERRY SAUCE**
⅔ cup dry red wine, such as Merlot
⅔ cup beef broth
⅔ cup fresh or frozen blackberries
2 tablespoons cold unsalted butter
Salt

1. Heat a large skillet over medium-high heat. Season the lamb chops lightly on both sides with pepper. Arrange in the skillet and brown one side of the chops; lower the heat to medium and cook the other side until medium-rare (6 to 8 minutes). If your skillet is not large enough, you will have to do this in two batches. Transfer the chops to a serving plate, tent with aluminum foil, and let rest while making the sauce.

2. Return the skillet to high heat. Pour the wine into the pan and let bubble for a minute or two to reduce by almost half. Add the broth to the reduced wine, bring to a boil, then reduce the heat to medium and allow the mixture to cook at a low boil for 2 minutes. Add the blackberries and butter. Swirl the pan around so the butter melts evenly and heat the berries for 1 minute (not too long or else the berries will break down; frozen berries will take a bit longer to cook than fresh). Season with salt. Place 2 chops per portion on dinner plates, then drizzle the sauce directly over the chops and serve.

# Dinnertime Classics:
# Pasta, Gnocchi, Polenta, and Rice

Pasta- and rice-based meals are universal crowd-pleasers and are likely to satisfy even the pickiest of palates. Pasta and rice can be prepared in an infinite variety of flavors, textures, and temperatures. They are fabulously inexpensive, and the choices of pasta shapes and rice varieties are seemingly infinite.

It is one of the mysterious elements of pasta to say what shape goes with what sauce. Of course, you are the master in your kitchen, but there are a few pointers that will help you in your creative judgment. Imported dried pasta is sturdier than fresh and so is good with thicker, bulkier sauces; fresh pasta is good for lighter sauces, such as cream sauces. Long noodles and spaghetti are good with fresh uncooked tomatoes, garlic, and olive oil; simple marinaras; butter sauces; pesto; and sautéed vegetables. The stubby tube pastas, such as penne and rigatoni, are best for baked dishes and chunky sauces. The fun shapes like fusilli, shells, radiatore, and orecchiette have ridges and grooves in which to collect sauces.

Cook pasta in an abundant amount of boiling water, and start tasting it for doneness a minute or two before the recommended time on the package. Don't rinse pasta with cold water after cooking unless you are using it in a pasta salad. Also, don't allow it to sit in the colander or it will become gummy and stick together. Return it to the pot right away and toss with a scant amount of butter, oil, or a few tablespoons of the sauce to prevent sticking. Serve as soon as possible.

Once risotto was an intimidating dish to master. No longer. With the miraculous help of the microwave oven, even the most timid cook can produce a nice risotto. Be sure to use Arborio (imported or domestic) or Carnaroli rice.

Italians serve risotto as a first course; I love the dish so much that I make it the main, with garlic bread and salad or steamed or sautéed vegetables. As with pasta, once risotto is cooked, it has to be served immediately or it will begin to change consistency. You want a nice soft risotto.

You may already know the secret ingredient for fried rice, but in case you don't, here it is: cold rice. Use directly out of the refrigerator or just-thawed frozen that you let sit on the counter for an hour. (Some people keep bags of frozen leftover rice just for fried rice.) When using cold rice, be sure to break up any lumps with your fingers as you add the rice to the skillet. If you use hot rice, your fried rice will turn to mush. You can use almost any kind of leftover plain, cooked rice, from brown jasmine, basmati, or Nepalese or Louisiana red rice to Forbidden (black) rice. You can make fried rice as simple or as exotic as you like; it's a fabulous way to use up leftover bits of vegetables and meats and get a fresh hot meal on the table quickly.

# Pasta with Pesto

**P**esto paste made with basil is the most common type of this sauce, but there are versions made with spinach, cilantro, parsley, mint, olives, sundried tomatoes, and even fiddlehead ferns, along with all manner of nuts. Remember that it is a preparation that depends on the balance of the ingredients. Make plenty of extra pesto and keep it in little freezer zipper-top plastic bags. You can easily break or cut off the amount you need, so you don't have to go to the trouble I used to in filling 2- to 4-tablespoon-capacity plastic Tupperware freezer containers, which would tumble off the freezer door all year long. Serve with a big mixed salad and crusty bread, if you wish. ○ *Serves 4*

**COOKING METHOD:** Stovetop
**PREP TIME:** 15 minutes
**COOK TIME:** About 10 minutes

1 clove garlic
¼ cup pine nuts
2 cups loosely packed fresh basil leaves (about 1 bunch)
¼ cup fresh flat-leaf parsley leaves
Pinch of salt, or to taste
½ cup extra virgin olive oil
½ cup grated Parmesan cheese, plus more for serving
2 to 3 tablespoons unsalted butter, softened
1 pound fresh or dried linguine or tagliatelle

**1.** Bring a large pot of salted water to a boil.

**2.** Combine the garlic and pine nuts in a small food processor and pulse to finely chop. Add the basil leaves, parsley, and salt; process until a coarse paste forms. With the machine running, slowly pour the olive oil through the feed tube, processing until a thick paste flecked with bits of basil forms. The pesto can also be made by hand using a mortar and pestle if you are feeling frisky, or in a blender. (Store in the refrigerator with a bit of olive oil poured over the top to preserve the color for up to 2 days, or freeze.)

**3.** When ready to serve, place the pesto in a mixing bowl and stir in the cheese. Mash in the butter.

**4.** Cook the pasta according to package directions. Drain, reserving about ½ cup of the cooking water, and transfer to a shallow serving bowl. Toss with the pesto until evenly distributed, using the cooking water, drizzled in little by little, to loosen the sauce. If you don't use all of the pesto, place little dabs over the top. Serve immediately, passing more cheese at the table.

**VARIATION**

# Spinach Pesto

This is a delicious variation of pesto that is perfect during the winter, when basil is less available. ❍ *Makes 1½ cups*

1 clove garlic
2 tablespoons pine nuts or walnuts
2 cups baby spinach leaves
½ cup fresh flat-leaf parsley leaves
1 teaspoon dried basil
Pinch of salt, or to taste
½ cup extra virgin olive oil

Combine the garlic and pine nuts in a small food processor and pulse to finely chop. Add the spinach, parsley, basil, and salt; process until a coarse paste forms. With the machine running, slowly pour the olive oil through the feed tube, processing until a thick paste flecked with bits of spinach forms. Cover and refrigerate or freeze as for basil pesto (left).

# Spaghetti with Zucchini, Basil, and Mint

Once I tasted the combination of fresh basil and mint, I was hooked. Then I found out the partnering has a long tradition in Italian country food. This is a lovely summer pasta, satisfying for those nights when you want something light and vegetable-y. Remember to only pack the cup measure loosely with the herbs; there will be plenty to flavor the entire bowl of pasta. You will need at least a 12-inch sauté pan or skillet for this dish, and it will be filled to capacity once you add the pasta. If your skillet is smaller, combine the zucchini and pasta in a shallow serving bowl instead. If you like, this can serve eight as a side dish to grilled or roasted chicken. ● *Serves 4*

**COOKING METHOD:** Stovetop
**PREP TIME:** 15 minutes
**COOK TIME:** About 30 minutes

1 pound semolina or whole wheat spaghetti

About ⅓ cup extra virgin olive oil

2 pounds small zucchini, cut into thin round slices on the diagonal

2 cloves garlic, finely minced

¼ cup loosely packed finely shredded fresh basil leaves

¼ cup loosely packed finely shredded fresh mint leaves

Salt and freshly ground black pepper

Grated Parmesan cheese for serving

**1.** Bring a large pot of salted water to a boil. Cook the pasta according to package directions.

**2.** Meanwhile, heat half of the olive oil in a large skillet over medium-high heat. Add half of the zucchini (you don't want to crowd it) and cook, stirring frequently, until golden on both sides. Do not overcook. Remove with a slotted spoon to a bowl and add the remaining oil and cook the remaining zucchini until golden. Add the garlic and cook for 30 seconds, then add the basil and mint. Add the reserved cooked zucchini back into the skillet, then season with salt and pepper. Stir and cook for 1 minute to wilt the herbs.

**3.** Drain the pasta and reserve ½ cup of the pasta water. Add the pasta to the skillet and gently toss with the zucchini; add a bit of pasta water if it looks too dry, then taste for salt. Divide among dinner plates, sprinkle with Parmesan, and serve immediately.

# Pasta with Broccoli Sauce

U sually a broccoli pasta sauce is chunky with broccoli florets, but here it is pureed and poured over, not tossed. I had this sauce at a birthday party for Patti, the vocalist of the singing duo Tuck and Patti. Years later I tracked down the caterer to get the recipe and found out they had made it up on the spot for the party. After more than two decades of obsessing over the sauce, here it is. Use fusilli or radiatore in place of the linguine, if you like. Serve with a side salad of layered sliced tomatoes and fresh mozzarella cheese, if desired. ● *Serves 4*

**COOKING METHOD:** Stovetop
**PREP TIME:** 15 minutes
**COOK TIME:** About 25 minutes

1½ to 1¾ pounds broccoli, cut into florets and stems trimmed,
     peeled, and sliced
3 strips lemon zest
¼ cup loosely packed chopped fresh flat-leaf parsley
½ cup vegetable broth
¼ cup plus 2 tablespoons extra virgin olive oil
1 medium-size white onion, chopped, or ¼ cup chopped shallots
Salt and freshly ground black pepper
Juice of 1 lemon
½ cup heavy cream or plain yogurt
1 pound whole wheat linguine, fresh if possible
¾ cup grated Parmesan cheese

**1.** Bring a large pot of salted water to a boil. Add the broccoli stems, cook for 1 minute, and then add the florets and cook for another 2 to 3 minutes only.

**2.** Meanwhile, in a food processor, pulse the lemon zest until finely ground, then add the parsley and process until smooth. Remove the broccoli from the cooking water with a slotted spoon and transfer to the food processor. (Leave the broccoli water in the pot for the pasta.) Add the vegetable broth and ¼ cup of the olive oil; pulse to make a coarse puree. Add some broccoli water if you want it a bit thinner.

**3.** Heat the remaining 2 tablespoons of olive oil in a large saucepan over medium-low heat and cook the onion until translucent, about 3 minutes. Remove the pan from the heat, pour the onion into the food processor, and pulse a few times. The sauce will not be smooth. Pour the broccoli sauce from the food processor into the saucepan. Place over low heat and season with the salt, pepper, and lemon juice. Whisk in the cream. Simmer for 10 minutes.

**4.** Bring the broccoli water back to a boil and add the linguine. Cook the pasta according to package directions. Drain and divide among individual dinner plates. Ladle over plenty of sauce, sprinkle with lots of Parmesan, and serve immediately.

# Better Fettuccine Alfredo

I adapted this more health-conscious version of the classic from a recipe that used to be served at the Rancho La Puerta spa (although I use way more Parmesan!). It is even better than the calorie-rich version and easier to make, too, since there is no cooking except for the pasta. All you need is yogurt and cottage cheese tossed with hot pasta. Purchase a thick yogurt without added gelatin, such as Greek yogurt. Balance the richness with a salad of crispy greens and cucumbers. ● *Serves 4*

**COOKING METHOD:** Stovetop
**PREP TIME:** 15 minutes
**COOK TIME:** About 20 minutes

1 clove garlic
One 4-inch strip lemon zest
¾ cup plain yogurt or milk
¾ cup low-fat or nonfat cottage cheese or ricotta cheese
1 pound fresh fettuccine
1 to 2 tablespoons olive oil
3 tablespoons chopped fresh flat-leaf parsley
½ cup grated Parmesan cheese, plus more for serving
Salt and freshly ground black pepper

**1.** Bring a large pot of salted water to a boil for the pasta.

**2.** Meanwhile, in a food processor, process the garlic and lemon by pulsing to chop. Add the yogurt and cottage cheese; process until smooth and creamy.

**3.** Cook the pasta according to package directions. Drain, reserving about ½ cup of the cooking water, then return to the hot pot in which it cooked; toss with the olive oil and leave over low heat. Pour the sauce over the pasta, add the parsley and the ½ cup Parmesan, then toss to combine, using a bit of the cooking water to loosen the sauce, if necessary. Season with salt and pepper. Pass more Parmesan at the table.

# Angel Hair with Tomatoes, Basil, and Garlic

C apelli d'angelo, or angel's hair, is the thinnest pasta. It takes nicely to very light vegetable sauces. You can also use capellini, which is slightly thicker. Here is the fastest tomato sauce in the world—it takes a mere 3 to 5 minutes—a specialty of my friend Sandra Lloyd, a standup comic/waitress at some of the finest restaurants (including Farallon in San Francisco) and now a doula. Use fresh tomatoes here, not canned, which means it is a summer pasta treat. This is all made in one pan, so be sure to use at least a 12-inch skillet or sauté pan; otherwise, pour the tomato mixture into a bowl and toss the pasta in there. Serve with crusty bread to mop up the juices. ❍ *Serves 4*

**COOKING METHOD:** Stovetop
**PREP TIME:** 15 minutes
**COOK TIME:** About 10 minutes

2 tablespoons unsalted butter
2 cloves garlic, thinly sliced
4 to 6 large Roma tomatoes, seeded and diced
Pinch of dried oregano
Salt and freshly ground black pepper
¾ cup low-sodium chicken broth
3 tablespoons minced fresh basil
1 pound angel hair pasta
3 ounces fresh soft goat's milk cheese, crumbled

**1.** Bring a large pot of salted water to a boil.

**2.** Meanwhile, heat the butter in a large skillet over medium heat. Add the garlic and cook for 30 seconds to 1 minute, then add the tomatoes, oregano, salt, and pepper; cook for 3 to 5 minutes. Add the chicken broth and basil to the skillet and bring to a simmer.

**3.** Cook the pasta according to package directions. Drain, then add the hot pasta to the skillet. Add the goat cheese and gently toss and stir to combine. Serve immediately.

# Penne Rigate Macaroni and Cheeses

**W**hen commercially packaged mac and cheese just won't do anymore, here is the real thing. While you can stick to the predictable curved elbows, I always make mine with straight penne rigate or mostaccioli tubes. You can also use whole wheat pasta, and feel free to be inventive with the cheese combinations. If you like, divide the mixture among 4 to 6 individual soufflé or gratin dishes and bake for only 15 minutes. Serve with a leafy green salad and a small bowl of canned stewed tomatoes. ● *Serves 4*

**COOKING METHOD:** Stovetop and oven
**PREP TIME:** 25 minutes
**COOK TIME:** About 40 minutes

1 pound penne rigate or mostaccioli

2 tablespoons cornstarch

1½ cups milk

1½ cups half-and-half (can be reduced-fat)

5 tablespoons unsalted butter

4 ounces Italian fontina or Muenster, cubed

4 ounces provolone or white sharp cheddar, cubed

2 ounces Bel Paese or cream cheese, diced

½ teaspoon salt

Freshly ground black pepper

Freshly ground nutmeg

2 egg yolks

2 slices bread, ground into fresh crumbs in the food processor

**1.** Preheat the oven to 350°F.

**2.** Bring a large pot of salted water to a boil. Cook the pasta according to package directions, taking care not to overcook because it will cook more in the oven. Drain and set aside.

**3.** In a small bowl, mix the cornstarch with 3 tablespoons of the milk. In a deep saucepan, whisk together the remaining 1 cup and 5 tablespoons milk, the half-and-half, and 4 tablespoons of the butter; bring to a low boil. Add the cornstarch mixture and whisk constantly over medium heat until thickened. Lower the heat to the lowest setting and add the cheeses, one at a time, and leave on the lowest heat to melt slowly, stirring occasionally, until smooth. Season with salt, pepper, and nutmeg. Remove from the heat and add the egg yolks one at a time, stirring constantly.

**4.** Place the cooked pasta in a 2½- to 3-quart baking dish or oversized gratin dish. Place one-third of the pasta in the dish, then pour one-third of the sauce over it. Make two more layers, then top with the bread crumbs and dot with the remaining 1 tablespoon butter (you can use olive oil, if you like).

**5.** Bake for 25 to 30 minutes, until browned and bubbling around the edges. Serve immediately.

# Seven-Vegetable and Rigatoni Pasticcio

I talian cuisine has an almost infinite repertoire of baked pastas, ranging from everyday spaghetti cakes and lasagnas that use leftovers to elegant molded *timballi* for special occasions. Although many are time-consuming to prepare, a few can be whipped up quickly for a hearty one-dish dinner. One of the most popular pastas *al forno* is baked rigatoni. Instead of layering the ingredients, in this casserole you toss the pasta with the cheeses and then simply cover it with an extra-chunky vegetable sauce. It is best made in a shallow casserole dish for fastest cooking. Pair this with some mixed greens and crusty bread.

○ *Serves 6 to 8*

**COOKING METHOD:** Stovetop and oven
**PREP TIME:** 25 minutes
**COOK TIME:** 35 to 40 minutes

5 tablespoons olive oil
¼ cup plain dry bread crumbs
Salt
1 large onion, diced
2 small zucchini, diced
1 green or red bell pepper (or ½ of each), seeded and diced
1 stalk celery, diced
1 Japanese eggplant, diced, or 6 spears asparagus cut into 1-inch pieces,
    or 4 ounces fresh mushrooms, diced
1 clove garlic, minced
1½ teaspoons Italian herb blend
Two 35-ounce cans Italian plum tomatoes, drained and chopped or
    crushed with your hands
1 cup frozen petite peas, thawed
Freshly ground black pepper
1 pound rigatoni
1 pound ricotta cheese
1½ cups grated Parmesan cheese
2 tablespoons chopped fresh flat-leaf parsley
2 tablespoons chopped fresh basil

1. Preheat the oven to 375°F. Brush a 3½-quart shallow baking dish with 1 table-spoon of the olive oil and coat with the bread crumbs, tapping out the excess. Bring a large pot of salted water to a boil for the pasta.

2. In a skillet, warm the remaining olive oil. Add the diced vegetables and garlic; sauté for 5 minutes. Add the herb blend; cook for 5 minutes more. Add the toma-toes and peas, bring the mixture to a boil, and then immediately remove from the heat. Season lightly with salt and pepper.

3. Meanwhile, cook the pasta until *al dente* (tender but still firm), taking care not to overcook since it will cook more in the oven. Drain well in a colander. Place the cooked pasta in the baking dish.

4. In a bowl, combine the ricotta, 1 cup of the Parmesan, the parsley, and the basil (alternatively, you can chop the parsley and basil in the food processor and mix in the cheeses); stir into the pasta and toss to evenly combine. Pour the hot vegetable sauce over the top of the pasta, covering it completely. Sprinkle with the remain-ing ½ cup Parmesan. Bake for 35 to 40 minutes, until bubbling around the edges. Serve immediately.

# Buddha's Delight with Buckwheat Noodles

Chinese cuisine features wonderful metaphorical names for dishes, and this one certainly grabs the attention of the diner. This stir-fry can change with the seasons, but it always contains a mixture of vegetables, sometimes up to 12 different ones. The basis is usually napa cabbage, also known as Chinese cabbage. Purely Chinese vegetables, such as fresh soybeans, water chestnuts, bamboo shoots, lotus roots, and mung bean sprouts, are encouraged. When you can find fresh water chestnuts, do indulge. I also like broccolini in this. You will need a steamer to make this dish. ○ *Serves 4*

**COOKING METHOD:** Stovetop
**PREP TIME:** 25 minutes
**COOK TIME:** About 25 minutes

12 ounces buckwheat noodles (soba), Chinese egg noodles, or Italian linguine

2 cups vegetable broth

2 tablespoons reduced-sodium soy sauce

2 tablespoons sugar or thawed frozen apple juice concentrate

Juice of ½ lemon

1 teaspoon grated fresh ginger

2 pinches red pepper flakes

1 clove garlic, crushed

2 tablespoons cornstarch

1½ teaspoons dark sesame oil, plus more for drizzling

1 large carrot, cut on the diagonal into ¼-inch slices

1 medium-size head broccoli, broken into small florets

1 medium-size zucchini, cut on the diagonal into ¼-inch slices

1 cup thawed frozen or fresh edamame

1 red bell pepper, cut into 1-inch cubes

4 ounces snow peas, strings zipped and pods halved on the diagonal

¼ cup sliced water chestnuts or ½ cup canned whole baby corn, rinsed

4 ounces baby shiitake mushrooms, sliced

2 to 3 cups chopped napa cabbage

½ cup chopped green onions (white part and some of the green)

**1.** Bring a large pot of salted water to a boil. Cook the pasta according to package directions. Drain well and rinse with hot water.

**2.** Meanwhile, in a small saucepan, combine the broth, soy sauce, sugar, lemon juice, ginger, red pepper flakes, and garlic. Whisk in the cornstarch. Bring to a boil over medium heat. Stir constantly until thickened, about 3 minutes, then stir in the sesame oil. Set aside, keeping warm.

**3.** In a large pan or wok with a steamer basket, or in a rice cooker with stacked steamers, fill the pan or rice cooker bowl one-quarter full with water and cover. Bring to a boil. Spray the steamer baskets with nonstick vegetable cooking spray or lay down some large cabbage leaves. Arrange the carrots, broccoli, zucchini, and edamame on the bottom tier of the steamer baskets. Arrange the pepper, snow peas, water chestnuts, mushrooms, and cabbage in the top tier. Place the baskets over the boiling liquid and cover. Steam for 10 to 15 minutes. If using a single steamer basket, steam the vegetables in three or four batches, depending on how much will fit in the basket at one time. Check for doneness by piercing a carrot or broccoli piece with the tip of a knife. You want the vegetables tender, but not mushy.

**4.** In a large warmed serving bowl, place the soba, then the vegetables, and pour the sauce over all, tossing gently to combine and evenly coat. Portion into individual shallow bowls and sprinkle with the green onions. Pass more sesame oil for drizzling.

# Down-to-Earth Linguine with Clams

C lams are high in protein and low in cholesterol and calories. This is a recipe adapted from my friend and fellow food writer Jan Nix, who also wrote a column at the San Jose *Mercury News*. There is *lots* of parsley here, almost as much as the clams, so no, that's not a typo. It is a delicious, satisfying pasta. No cheese, please, with seafood pasta sauces. ○ *Serves 4*

**COOKING METHOD:** Stovetop
**PREP TIME:** 15 minutes
**COOK TIME:** About 20 minutes

¼ cup extra virgin olive oil
4 cloves garlic, minced
½ cup dry white wine
Three 6½-ounce cans chopped clams, undrained
1 tablespoon minced fresh basil
1 tablespoon minced fresh oregano
1¼ cups loosely packed chopped fresh flat-leaf parsley (1 bunch)
1 pound fresh linguine
Salt and freshly ground black pepper
Lemon wedges for serving

**1.** Bring a large pot of salted water to a boil.

**2.** Meanwhile, heat the olive oil in a large saucepan over medium-low heat and cook the garlic until it just turns golden, 1 to 2 minutes; do not allow to darken or burn. Add the wine and simmer for 5 to 6 minutes, to reduce a little bit and burn off some alcohol. Drain the juice of the canned clams into the saucepan. Add the basil, oregano, and parsley; simmer for 5 minutes. Add the clams and leave over the lowest heat while the pasta cooks.

**3.** Cook the pasta according to package directions. Drain and place in a warmed shallow serving bowl. Top with the sauce and toss gently to combine. Add salt and pepper and toss again. Serve pronto with the lemon wedges.

# Shells with Tuna and Tomato Sauce

C anned tuna and tomatoes cook up into a lovely traditional pasta sauce in 30 minutes. I use a cuplike pasta, such as medium-size shells, to hold the sauce. There is only a whisper of anchovy paste, which dissolves into the sauce. It is actually the secret ingredient in many Italian sauces. ○ *Serves 4*

**COOKING METHOD:** Stovetop
**PREP TIME:** 15 minutes
**COOK TIME:** About 30 minutes

2 tablespoons olive oil
2 cloves garlic, minced
¼ teaspoon anchovy paste
One 16-ounce can Italian plum tomatoes, pureed in a food processor
1 tablespoon dry white wine
½ teaspoon red pepper flakes
2 tablespoons capers, rinsed
Freshly ground black pepper
One 7-ounce can water-packed tuna, drained and separated into chunks
¼ cup loosely packed chopped fresh flat-leaf parsley
1 pound medium-size shells

1. Bring a large pot of salted water to a boil.

2. Meanwhile, heat the olive oil in a large saucepan over medium-low heat and cook the garlic for 30 seconds. Remove the pan from the heat and add the anchovy paste to the hot oil. Add the tomatoes, wine, red pepper flakes, capers, and black pepper to taste. Simmer for 20 minutes.

3. Add the tuna and parsley; simmer for another 10 minutes.

4. Cook the pasta according to package directions. Drain and place in a warmed shallow serving bowl. Pour all of the sauce over the pasta and toss gently. Serve immediately.

# Pappardelle with
# Chunky Red Wine Meat Sauce

From the simplest pomodoro sauce of crushed tomatoes and basil to the long-simmered meat ragu, the family of Italian tomato sauces is now pure Americana, as it has become so integral to our melting pot cuisine. Here is a hearty sauce that combines the convenience of fast cooking with the flavor of having simmered for hours. The secret is a jar of your favorite marinara. Please, no added salt here; the jarred marinara has plenty. Keep tubes of imported tomato paste in your refrigerator; it is a high-quality convenience product. ○ *Serves 4*

**COOKING METHOD:** Stovetop
**PREP TIME:** 20 minutes
**COOK TIME:** About 30 minutes

1 pound ground beef chuck or ground turkey

1 medium-size yellow onion, chopped

2 cloves garlic, crushed

One 28-ounce jar marinara sauce

⅔ cup dry red wine

2 tablespoons tomato paste

¼ cup sliced black olives

6 ounces fresh white mushrooms, thinly sliced

2 tablespoons chopped fresh basil

⅛ teaspoon red pepper flakes

1 to 2 tablespoons extra virgin olive oil

1 pound pappardelle

Grated Parmesan-Romano cheese blend for serving

1. Bring a large pot of salted water to a boil.

2. Meanwhile, heat a large skillet over medium-high heat and brown the beef and onion, about 8 minutes. Remove the mixture from the skillet and rinse in a colander or dab with paper towels to remove extra fat. Add the garlic to the empty skillet and cook for 30 seconds. Transfer the beef and garlic to a deep saucepan and add the marinara sauce, wine, tomato paste, olives, mushrooms, basil, and red pepper flakes. Bring to a low boil, then immediately reduce the heat and simmer for about 20 minutes, stirring a few times.

3. Drizzle in the olive oil.

4. Cook the pasta according to package directions. Drain and portion onto shallow plates. Ladle the sauce over the pasta. Serve with the Parmesan-Romano.

# Italian Pasta and Turkey Meatballs

Americans have taken the art and craft of meatball-making a step further by using ground turkey instead of the traditional beef. You can serve these turkey meatballs over spaghetti or penne (with more Parmesan all over the top), over rice, or piled into a sweet French roll for a hearty sandwich. Note the technique for patting the meat into a rectangle and cutting it into squares to form equally portioned meatballs. These are from the kitchen of my sister, Amy.

**o** *Serves 2 with leftovers*

**COOKING METHOD:** Oven and stovetop
**PREP TIME:** 30 minutes
**COOK TIME:** About 30 minutes

### MEATBALLS

¼ large yellow onion, finely chopped
3 cloves garlic
About ¼ cup chopped fresh flat-leaf parsley
1 pound ground dark turkey meat
½ cup dry bread crumbs
⅓ cup grated Parmesan cheese, plus a few more tablespoons for rolling the meatballs
1 egg, beaten
½ teaspoon dried oregano
½ teaspoon salt
½ teaspoon freshly ground black pepper

### SAUCE

3 tablespoons olive oil
1 medium-size yellow onion, finely chopped
One 28-ounce can diced tomatoes in juice, undrained
4 tablespoons tomato paste
½ cup chicken broth
½ teaspoon salt
Freshly ground black pepper

1 pound spaghetti or penne
Grated Parmesan cheese for serving

**1.** Preheat the oven to 400°F.

**2.** To make the meatballs, place the onion, garlic, and parsley in a food processor and pulse to finely chop. Place the turkey in a medium-size mixing bowl, breaking it up a bit with your fingers or a large fork. Add the bread crumbs, Parmesan, onion-parsley mixture, egg, oregano, salt, and pepper. Mix well using your hands or a large fork. Be careful not to compact the meat, which will make your meatballs tough.

**3.** On a cutting board, lightly pat the meat mixture into a thick rectangle, about 8 by 6 inches. With a table knife, cut a cross, dividing the rectangle into 4 equal portions; further divide the 4 portions in half, to make 8 equal portions. Gently shape each portion into a meatball, each a bit bigger than a golf ball. Roll the meatballs in some Parmesan cheese and place on a parchment paper–lined baking sheet. Bake for 25 to 30 minutes, until firm.

**4.** While the meatballs are baking, make the sauce. Heat the olive oil in a medium-size saucepan over medium heat. Add the onion and cook until soft but not browned, about 3 minutes. Add the tomatoes, tomato paste, broth, salt, and pepper. Stir to blend, partially cover, and simmer for 20 minutes.

**5.** Meanwhile, bring a large pot of salted water to a boil. Cook the spaghetti according to package directions. Drain.

**6.** Lift the meatballs off the baking sheet with a slotted spoon and add to the hot sauce, spooning some sauce over them. Cover and keep on low heat until ready to serve. Portion the pasta onto shallow plates, place 4 meatballs on top, and pour some sauce over the meatballs and pasta. Serve immediately with cheese on the side.

# Little Ear Pasta with Sausage and Red Peppers

T his recipe uses orecchiette, a pasta very popular in Italy, which translates to "little ears," a shape sort of like a half shell with one side a dash thicker than the other. Toss a green salad to accompany this dish and serve with a nice crusty baguette or some breadsticks with butter. ○ *Serves 4*

**COOKING METHOD:** Stovetop
**PREP TIME:** 20 minutes
**COOK TIME:** About 25 minutes

¼ cup olive oil
4 cloves garlic
1½ pounds sweet Italian turkey sausage, casings removed
1 medium-size red bell pepper, diced
1 medium-size green or yellow bell pepper, diced
1 pound orecchiette or medium-size shells
Salt and freshly ground black pepper
Grated Parmesan cheese for serving

**1.** Bring a large pot of salted water to a boil.

**2.** Meanwhile, heat a large skillet over medium-low heat and add the oil. Add the whole garlic cloves and cook until golden, 6 to 8 minutes; discard the garlic. Increase the heat to medium-high and add the sausage and peppers. Brown the sausage until no pink remains, about 8 minutes, breaking it apart as it cooks.

**3.** Cook the pasta according to package directions. Drain, reserving ½ cup of the cooking water, and return to the cooking pot. Add the sausage and peppers plus enough cooking water to evenly moisten the pasta. Season with salt and pepper. Portion onto shallow plates and serve with the Parmesan.

# Chinese Spaghetti with Pork Sauce

One of the classics of Chinese cuisine is a thick sauté of ground pork and assertive spices poured over thin noodles and eaten with chopsticks. This lovely shift of the predictable Mediterranean flavors to the prominent flavors of soy sauce and vinegar is positively addicting. While many Asian noodles are boiled, then pan-fried, in this dish they have been simply boiled and then tossed with the extra-thick meat sauce, a style called lo mein. This dish of pork and noodles is so popular that it has its own melodic name, which translates to "ants climbing a tree." You can get fresh thin Chinese noodles in the refrigerated case, or just use Italian vermicelli or angel hair pasta. ● *Serves 4*

**COOKING METHOD:** Stovetop
**PREP TIME:** 20 minutes
**COOK TIME:** About 25 minutes

1½ pounds ground pork
1 large onion, finely chopped
3 cloves garlic, minced
¾ cup tomato-based chili sauce (look next to the ketchup in the market)
⅓ cup water
5 tablespoons reduced-sodium soy sauce
2 tablespoons cider vinegar or Chinese black vinegar
Freshly ground black pepper
1 pound fresh vermicelli or angel hair pasta
1 medium-size cucumber, peeled, seeded, and diced
4 green onions (white part and 3 inches of the green), chopped

1. Bring a large pot of salted water to a boil.

2. Meanwhile, heat a large skillet over medium-high heat and brown the pork, about 10 minutes. Drain or dab with paper towels to remove extra fat. Add the onion and garlic, cooking for 3 minutes, then add the chili sauce, water, soy sauce, vinegar, and pepper to the pan. Cook, uncovered, for 8 to 10 minutes.

3. Meanwhile, cook the pasta according to package directions. Drain and place in a warmed shallow serving bowl. Pour the pork sauce over the pasta, then sprinkle with the cucumber and green onions. Serve immediately.

# Empress Chili and Spaghetti

Empress chili is sort of famous, in a chili sort of way. It refers to John Kiradjieff's Cincinnati chili, which he served in that town's first chili parlor, the Empress. It is a chili that has its roots in the Greek population in urban Midwest communities. They add cinnamon and allspice to their chili, just like they do to their moussaka meat sauce, sweeten it with sherry wine, give it depth with a dash of unsweetened cocoa powder, and serve it over spaghetti. Topped with a spoonful of red kidney beans, cheddar cheese, and chopped raw onion, it is then known as "five-way chili." ○ *Serves 4*

**COOKING METHOD:** Stovetop
**PREP TIME:** 20 minutes
**COOK TIME:** About 30 minutes

2 tablespoons olive oil

1 pound beef chuck, ground for coarse chili grind, if possible

1 medium-size yellow onion, chopped

1 large red bell pepper, diced

1 large green bell pepper, diced

1 tablespoon chili powder, or to taste

2 teaspoons unsweetened cocoa powder

½ teaspoon ground cinnamon

¼ teaspoon ground allspice

Pinch of cayenne pepper

One 28-ounce can diced tomatoes in juice, undrained

2 tablespoons tomato paste

¼ cup dry sherry

2 teaspoons Worcestershire sauce

1 teaspoon salt, or to taste

1 pound spaghetti

About ¾ cup sour cream, for serving

1. Bring a large pot of salted water to a boil.

2. Meanwhile, heat a large skillet over medium-high heat and add the oil. Brown the beef and onion, about 8 minutes. Add the peppers to the skillet and cook for 5 to 8 minutes, until soft. Add the chili powder, cocoa, cinnamon, allspice, and cayenne; cook, stirring, for 1 minute. Add the tomatoes and their juice, tomato paste, sherry, and Worcestershire sauce. Bring to a low boil, then immediately reduce the heat and simmer for about 15 minutes to thicken, stirring a few times. Season with salt.

3. Cook the pasta according to package directions. Drain and portion onto shallow plates. Spoon the sauce over the pasta and top with sour cream.

# Ravioli with Quick Tomato Basil Sauce

**I** have loved ravioli since I was a kid and always ordered it whenever going out to dinner in an Italian restaurant. Today there are many different fillings to choose from, anything from plain ricotta cheese to artichoke to prosciutto; there's even ravioli with nondairy tofu filling. This is one of the simplest sauces, and it is excellent on ravioli. You can use an immersion blender in lieu of the food processor, if you like. ● *Serves 4*

**COOKING METHOD:** Stovetop
**PREP TIME:** 15 minutes
**COOK TIME:** About 15 minutes

One 32-ounce can Italian plum tomatoes in juice, undrained
1 shallot, quartered
⅓ cup fresh basil leaves
Salt and freshly ground black pepper
2 tablespoons extra virgin olive oil
Two 9-ounce packages ravioli of your choice
⅔ cup grated Romano or Parmesan cheese

**1.** Combine the tomatoes, shallot, and basil in a food processor and pulse to puree. Season with salt and pepper. Pour into a saucepan and simmer for 15 minutes, uncovered. Stir in the olive oil.

**2.** Meanwhile, bring a large pot of salted water to a boil. Cook the ravioli according to package directions. Drain and portion onto shallow plates. Top with some sauce and pass the cheese at the table.

# Ravioli with Mushrooms and Sweet Peas

This has to be the ravioli I make the most. I originally made it with frozen peas for catering, but you can make this extra special by using fresh peas. This is a sauceless pasta dish that is really delicious in its simplicity. ● *Serves 4*

**COOKING METHOD:** Stovetop
**PREP TIME:** 20 minutes
**COOK TIME:** About 15 minutes

Two 9-ounce packages meat or cheese ravioli
5 tablespoons unsalted butter
2 shallots, minced
12 ounces fresh white mushrooms, thinly sliced
2 cups frozen petite peas, thawed
Salt and freshly ground black pepper
½ cup grated Parmesan cheese

**1.** Bring a large pot of salted water to a boil. Add the ravioli and cook according to package directions. Drain and set aside.

**2.** In a large skillet, melt the butter over medium-high heat. Add the shallots and mushrooms. Cook to brown the mushrooms and evaporate the liquid, about 10 minutes. Add the peas and cook for a few minutes to heat them.

**3.** Add the ravioli to the skillet, tossing well to combine and heat through. Season with salt and pepper. Portion onto shallow plates and sprinkle with the cheese. Serve immediately.

# Gnocchi with Lamb Ragu

R*agu* is a derivative of the French word *ragoûter*, meaning "the arousing or enhancing of taste." Chunky meat sauces are good on the larger pasta types like pappardelle, on ridged pasta tubes, or, as here, on gnocchi, once available only in Italian neighborhood delis or homemade, but now readily found in the fresh pasta section of the supermarket. Make this when you see really fresh ground lamb. Serve with a green salad or steamed green beans. Gnocchi are also good pan-fried in olive oil and served as a side dish to steak and poultry.

○ *Serves 4*

**COOKING METHOD:** Stovetop
**PREP TIME:** 20 minutes
**COOK TIME:** About 45 minutes

2 tablespoons olive oil
1 medium-size yellow onion, finely chopped
2 cloves garlic
1 pound ground lamb
One 28-ounce can crushed tomatoes in heavy puree
2 tablespoons tomato paste
2 tablespoons dry white wine
1 bay leaf, broken in half
Salt and freshly ground black pepper
1 pound potato gnocchi
1 cup grated Romano or Parmesan cheese

**1.** In a large skillet, heat the olive oil over medium heat. Add the onion and sauté for 5 minutes, or until the onion is tender. Place the whole garlic cloves on toothpicks (for easy retrieval later), add them to the pan, and cook for 1 minute more. Stir in the lamb and cook for 10 minutes, stirring frequently to break up any lumps, until it is no longer pink. Add the tomatoes, tomato paste, wine, bay leaf, and salt and pepper. Bring the sauce to a simmer and reduce the heat to low. Cook, stirring occasionally, until the sauce is thickened, about 30 minutes. Discard the garlic and bay leaf.

**2.** Bring a large pot of salted water to a boil. Cook the gnocchi according to package directions. Drain. Ladle the sauce over the gnocchi and sprinkle with the cheese.

Polenta is a fancy name for cornmeal. Polenta is made from regular cornmeal or a coarse cornmeal and cooks in milk, water, or broth. For the traditional version, it takes a bit of cooking and constant stirring for at least 20 minutes to get it to its nice creamy texture. For weeknights, go for the imported instant polenta; those grains are plumped and ready in 5 minutes. Use a whisk to stir it into the liquid to prevent lumping, or stir with a wooden spoon for that traditional touch. A perfect polenta splatters and spits a bit as it bubbles. If you don't want to fuss with making the polenta, it comes ready-made in sausage-shaped tubes (though that version is often high in sodium). You can use this recipe as a foundation for many Italian tomato-based sauces for quick, delicious dinners.

## Creamy 5-Minute Polenta

Remember that polenta, which is ground cornmeal, should always smell fresh before cooking and be stored in the refrigerator or freezer. It blends well with all manner of sauces and even sautéed vegetables or a drizzle of olive oil. It is incredibly versatile and can be served as a side dish to homespun dishes like sautéed pork chops, sausages, or chicken cacciatore. If you wish to serve it with a melting cheese, such as fontina, spoon half the portion onto a plate, sprinkle with the cheese, and top with the rest of the portion of polenta, layering instead of stirring it into the mass. It is amazing when mixed with crumbled blue cheese and walnuts and served as a side dish to chicken or beef. **◉ Serves 4**

2 cups water
2 cups chicken broth
1¼ cups instant polenta
2 tablespoons unsalted butter
⅓ cup grated Parmesan cheese

In a medium-size saucepan, bring the water and the broth almost to a boil over medium heat. Pour in the polenta in a slow stream, whisking constantly to avoid clumping. Reduce the heat to low. Cook, stirring frequently, until smooth and thick, about 5 minutes. The polenta will make soft mounds and splatter a bit while cooking. Stir in the butter and cheese. Spoon onto plates and serve immediately.

Alternatively, you can spread the polenta in a greased 8-inch square baking pan and refrigerate to firm up. You can warm this firm version in a low oven to reheat, or you can pan-fry slices to serve as a bed for sauces and other toppings or as a simple side dish.

# Creamy Polenta and
# Weeknight Bolognese Sauce

B olognese is the epitome of the long-simmered Italian tomato sauce. But I don't have hours for simmering on a weeknight. Here is the quick version, and it is every bit as good as the long-simmered version. Bolognese has the addition of milk to tenderize the meat, which is an odd ingredient, and I always think it will not work, but it does. Pour lots of this sauce over a pile of polenta (or pasta) and luxuriate in the taste sensation. Serve with a big green salad.  ○ *Serves 4*

**COOKING METHOD:** Stovetop
**PREP TIME:** 20 minutes
**COOK TIME:** About 40 minutes

¼ cup olive oil
1¼ pounds ground beef chuck or ground turkey
2 shallots, minced
3 tablespoons minced carrot
1 stalk celery, minced
½ cup milk
One 14½-ounce can vegetable broth
⅔ cup dry white wine
1½ cups crushed tomatoes in heavy puree
Salt and freshly ground black pepper
1 recipe Creamy 5-Minute Polenta (left)
Parmesan cheese for serving (optional)

**1.** In a deep saucepan, heat the olive oil over medium-high heat. Add the beef, shallots, carrot, and celery, and cook until all the pink is gone from the meat, breaking up the clumps, 3 to 5 minutes. Add the milk and reduce the heat to medium, cooking until the milk is absorbed, 3 minutes. Add the broth, wine, and tomatoes and adjust the heat to high, bringing to a boil, then reduce the heat to low. Season with salt and pepper. Simmer, uncovered, stirring occasionally, until thick, 30 minutes.

**2.** Meanwhile, prepare the polenta. Divide the polenta among dinner plates and spoon the sauce over the top. Pass a bowl of Parmesan, if you wish.

# Not Your Mother's Microwave Risotto with Asparagus and Mushrooms

**P**urists might declare this a travesty, but when time is of the essence, risotto made in the microwave is just one of those surprise modern technique substitutions that really works. I love risotto, but often, especially on weeknights, I do not want to take the time to stand, chained to the stove, stirring and stirring for 45 minutes. The technique used here is precise, but very easy. This recipe was created by Sam Gugino, who was my first food editor at the San Jose *Mercury News* in the late 1980s. He was, and still is, an inspired cook and food writer, bringing to the readership many wonderfully practical and enduring recipes and recommendations. ○ *Serves 4*

**COOKING METHOD:** Microwave oven
**PREP TIME:** 10 minutes
**COOK TIME:** About 25 minutes

2 tablespoons unsalted butter
2 tablespoons olive oil
3 tablespoons minced shallots
1½ cups Arborio or Carnaroli rice
3¾ cups low-sodium chicken broth, heated
6 ounces fresh mushrooms of your choice, sliced
12 ounces asparagus spears, cut into 2-inch pieces on the diagonal
Salt and freshly ground black pepper
¾ cup grated Parmesan cheese

**1.** Place the butter and oil in a deep 9-inch round or square microwave-safe dish. Heat, uncovered, for 2 minutes on High to melt and warm. Add the shallots and stir to coat; cook for 4 minutes. Add the rice and stir to coat all the grains; cook on High for 2 minutes. Pour in the hot broth and cook on High for 10 minutes. Add the mushrooms and asparagus (the mixture will be undercooked and a bit soupy at this point); cook on High for 8 minutes.

**2.** Taste for texture (risotto should be tender and creamy, yet at the same time chewy) and season with salt and pepper. If not tender, continue to cook on High in 2-minute intervals, adding a tablespoon or two of hot broth, if necessary. Remove the dish from the microwave, stir in the cheese, and serve immediately.

# Golden Risotto with
# Fresh Corn and Ginger

F resh corn risotto is such a guiltless pleasure. Use one of those fabulously convenient corn zippers (great name) for cutting the corn off the cob. You can order one at www.williams-sonoma.com. You will have some of the milk from the corn, as well, and that will contribute to the creaminess of the finished risotto. If you like, garnish the top with some strips of prosciutto, sautéed scallops, or cooked shrimp. ● *Serves 4*

**COOKING METHOD:** Microwave oven
**PREP TIME:** 10 minutes
**COOK TIME:** About 25 minutes

3 tablespoons olive oil
½ white onion, minced
1 clove garlic, minced
One 1-inch chunk fresh ginger, grated
1½ cups Arborio or Carnaroli rice
4 cups low-sodium chicken broth, heated
1 cup fresh corn kernels (from 2 to 3 ears)
Salt and freshly ground black pepper
1 cup grated Parmesan cheese
2 tablespoons unsalted butter

**1.** Place the oil in a 9-inch round or square microwave-safe dish. Heat in the microwave, uncovered, for 2 minutes on High to melt and warm. Add the onion, garlic, and ginger, and stir to coat; cook on High for 2 minutes. Add the rice and stir to coat all the grains; cook on High for 4 minutes. Pour in the hot broth and cook on High for 10 minutes. Add the corn (the mixture will be undercooked and a bit soupy at this point); cook on High for 8 minutes.

**2.** Taste for texture (the risotto should be tender and creamy, yet at the same time chewy) and season with salt and pepper. If not tender, cook on High in 2-minute intervals, adding a tablespoon or two of hot broth, if necessary. Remove the dish from the microwave, stir in the cheese and butter, and serve immediately.

Many dishes transform into a complete meal with a bit of starch on the side. Here are five excellent, and fast, rice recipes that will complement a wide variety of dishes. You will notice I call for white rice in the following recipes. That is because of their quick cooking time. If you wish to use brown rice, use instant brown rice, unless you are able to wait the 45 minutes cooking time (it takes approximately double the amount of time as white rice) or have a stash of cooked rice in little bags waiting in the freezer. There is now even an instant wild rice from Lundberg, as well as some white and wild rice mixes from Uncle Ben's from which to choose. I also use some of the packaged rice mixes, especially yellow rice, on occasion. Don't pass up black Forbidden rice or red Bhutanese rice, both packaged by Lotus Foods; they are a delightful change from regular rice, and they cook in 30 minutes.

## Fragrant Coconut Rice

There is coconut rice made with shredded coconut and coconut rice made with coconut milk. This is in the latter category. Serve with stir-fries or Indian- or Thai-inspired dishes.

**○ Serves 4**

One 14-ounce can coconut milk
⅓ cup water
Zest of ½ lemon
¼ teaspoon freshly grated nutmeg
4 whole cloves
1 cup long-grain white rice
Pinch of salt

Bring the coconut milk, water, zest, nutmeg, and cloves to a slow boil in a small saucepan. Add the rice and salt. Reduce the heat to the lowest setting, cover tightly, and simmer until all the liquid is absorbed, 20 to 25 minutes. Remove from the heat and let stand for 10 minutes, covered, then serve.

## Sauté of Corn, Rice, and Fresh Basil

Adapted from my rice cooker cookbook and a knockout favorite, this is one of the best ways to use fresh corn cut off the cob. It is basically a fried rice, American style. You will love this with fish or poultry. **○ Serves 4**

2 tablespoons unsalted butter

2 tablespoons olive oil

2 tablespoons minced shallots

6 to 7 medium-size ears white corn, kernels removed, or one 12-ounce bag frozen baby white corn, thawed (3 to 3½ cups)

2 cups cooked, cooled rice

3 tablespoons drained and minced sun-dried tomatoes packed in oil

¼ cup minced fresh basil leaves

Salt and freshly ground black pepper

In a large skillet, heat the butter and oil over medium-high heat. Add the shallots and sauté for 1 minute, until soft. Add the corn and cook for 1 to 2 minutes. Add the rice to the skillet, breaking up any clumps, if necessary. Sauté the rice and corn for 2 minutes, allowing it to heat up and grow fragrant. Add the sun-dried tomatoes and basil; keep stirring. Cook for another few minutes to heat all the ingredients. Season with salt and pepper, and serve hot.

## Rice Pilaf with Raisins and Almonds

Properly made rice pilaf, here with the touch of almonds and raisins, is one of the best ways to prepare rice as a side dish to plain chicken or Indian- or Moroccan-spiced dishes.  ◐ Serves 4

1 tablespoon unsalted butter

3 tablespoons finely chopped onion

¼ cup slivered blanched almonds

1 cup basmati rice, rinsed until water runs clear

1 heaping tablespoon dark or golden raisins

1½ cups chicken broth

Pinch of salt

In a small saucepan over medium heat, melt the butter. Add the onion and almonds; cook until the onions are wilted and the almonds are a bit golden. Add the rice and raisins; stir until the rice is evenly coated. Add the broth and salt. Bring to a boil, then reduce the heat to the lowest setting. Cover tightly and simmer for 20 minutes, until all the liquid is absorbed and the rice is tender. Remove from the heat and let stand for 10 minutes, covered, then serve.

## Saffron Rice with Green Onions

Saffron rice is so delicate and versatile that it goes with just about every stew, curry, and stir-fry I make. Use 2½ cups of liquid if you are using converted rice. ● Serves 4

2 cups chicken or vegetable broth
1 cup long-grain white rice
Pinch of salt (optional)
1 tablespoon unsalted butter
Pinch of saffron threads or ⅛ teaspoon ground turmeric
2 tablespoons finely chopped green onions or chives

Bring the broth to a boil in a small saucepan. Add the rice, salt, if using, butter, and saffron. Reduce the heat to the lowest setting, cover tightly, and simmer until all the liquid is absorbed, 20 to 25 minutes. Remove from the heat and sprinkle with the green onions. Let stand for 10 minutes, covered, then serve, stirring the green onions into each portion.

## Lemon Rice

Lemon rice is perfect for serving with all types of fish, poultry, or vegetable dishes. Once you try it, you will find yourself making it once a week. ● Serves 4

3 cups water or chicken broth
1½ cups long-grain white rice
Pinch of salt
6 tablespoons (¾ stick) unsalted butter
1 clove garlic
Grated zest and juice of 1 lemon
2 tablespoons minced fresh flat-leaf parsley

Bring the water to a boil in a heavy saucepan. Add the rice, salt, and 1 tablespoon of the butter. Place the whole clove of garlic on top. Reduce the heat to the lowest setting. Cover tightly and simmer for 20 to 25 minutes, until all the liquid is absorbed. Let stand for 10 minutes, covered. Remove the garlic and discard if desired. Stir in the remaining 5 tablespoons butter, the lemon zest and juice, and the parsley. Serve immediately.

# Italian Sausage and
# Red Sauce with Rice

T his is real home cooking, but it is home cooking in Europe as well as in the United States. I love red sauce of any type over rice. To my surprise, my friend in France agreed with me. "Oh, we eat *riz et tomates* all the time!" she exclaimed. My love affair with the local market's homemade Italian sausage inspired me to add that to this sauce, and I vary the cheese, sometimes using Parmesan, other times Asiago or Pecorino-Romano. You don't even need the vegetables if you don't want them. There is a dash of juggling here: Make the sauce first, then put on the rice, and finally cook the sausage. ○ *Serves 4*

**COOKING METHOD:** Stovetop
**PREP TIME:** 20 minutes
**COOK TIME:** About 35 minutes

3 tablespoons olive oil

½ cup chopped onion

1 medium-size zucchini, diced, or 4 ounces fresh white mushrooms, sliced

One 32-ounce can tomato puree

One 6-ounce can tomato paste

Pinch of dried oregano or 1 teaspoon chopped fresh oregano or basil

3½ cups plus 3 tablespoons water

1¾ cups long-grain white rice

1½ pounds Italian pork or turkey sausage (half mild and half hot), casings removed

Salt and freshly ground black pepper

¾ cup grated Romano, Parmesan, or Asiago cheese

**1.** In a deep saucepan, heat 2 tablespoons of the olive oil over medium heat and sauté the onion until very soft, about 5 minutes. Add the zucchini and sauté a minute or two to soften. Add the tomato puree, tomato paste, and oregano. Bring to a boil, then simmer, uncovered, for 15 minutes.

**2.** In a medium-size saucepan, bring the 3½ cups water to a boil. Add the remaining 1 tablespoon olive oil. Add the rice, cover, and cook until the water is absorbed and the rice is tender, 20 minutes.

**3.** In a large skillet over medium heat, cook the sausage with the 3 tablespoons water. Cover and cook for 5 to 7 minutes, until lightly browned, breaking it apart as it cooks. Remove the sausage with a slotted spoon, draining off any fat, and add it to the tomato sauce. Season with salt and pepper. Cook the sauce for 10 more minutes, or until the rice is done.

**4.** Ladle the rice into shallow bowls, top with some sauce, and pass the cheese at the table.

# Suppertime Fried Rice
# with Tofu and Vegetables

O nce you find out how convenient and tasty a tofu and vegetable fried rice is, I guarantee that you will make it more often for dinner. Quick-cooking vegetables can be added raw, like napa cabbage, bok choy, mushrooms, celery, zucchini, green peas (these can go in straight from the freezer), shredded carrot, and canned vegetables such as bamboo shoots and water chestnuts. For veggies that take longer to cook, such as broccoli or carrots, cut into small pieces. To save time, use pre-washed and pre-cut packaged vegetables that are often labeled especially for stir-fry. Don't use too many vegetables, or too much of one kind, though; you don't want to overwhelm the rice. ○ *Serves 4*

**COOKING METHOD:** Stovetop
**PREP TIME:** 20 minutes
**COOK TIME:** About 20 minutes

3 to 4 tablespoons canola oil, light olive oil, or peanut oil

2 large or extra-large eggs, lightly beaten (you can add another egg or two, if you like)

¼ red onion, diced

½ cup diced bell pepper of your choice

4 ounces fresh mushrooms of your choice, sliced

8 ounces baked flavored tofu (optional), cut into 1-inch cubes

2 cups assorted stir-fry vegetables in any combination, such as coarsely grated carrot, finely diced celery, finely diced zucchini, chopped broccoli, chopped bok choy, shredded napa cabbage, sliced water chestnuts, chopped green beans, snow peas, or frozen peas

2 cloves garlic, minced

1 tablespoon minced fresh ginger

4 cups cold cooked rice (any variety)

4 tablespoons reduced-sodium soy sauce

4 tablespoons oyster sauce

1 tablespoon Asian sesame oil

¼ cup sliced almonds (optional), toasted

2 to 3 green onions (optional), minced

**1.** Spray a large nonstick wok or skillet twice with nonstick cooking spray. Heat 1 tablespoon of the oil and pour in the eggs. When they have set, turn the omelet over with 2 spatulas; cook briefly on the second side, but do not brown. Slide the omelet out of the pan onto a plate; cut into thin strips with kitchen shears. Set aside.

**2.** In the same wok or skillet, add the remaining 2 to 3 tablespoons oil and add the onion, then stir-fry for a few minutes to soften. Add the bell pepper and mushrooms, cooking for 2 minutes. If using tofu, add it here and cook for 2 minutes. Add the other vegetables, garlic, and ginger, stirring so all the ingredients are mixed together. Add the rice, soy sauce, oyster sauce, and sesame oil to the skillet, breaking up any clumps. Continue cooking, allowing the rice to heat up and grow fragrant. When the vegetables are tender, add the egg strips. Serve hot, sprinkled with the sliced almonds and green onions, if using.

# Vegetarian Paella

**P**aella, a rice dish similar to Creole jambalaya and Mexican *arroz con pollo*, is usually a bit of an extravagance both in terms of ingredients and time. But here I have taken the Spanish signature dish and adapted it enthusiastically into a fast, satisfying, vegetarian one-dish weeknight meal, using quick-cooking brown rice. You can make up your own vegetable combination each time you make the paella once you become comfortable with the technique, just keep the peppers, artichokes, saffron or turmeric, and olives as the base. If you are a purist, get a bottle of Spanish olive oil, which has a slightly different flavor than that of Italian and domestic olive oils.

I have a Calphalon paella pan; it can be used both on the stovetop and in the oven, and I like to use it every chance I get. But you can certainly prepare this dish in a 12-inch cast-iron skillet or even a large Dutch oven. ○ *Serves 4*

**COOKING METHOD:** Stovetop and oven
**PREP TIME:** 30 minutes
**COOK TIME:** About 45 minutes

AIOLI
3 cloves garlic, crushed
2 tablespoons extra virgin olive oil
2 teaspoons fresh lemon juice
¾ cup mayonnaise

3 tablespoons extra virgin olive oil
1 large yellow or white onion, diced
½ green bell pepper, cut into thin strips and halved
½ red bell pepper, cut into thin strips and halved
1 medium-size zucchini, halved lengthwise and sliced
2 cloves garlic, minced
3 cups quick-cooking brown rice
2 cups vegetable broth
1 cup water
2 tablespoons chopped fresh flat-leaf parsley

¼ teaspoon saffron threads, crushed, or ½ teaspoon ground turmeric

2 fresh plum tomatoes, seeded and diced, or 3 canned plum tomatoes, drained and diced

One 12-ounce package frozen artichoke hearts, thawed and coarsely chopped

½ cup frozen petite peas, thawed

⅓ cup coarsely chopped pimento-stuffed green olives

½ teaspoon salt

Freshly ground black pepper

1 lemon, cut into thick wedges, for serving

**1.** To make the aioli, in a small bowl, combine the garlic, olive oil, lemon juice, and mayonnaise; stir until smooth. Refrigerate until serving.

**2.** Preheat the oven to 325°F.

**3.** In a large ovenproof skillet or paella pan, heat the olive oil over medium-high heat and sauté the onion until slightly browned, about 8 minutes. Add the pepper strips and zucchini, cooking until they soften, 3 minutes. Add the garlic and cook for 30 seconds. Add the rice and stir until hot. Add the broth, water, parsley, and saffron; bring to a boil, then reduce the heat to low to simmer. Cover tightly with aluminum foil and cook over low heat for 10 minutes. During the cooking time, move the pan back and forth on the burner for even cooking, if necessary.

**4.** Remove the foil and arrange the tomatoes, artichokes, peas, olives, and a sprinkle of salt and pepper over the top of the rice; press into the rice.

**5.** Place the pan on the lower oven rack and bake for about 20 minutes, until the rice is tender, having absorbed all the liquid, and the vegetables are cooked. Remove from the oven and let stand for 5 to 10 minutes before serving. Serve the paella out of the pan, with bowls of aioli and lemon wedges on the side.

# The Soup Kitchen

After a long day away from home it's easy to resort to take-out or fast food for dinner. But in the time it would take you to fight the extra traffic involved in reaching yet another destination, you can make a pot of comforting homemade soup.

A bowl of aromatic, substantial, almost effortless soup for dinner? Is there such a thing? Yes, and here is a chapter devoted to some of the fastest delectable homemade soup recipes for creating a simple meal.

Often soups are relegated to a first course or lunch. But I like to make main-dish soups, served in a big bowl, that are hearty and filling.

There are few things more satisfying than a good bowl of soup. The combinations made with ingredients such as meat, seafood, vegetables, beans, or pasta in water, milk, or broth are almost limitless. In reality, you don't have to be strict about proportions with soup, which is convenient if you have to make substitutions or are in a hurry. I think whole populations have existed on soups at times, since a few ingredients can go a long way when combined with broth or water, hence the lovely traditional potages of the French and the hearty borschts of Eastern Europe.

If you do not make your own stocks, there are a multitude of commercial broths on the market, in cans, frozen concentrates, and aseptic boxes. You can choose from chicken, beef, and vegetable broths. If you make your own stocks and keep them in the freezer, all the better, but a good bowl of homemade soup should not be passed over just because you are using canned broth.

Soup is a lighter main dish and perfect for many weeknights. You may complement any of the recipes in this chapter with some fresh bread (or the Garlicky Dinner Rolls on page 181), or good crackers and cheese, and a substantial salad using the greens and vegetables of your choice. These recipes are also designed so that there will not be any leftovers, so if you want leftovers, double the recipes.

# Roasted Red Pepper Soup

I was lucky to get this recipe. We had a popular eatery adjacent to a motel in Palo Alto called Fresco's. Everyone went to Fresco's for the red pepper soup. Eventually Fresco's closed, but the restaurant that took its place was besieged with so many requests for the red pepper soup that they had to put it on the menu. A friend sent me a copy of the recipe that must have appeared in the local free newspaper. If you have time and love peppers, roast fresh peppers instead of using the jarred variety. Char the skins over a gas flame or under the broiler. Place in a plastic bag and close the bag to steam off the skins. Remove the blistered skin and seeds under running water. This soup is divine, probably from the heavy cream and butter. I switched the amounts of broth and cream compared to the original recipe, but if you are a hedonist, absolutely switch the proportions back. ○ *Serves 4*

**COOKING METHOD:** Stovetop
**PREP TIME:** 10 minutes
**COOK TIME:** 35 to 40 minutes

¼ cup (½ stick) unsalted butter
½ cup chopped yellow or white onion
One 16-ounce jar roasted red peppers, drained, or 6 fresh red bell peppers, roasted
1 jalapeño chile
1 teaspoon Worcestershire sauce, or to taste
4 cups chicken broth
2 cups heavy cream
Salt

1. Melt the butter in a large saucepan or Dutch oven over medium heat and sauté the onion until limp, about 6 minutes. Do not brown. Add the peppers, jalapeño, Worcestershire sauce, and broth. Bring to a boil, then reduce the heat and simmer, partially covered, for 25 minutes.

2. Puree the soup in batches in a food processor, or use an immersion blender (my preference). Slowly add the cream and then season with salt. Simmer for 5 to 10 minutes, until steaming hot. Do not boil. Serve immediately.

# Curried Carrot Yogurt Soup

**I** have a particular fondness for carrot soup in its many guises. This version is velvety smooth, as well as nutritious and incredibly delicious. It is also a beautiful orange color, naturally sweet, and good hot or cold. ● *Serves 4*

**COOKING METHOD:** Stovetop
**PREP TIME:** 15 minutes
**COOK TIME:** About 30 minutes

6 medium-size carrots, scrubbed or peeled and cut into chunks

2 medium-size russet potatoes, peeled and chopped

1 medium-large white onion, chopped

3 cups chicken or vegetable broth

2 teaspoons hot curry powder

One 1-inch piece fresh ginger, grated

1 teaspoon ground coriander

1 cup plain yogurt

Salt and freshly ground white pepper

4 thin slices lemon, seeded

2 tablespoons thinly sliced green onion

**1.** Combine the carrots, potatoes, onion, broth, curry powder, ginger, and coriander in a large saucepan or Dutch oven over medium-high heat; bring to a boil. Cover and simmer until the carrots and potatoes are tender when pierced, 15 to 20 minutes.

**2.** Allow the soup to cool, uncovered, for 10 minutes, then transfer the solids and some of the broth to a blender or food processor. Add ¾ cup of the yogurt and puree, in batches if necessary, or use an immersion blender right in the pot; you want to obtain the smoothest puree possible. Return to the saucepan. Season with salt and pepper and bring back to a simmer to heat through.

**3.** Serve the soup hot, garnished with a spoonful of the remaining ¼ cup yogurt, the lemon slices, and the green onions.

# Broccoli and Cheddar Soup

**T**his broccoli soup will become one of your favorite from-the-garden soups. Just wait until you taste it—it is pure comfort. The soup tastes best freshly made. Serve with Olive Oil Cornbread (page 248). ● *Serves 4*

**COOKING METHOD:** Stovetop
**PREP TIME:** 15 minutes
**COOK TIME:** About 30 minutes

1 tablespoon olive oil
1 tablespoon unsalted butter
1 medium-size white onion, chopped
1 leek, washed and white part chopped
2 cloves garlic, crushed
2 heads broccoli, cleaned and chopped, including stems
6 cups chicken broth
1 cup half-and-half or heavy cream
2 cups shredded sharp cheddar cheese
Salt and freshly ground black pepper

**1.** Heat the oil and butter in a large saucepan or Dutch oven over medium heat. Add the onion and leek. Cook, stirring occasionally, until softened but not browned, about 5 minutes. Add the garlic; cook for 1 minute. Add the broccoli and broth. Increase the heat to high and bring to a boil. Immediately reduce to a simmer, partially cover, and cook until the broccoli is soft, 20 minutes.

**2.** Add the half-and-half and cheese; stir until melted. Season with salt and pepper and serve immediately.

# Cream of Mushroom Soup

T here is nothing in a can that comes even close to homemade cream of mushroom soup. This is such a delicious soup that it is almost a revelation. You don't need to have any special mushrooms; domestic white mushrooms are fine. Look for lovely, fresh, firm white caps and then go make this soup immediately. Serve with Garlicky Dinner Rolls (recipe follows). ● *Serves 4*

**COOKING METHOD:** Stovetop
**PREP TIME:** 15 minutes
**COOK TIME:** About 40 minutes

Juice of 1 lemon
1¼ pounds white mushrooms, sliced or coarsely chopped
¼ cup (½ stick) unsalted butter
1 medium-size yellow or white onion, finely chopped
2½ tablespoons all-purpose flour
½ teaspoon salt
Pinch of freshly ground black or white pepper
½ cup dry white wine
6 cups chicken broth
½ cup heavy cream
2 egg yolks
3 tablespoons dry sherry

1. In a bowl, squeeze the lemon over the mushrooms; set aside.

2. Melt the butter in a large saucepan or Dutch oven over medium heat and sauté the onion until limp, about 6 minutes. Sprinkle with the flour and cook, stirring, for 1 to 2 minutes. Add the mushrooms and increase the heat to medium-high; stir to coat the mushrooms. Add the salt and pepper. Add the wine and cook until the liquid is absorbed. Add the broth. Bring to a boil, then reduce the heat and cook, partially covered, for 20 minutes, until the mushrooms are tender.

3. In a medium-size bowl, combine the cream and egg yolks and mix well with a whisk. Ladle in a little bit of the soup, working up to 2 cups total and whisking

constantly to prevent curdling, to heat up the mixture. Pour back into the soup pot and stir well to combine; add the sherry. Simmer for 5 to 10 minutes, until steaming hot, but do not boil. Serve immediately.

# Garlicky Dinner Rolls

**◉ *Makes 8 rolls***

½ teaspoon coarse kosher or sea salt
1 tablespoon water
1 teaspoon minced fresh garlic
2 teaspoons finely chopped fresh flat-leaf parsley
¼ cup olive oil
8 store-bought bake-and-serve dinner rolls, preferably American style,
    such as Parker House or cloverleaf

**1.** In a small bowl, stir the salt into the water. Let stand for 5 minutes to dissolve the salt, then stir again. Stir in the garlic, parsley, and oil; mix well.

**2.** Bake the dinner rolls according to package directions.

**3.** Place the hot rolls close together in a parchment paper–lined basket or in a shallow dish and drizzle the garlicky oil mixture evenly over the top. Serve at once.

# Crème of Asparagus Soup

A sparagus soup is an ode to spring. The proportions in this soup are so basic that you can use it for any fresh single vegetable soup—carrot, zucchini, celery, etc. But it is especially nice with asparagus. ● *Serves 4*

**COOKING METHOD:** Stovetop
**PREP TIME:** 5 minutes
**COOK TIME:** About 30 minutes

2 pounds fresh asparagus, ends trimmed
3 tablespoons unsalted butter
1 medium-size white onion, chopped
5 cups chicken broth
⅔ cup crème fraîche, store-bought or homemade (page 185)
Juice of ½ lemon
Salt and freshly ground black pepper

1. Cut off the tips of a dozen asparagus spears and reserve them for the garnish. Coarsely chop the remaining asparagus into approximately ½-inch chunks.

2. Melt the butter in a large saucepan or Dutch oven over medium heat and sauté the onion until limp, about 5 minutes. Add the chopped asparagus and cook for a minute or two. Add the broth and simmer, partially covered, until the asparagus is very tender, about 25 minutes.

3. While the soup is simmering, blanch the reserved asparagus tips in lightly salted boiling water for a couple of minutes, or cook in the microwave, until crisp-tender. Drain and reserve.

4. Transfer the solids with a slotted spoon and some of the broth to puree in a blender or food processor, in batches if necessary, or use an immersion blender right in the pot; you want to obtain the smoothest puree possible. Return to the saucepan. Stir in the crème fraîche and lemon juice. Season with salt and pepper and bring back to a simmer. Ladle into bowls and garnish with the asparagus tips. Serve hot.

# Country Vegetable Chowder

**S**erve this deliciously creamy, rich, and filling wonder with round kaiser or sesame seed rolls, split in half and toasted in a skillet with butter and garlic. Fantastic! ○ *Serves 4*

**COOKING METHOD:** Stovetop
**PREP TIME:** 15 minutes
**COOK TIME:** About 40 minutes

2 tablespoons unsalted butter
2 medium-size leeks, washed, white part only thinly sliced into rounds, then cut in half
2 tablespoons all-purpose or whole wheat pastry flour
2 stalks celery, diced
3 new potatoes, diced
1 teaspoon dried crumbled herbs, such as basil, thyme, or Italian blend
2 cups chicken or vegetable broth
One 14½-ounce can diced tomatoes, undrained
One 16-ounce package frozen baby lima beans, thawed
6 ounces fresh baby spinach leaves (about 3 large handfuls)
1½ cups half-and-half or plain soy milk
Salt

**1.** Melt the butter in a large saucepan or Dutch oven over medium heat and sauté the leeks until limp, about 8 minutes. Sprinkle the leeks with the flour and cook, stirring, for 30 seconds. Add the celery, potatoes, herbs, broth, and tomatoes and their juice. Increase the heat to high and bring to a boil. Reduce the heat, partially cover, and simmer for 20 minutes, until the vegetables are tender.

**2.** Add the lima beans, spinach, and half-and-half. Season with salt and simmer for 10 minutes, until steaming hot. Serve immediately.

# Peggy's Chipotle Sweet Potato Soup

R idiculously easy and ever so satisfying, this soup has that lovely velvety feel on the tongue. My friend Peggy Fallon, who has an impeccable food palate, combined sweet potatoes with smoky chipotle chile peppers, to the best advantage of each. Remove as many chiles as you need from the open can, transfer the remaining chipotles and adobo sauce to a small jar with a tight-fitting lid or a plastic bag, then refrigerate or freeze. ○ *Serves 4*

**COOKING METHOD:** Stovetop
**PREP TIME:** 15 minutes
**COOK TIME:** About 40 minutes

2 tablespoons olive oil
1 large yellow onion, chopped
3 pounds sweet potatoes, peeled and cut into 2-inch chunks
4½ cups chicken or vegetable broth, or more as needed
1 to 2 canned chipotle chiles in adobo sauce, coarsely chopped
½ to 1 cup crème fraîche, store-bought or homemade (right), plus more for garnish
Juice of 2 fresh limes
Salt
Coarsely chopped fresh cilantro

**1.** Heat the oil in a large saucepan or Dutch oven over medium heat. Add the onion and cook, stirring occasionally, until softened but not browned, 3 to 5 minutes. Add the sweet potatoes and enough broth to cover. Increase the heat to high and bring to a boil. Reduce to a simmer, partially cover, and cook until the sweet potatoes are tender when pierced with the tip of a sharp knife, about 30 minutes. Stir in the chipotle chiles and adobo sauce.

**2.** Using an immersion blender, puree the soup until smooth. (Alternatively, let the soup cool for 10 minutes. Then, working in several batches, puree in a blender or food processor; return the mixture to the soup pot.) Cooking over medium-low heat, gently whisk in the crème fraîche and lime juice until well blended and hot. Season to taste with salt and more lime juice, if needed. Top each serving with a small spoonful of crème fraîche and a sprinkling of cilantro. Serve at once.

## · · Homemade Crème Fraîche · ·

There are many ways to make homemade crème fraîche, simply a thickened cream that is used in place of sour cream or heavy cream in recipes. Here are two easy ways.

## Traditional Crème Fraîche

This is the most authentic method, since the mixture sits to ripen and thicken. The recipe can be doubled or tripled with no problem. This is really tasty stuff and will not separate when stirred into hot soup. **○ Makes 1½ cups**

1 cup heavy or whipping cream, not ultra-pasteurized if possible
⅓ cup regular sour cream (not reduced-fat or imitation) or cultured buttermilk
2 tablespoons plain yogurt with acidophilus cultures

1. In a small bowl, combine the heavy cream, sour cream, and yogurt; whisk until smooth. Leave in the bowl or pour into a clean jar or small crock, preferably sterilized in the dishwasher. Cover with plastic wrap. Let stand at room temperature for 6 to 8 hours, or overnight, until thickened. Let stand a few hours longer if you want it a bit thicker.

2. Cover and refrigerate until ready to use. It will continue to thicken as it chills. This keeps in the refrigerator for up to 1 week.

## Fast Low-Fat Crème Fraîche

Ready instantly, this version has a completely different texture from the first, but it works just as well in soups. Use a thick whole-milk yogurt, please. Greek-style yogurt is really good here, since it is strained. **○ Makes 1½ cups**

½ cup whole milk
1 cup thick plain yogurt with acidophilus cultures

In a small bowl, vigorously whisk together the milk and yogurt, or mix with an immersion blender. Cover and refrigerate until ready to use. This keeps in the refrigerator for 2 to 3 days.

# Garlicky Tortellini Soup with Tomato and Spinach

T his is one of my favorite on-the-spot pasta and vegetable soup dinners, the creation of my friend, food writer Peggy Fallon. It uses a package of those wonderful fresh cheese tortellini that grace the refrigerated section of the supermarket. This main-course soup needs only a tossed salad and fresh crusty bread.

○ *Serves 4*

**COOKING METHOD:** Stovetop
**PREP TIME:** 10 minutes
**COOK TIME:** About 25 minutes

2 tablespoons olive oil
6 cloves garlic, finely chopped
5 cups chicken broth or a combination of broth and water
⅛ teaspoon red pepper flakes
1 package (about 9 ounces) fresh or frozen cheese tortellini
One 14½-ounce can diced tomatoes, undrained
12 ounces fresh baby spinach leaves (about 6 large handfuls)
Salt
Freshly shaved or grated Parmesan cheese

Heat the oil in a large saucepan or Dutch oven over medium heat. Add the garlic and cook, stirring, until just fragrant, 30 seconds to 1 minute; do not brown or it will get bitter. Add the broth and pepper flakes. Increase the heat to high and bring to a boil. Add the tortellini and cook about half as long as the package directs. Add the tomatoes and their juice. Reduce the heat to medium-low and cook until the tortellini is tender. Stir in the spinach and cook until just wilted, about 1 minute. Season with salt and serve, passing the cheese at the table.

# Chinese Dumpling Soup with Shiitake Mushrooms, Greens, and Tofu

I saw a version of this soup on one of the TV cooking shows and immediately had to experiment. I adore bok choy and spinach, and those stuffed Chinese pot stickers, and here they are all just tossed into a pot of hot broth. I added mushrooms and tofu to the greens. The fresh shiitake mushrooms are thick and meaty and make a rich, brothy soup. This is so quick and impressive.

○ *Serves 4*

**COOKING METHOD:** Stovetop
**PREP TIME:** 10 minutes
**COOK TIME:** About 30 minutes

Three 14½-ounce cans chicken or vegetable broth
3 cups water
8 medium-size shiitake mushrooms, stemmed and sliced
2 baby bok choy, outer leaves discarded
6 ounces fresh baby spinach leaves (about 3 large handfuls)
6 green onions (white and green parts), sliced on the diagonal into ¼-inch slices
2 cloves garlic, minced
One 3-inch piece fresh ginger, cut into thin slivers
One 12-ounce package Chinese pot stickers stuffed with pork and vegetables,
    or chicken and vegetables, as desired
6 ounces extra-firm tofu, cut into ½-inch cubes
Reduced-sodium soy sauce
Hot chile oil

1. In a large saucepan over medium-high heat, combine the broth and water; bring to a boil. Add the mushrooms, bok choy, spinach, green onions, garlic, and ginger. Return to a boil, then reduce the heat and simmer for 15 minutes, until the vegetables are tender.

2. Add the dumplings and cook according to the package directions. Add the tofu and cook for 5 minutes to heat through. Serve immediately, with cruets of soy sauce and hot chile oil for drizzling.

# Italian Potato Leek Soup

I always describe potato leek soup as the workhorse of the French kitchen, and not surprisingly it is made all over Europe as well. This version has the unexpected additions of rice and cheese, which add plenty of texture and flavor to this gloriously satisfying soup. Don't worry about proportions; just use a leek for every potato. It tastes just as good made with water as with broth, and you simply cook the vegetables until they are mushy, add the rice, then the cheese, and your old-fashioned soup is ready for dinner. Bet you eat two full bowls!

**o** *Serves 4*

**COOKING METHOD:** Stovetop
**PREP TIME:** 10 minutes
**COOK TIME:** About 45 minutes

¼ cup (½ stick) unsalted butter
1 medium-size yellow onion, chopped
3 medium-size leeks, washed and thinly sliced (white part only)
3 medium-size russet potatoes, peeled and cut into chunks
About 6 cups water or vegetable, beef, or chicken broth
¼ cup Arborio or Carnaroli rice
3 tablespoons chopped fresh flat-leaf parsley or chervil
⅓ cup grated Parmesan cheese, plus more for serving
Salt and freshly ground black pepper

**1.** Melt the butter in a large saucepan or Dutch oven over medium heat. Add the onion and cook, stirring occasionally, until softened but not browned, about 5 minutes. Add the leeks, potatoes, and enough water to cover. Increase the heat to high and bring to a boil. Reduce to a simmer, partially cover, and cook until the potatoes are tender, about 20 minutes.

**2.** Using an immersion blender, give a few pulses to coarsely puree the soup. Add the rice and parsley; cook for about 20 minutes, until the rice is soft.

**3.** Stir in the cheese and salt and pepper. Serve immediately, with more cheese on the side.

# Red Lentil Vegetable Soup

T he family of lentils is a lot larger than one can imagine, and they are prominent in Middle Eastern and Indian cuisines. While the humble German brown lentil is the most common in European-style cuisine, brown ones take well over an hour to cook properly. Enter the red lentil, a bit smaller and a lovely salmon color; it cooks in less than half an hour. Be sure to chop the vegetables smaller than usual so they are consistent with the smaller size of the lentil and cook faster as well. Serve with toasted pita bread. ○ *Serves 4*

**COOKING METHOD:** Stovetop
**PREP TIME:** 10 minutes
**COOK TIME:** About 40 minutes

4 tablespoons olive oil
1 medium-size yellow or white onion, finely chopped
2 stalks celery, finely chopped
2 medium-size carrots or parsnips, finely chopped
2 medium-size zucchini, finely chopped
3 tablespoons chopped fresh cilantro stems
½ teaspoon ground cumin
½ teaspoon ground turmeric
One 14½-ounce can diced tomatoes, undrained
5 leaves Swiss chard, chopped
5 cups water
Salt and freshly ground black pepper
Chopped fresh cilantro leaves for serving

**1.** Heat the oil in a large saucepan or Dutch oven over medium heat. Add the onion and cook, stirring occasionally, until softened but not browned, about 5 minutes. Add the celery, carrots, zucchini, and cilantro stems; cook for 5 minutes. Sprinkle with the cumin and turmeric, and cook for another minute. Add the tomatoes, Swiss chard, and water. Increase the heat to high and bring to a boil. Reduce to a simmer, partially cover, and cook until soft, about 30 minutes.

**2.** Season with salt and pepper and serve immediately, sprinkled with cilantro.

# Black Bean Soup

**I** really learned about beans (other than baked beans) when I traveled in Mexico and Central America, since people in these countries eat plenty of beans. When I hit Guatemala, I became instantly hooked on black beans. In the years since, beans have regained an honored place in American cooking, especially with all the artisan beans now available. But black beans, a hallmark of Cuban cooking as well, are among the tastiest. Remember to smash a portion of the beans before serving; it makes the soup nice and thick. If I happen to have a leftover sweet potato, I will add ¼ cup diced. The soup is fine as it is, but it is also good topped with some plain yogurt or sour cream. Or serve it with Sour Cream Cornbread with Cheddar and Corn Kernels (page 249). ● *Serves 4*

**COOKING METHOD:** Stovetop
**PREP TIME:** 5 minutes
**COOK TIME:** About 30 minutes

3 tablespoons olive oil

1 medium-size white onion, chopped

1 large carrot, chopped

1 stalk celery, chopped

1½ teaspoons curry powder of your choice

½ teaspoon ground coriander

Two 15-ounce cans black beans, rinsed and drained

3 cups vegetable broth

Freshly ground black pepper

8 sprigs fresh cilantro, leaves chopped

Juice of 1 lemon or lime

**1.** Heat the oil in a large saucepan or Dutch oven over medium heat. Add the onion, carrot, and celery; cook, stirring occasionally, until softened but not browned, 5 to 8 minutes. Sprinkle in the curry powder and coriander while cooking the vegetables to heat up the spices. Add the beans, broth, pepper, and cilantro leaves. Increase the heat to high and bring to a boil. Reduce to a simmer, partially cover, and cook for 20 minutes.

**2.** Using a slotted spoon, transfer half of the solids to a food processor and puree, or use an immersion blender with a few pulses, or mash by hand against the side of the pot with a fork; stir to combine. Stir in the lemon juice and serve immediately.

# White Bean Soup with Greens

I am always looking for ways to cook greens. This southern Italian soup features creamy white beans and a big bunch of fresh greens. You will adore it for its tastiness with so few ingredients, characteristic of *cucina povera*, which uses the simplest foods in a loving and clever manner. Choose from Great Northern beans or cannellini beans. Do not add the salt before the soup has finished cooking, or it may become too salty. ● *Serves 4*

**COOKING METHOD:** Stovetop
**PREP TIME:** 10 minutes
**COOK TIME:** About 30 minutes

1½ pounds Swiss chard or escarole, ends trimmed
6 cups chicken broth
1 clove garlic, crushed
One 15-ounce can white beans of your choice, rinsed and drained
½ teaspoon salt
⅛ teaspoon freshly ground white pepper
Freshly grated Parmesan cheese
Red pepper flakes

1. Bring a large saucepan of water to a boil over medium-high heat. Add the greens and cook for 5 to 7 minutes, or until barely tender. Drain the greens into a colander, squeezing out as much water as possible. It is not necessary to cut the greens, because they will break apart while they cook in the soup.

2. Add the broth to the saucepan and bring to a simmer over medium-high heat. Add the garlic, beans, and greens. Simmer gently, partially covered, for 20 minutes. Add the salt and the pepper, stir, and serve hot. Pass the cheese and pepper flakes at the table.

# Corn Chowder

W ith many corn chowders, it always seemed to me like something was missing. Well, here are the missing ingredients, as far as I'm concerned—more vegetables and a dash of spicy red pepper flakes. ○ *Serves 4*

**COOKING METHOD:** Stovetop
**PREP TIME:** 10 minutes
**COOK TIME:** About 35 minutes

2 tablespoons olive oil
1 medium-size yellow or white onion, chopped
¼ teaspoon red pepper flakes
2 medium-size russet potatoes, peeled and diced
4 stalks celery, chopped
One 12-ounce bag frozen baby white corn kernels,
    thawed, or 2 cups fresh corn cut off the cob
½ red bell pepper, finely chopped
3 cups chicken broth
One 15-ounce can cream-style corn
1 cup milk
2 tablespoons chopped fresh flat-leaf parsley or cilantro
Salt and freshly ground black pepper

**1.** Warm the oil in a large saucepan or Dutch oven over medium heat. Add the onion and red pepper flakes; cook for about 2 minutes. Add the potatoes, celery, corn kernels, bell pepper, and broth; bring to a boil. Reduce the heat to a simmer and partially cover. Cook for 20 minutes, until the vegetables are tender.

**2.** Add the creamed corn, milk, and parsley; simmer for 10 minutes to heat through. Season with salt and pepper and serve hot.

# Vegetarian Beet and Cabbage Borscht

T he ruby-red beet is very old-fashioned, and variations of this soup have been made all over Europe in winter for generations. I adore the addition of the beet greens. This soup is incredibly easy to make and will become a permanent part of your soup repertoire very quickly. ● *Serves 4*

**COOKING METHOD:** Stovetop
**PREP TIME:** 20 minutes
**COOK TIME:** About 40 minutes

2 tablespoons olive oil
1 medium-size yellow onion, chopped
1½ pounds red beets (3 to 4 beets), peeled and chopped, with
    greens, rinsed and chopped
2 medium-size russet potatoes, peeled and chopped
2 large carrots, thickly sliced
¼ head napa cabbage, shredded
1 teaspoon dried dillweed
2 tablespoons dry red wine, such as Merlot
1 tablespoon tomato paste
Salt
Cold sour cream or plain yogurt for serving

Warm the oil in a large saucepan or Dutch oven over medium heat. Add the onion and cook until soft, 5 minutes. Add the beets, beet greens, potatoes, carrots, cabbage, dillweed, wine, and tomato paste, and then add water to cover by 1 inch. Increase the heat to high and bring to a boil. Reduce the heat, partially cover, and simmer for 30 minutes, until the vegetables are tender but not falling apart. Season with salt and serve topped with spoonfuls of sour cream.

# Tomato Vegetable Soup

**H**ere is the companion to the Chicken Noodle Soup (page 200) that my mother clipped from an article on making a homemade soup to compete with commercial canned soups. If you wish to make this vegetarian, substitute the chicken broth with vegetable broth. I doubled the original recipe and I added a few more vegetables, since I like a big bowl of chunky vegetable soup for dinner.

**○ *Serves 4***

**COOKING METHOD:** Stovetop
**PREP TIME:** 15 minutes
**COOK TIME:** About 45 minutes

One 28-ounce can diced tomatoes, undrained
Three 14½-ounce cans chicken broth
2 cups water
2 medium-size carrots, chopped
1 medium-size yellow onion, diced
2 stalks celery, diced
2 red potatoes, diced
1 cup 1-inch-long pieces green beans
1 cup frozen petite peas
1 cup frozen baby lima beans
1 clove garlic, minced
½ teaspoon salt, or to taste
½ teaspoon dried marjoram
½ teaspoon dried thyme
¼ cup alphabet pasta, mini-bows, or *semi di melone* (optional)

**1.** In a large saucepan over medium-high heat, combine the tomatoes and their juice, the broth, and the water; bring to a boil. Add all of the vegetables, the garlic, salt, marjoram, and thyme. Return to a boil. Reduce the heat and simmer for 40 minutes, until the vegetables are tender.

**2.** If you want to add some alphabet pasta, do so and cook for 5 minutes. Serve immediately.

# Pumpkin and Hominy Tortilla Soup

**I** love creamy pumpkin soup, and this version also contains hominy, which adds a wonderful depth of flavor and texture. It is assembled and cooked in a flash, then served with an assortment of condiments. While the soup is cooking, bake the tortillas strips, make a simple salsa, and then assemble the bowls of garnishes so that diners can add what they wish to the soup. ● *Serves 4*

**COOKING METHOD:** Stovetop
**PREP TIME:** 10 minutes
**COOK TIME:** About 30 minutes

2 tablespoons olive oil
1 medium-size yellow or white onion, chopped
2 cloves garlic, minced
One 15-ounce can whole white hominy, drained
4 cups chicken or vegetable broth
1 teaspoon ground cumin
One 32-ounce can pumpkin puree
1 teaspoon salt
Freshly ground black pepper

**GARNISHES**
6 yellow or white corn tortillas
3 tablespoons olive oil
4 plum tomatoes, chopped
3 green onions (white part and some of the green), chopped
One 2-ounce can roasted chopped green chiles, drained
Pinch of garlic salt
1 avocado, sliced
Shredded Monterey Jack or Mexican white cheese
Fresh cilantro sprigs

**1.** Warm the oil in a large saucepan or Dutch oven over medium heat. Add the onion and cook until transparent, about 8 minutes. Add the garlic and cook, stirring, until just fragrant, 30 seconds. Add the hominy, broth, and cumin; bring to a boil. Reduce to a simmer and partially cover. Cook for 20 minutes.

**2.** Transfer the solids and some of the broth to a blender or food processor to puree, in batches if necessary, or use an immersion blender right in the pot; you want to obtain the smoothest puree possible. Return to the saucepan and add the pumpkin; stir to combine well. Add the salt and pepper and return to a high simmer.

**3.** While the soup is cooking, preheat the oven to 400°F.

**4.** Lightly brush both sides of each tortilla with the oil. With a knife or kitchen shears, cut the tortillas into 2½ by 1-inch strips. Spread the tortilla strips onto a parchment paper–lined baking sheet. Bake until crisp but not browned, 8 to 12 minutes, turning once halfway through baking.

**5.** In a small bowl, combine the tomatoes, onions, green chiles, and garlic salt. Place the tortillas, salsa, avocado, grated cheese, and cilantro in separate bowls. To serve, ladle the hot soup into big bowls. Serve immediately with all of the garnishes for topping.

# White Clam Chowder

**T**his classic American soup is divinely simplistic in its ingredients and technique. It is a thin soup rather than a thick one, and for that reason you should plan on large servings. Of course, you could plan on leftovers instead, if you prefer. The Pumpernickel Croutons really jazz this up. ○ *Serves 4*

**COOKING METHOD:** Stovetop
**PREP TIME:** 10 minutes
**COOK TIME:** About 40 minutes

6 to 8 slices bacon, cut into ¼-inch strips

2 large white onions, sliced and quartered

4 russet potatoes, peeled and diced

3 stalks celery, chopped

One 6½-ounce can minced clams, undrained

One 6½-ounce can chopped clams, undrained

2 quarts milk

2 teaspoons Worcestershire sauce

Few drops of Tabasco sauce

1 to 2 tablespoons unsalted butter

Salt and freshly ground black or white pepper

PUMPERNICKEL CROUTONS

3 cups cubed (about 1 inch square) pumpernickel rye bread, crusts removed

3 to 4 tablespoons olive oil or unsalted butter, melted

¼ cup chopped fresh flat-leaf parsley

**1.** In a large saucepan or Dutch oven over medium-high heat, fry the bacon and onions until just golden, about 8 minutes. Add the potatoes, celery, clams with their liquid, and milk. Reduce the heat to low and simmer, uncovered, for 30 minutes, until the potatoes are tender. Do not allow to boil. Halfway through cooking, stir in the Worcestershire sauce, Tabasco, butter, and salt and pepper.

**2.** While the soup is cooking, make the croutons. Preheat the oven to 400°F.

**3.** Place the bread cubes on an ungreased baking sheet. Drizzle with the olive oil and stir to coat. Toast in the oven until dry and slightly browned, stirring about every 5 minutes to keep from burning. Set aside at room temperature until serving. These are best used the same day they are made.

**4.** Ladle the soup into bowls and sprinkle with lots of parsley and the croutons.

# Chicken Noodle Soup

T wenty years ago my mother clipped out two recipes from *Consumer Reports* magazine, of all places. There was an article about making quick homemade soups that were better than the canned versions. This is one of those recipes, a great little chicken noodle soup and a boon to have around for when you are sick or have children visiting. Everyone loves egg noodles, true comfort food, especially the dried ones you buy in the kosher food section. Get the biggest still-on-the-bone chicken breast half you can find and leave the skin on; that is where the flavor comes from. If you have fresh thyme and marjoram in your garden, by all means, use those instead of the dried. Don't be tempted to add more ingredients. This recipe is perfect in its simplicity. ○ *Serves 2 to 3*

**COOKING METHOD:** Stovetop
**PREP TIME:** 10 minutes
**COOK TIME:** About 45 minutes

One 12-ounce bone-in chicken breast half, skin on
¼ cup finely chopped shallots
4 cups water
2½ cups chicken broth
2 stalks celery, sliced
1½ teaspoons salt, or to taste
¼ teaspoon dried marjoram
¼ teaspoon dried thyme
4 ounces medium-width egg noodles or orzo

**1.** In a large saucepan over medium heat, brown the chicken breast, skin side down, to render some of the fat, about 5 minutes. Remove the chicken. Add the shallots and cook until soft; do not brown. Return the chicken to the pan. Add the water, broth, celery, salt, marjoram, and thyme. Increase the heat and bring to a boil. Reduce the heat and simmer for 30 minutes, until the chicken is cooked through and tender.

**2.** Remove the chicken and let cool slightly. Add the noodles to the hot broth and cook for about 8 minutes, until soft. Dice or shred the chicken, discard the skin and bones, and return the chicken to the pan to heat through. Serve immediately.

# Escarole Sausage Soup

**T**his thick and hearty soup comes courtesy of Julia Wiley, a modern-day farmer who owns Mariquita Farm with her husband (www.mariquita.com). I got it from their charming e-newsletter called *The Ladybug Letter*. Escarole, with its head of broad pale green leaves, is a boutique vegetable these days in the sense that old becomes new again. It is a mild-flavored member of the endive family and is a green greatly favored in European-style soups for its flavor. ○ *Serves 4*

**COOKING METHOD:** Stovetop
**PREP TIME:** 10 minutes
**COOK TIME:** About 40 minutes

1 pound mild or hot Italian sausage (pork or turkey), casings removed
1 large yellow onion, chopped
2 to 4 cloves garlic, to taste, minced
3 cups chicken broth
One 14½-ounce can diced tomatoes, undrained
One 15-ounce can white beans, pinto beans, or garbanzo beans, rinsed and drained
One 3- to 4-inch hunk Parmesan rind (optional)
1 large bunch escarole or other cooking green such as chard, dandelion, kale,
     or spinach, cleaned under running water and coarsely chopped
Salt and freshly ground black pepper

**1.** In a large saucepan or Dutch oven over medium-high heat, cook the sausage until no pink remains. Drain off most of the fat, if any, and remove the meat to a bowl.

**2.** Add the onion to the sausage drippings and cook until transparent, about 5 minutes. Add the garlic and cook, stirring, until just fragrant, 30 seconds. Add the broth, tomatoes with their juice, beans, and cheese rind, if using; bring to a low boil and return the sausage to the soup pot. Reduce to a simmer and partially cover. Cook for about 20 minutes.

**3.** Add the escarole and simmer, partially covered, for 5 to 8 minutes, until the greens are wilted. Season with salt and pepper and serve hot.

# Thai Chicken Soup

O nce you taste this lovely soup you will be a convert. Chicken simmered in coconut milk and ginger makes one of the great soups of the world. Coconut milk is used like cream in Southeast Asian cuisine. This is a streamlined version, ready in a mere 20 minutes. You can grate the ginger on a small ceramic grater, available in Asian groceries, or dice it and process in a small food processor.

*o Serves 4*

**COOKING METHOD:** Stovetop
**PREP TIME:** 5 minutes
**COOK TIME:** About 20 minutes

4 cups canned unsweetened coconut milk
Three 14½-ounce cans chicken broth
Two 4-inch pieces fresh ginger, grated (4 to 5 tablespoons)
Two 6- to 8-ounce boneless, skinless chicken breasts, cut into finger-size strips
1 cup canned sliced bamboo shoots, drained
½ cup fresh lime juice
5 tablespoons Thai fish sauce
Pinch of red pepper flakes
Chopped fresh cilantro leaves

**1.** In a large saucepan over medium heat, heat the coconut milk, broth, and ginger to a low simmer; simmer for 5 to 10 minutes. Do not boil.

**2.** Add the chicken, bamboo shoots, lime juice, and fish sauce. Slowly bring just to a low boil and then simmer for 5 minutes, until the chicken is cooked through. Do not overcook or the chicken will dry out.

**3.** Stir in the red pepper flakes. Serve immediately, sprinkled with lots of cilantro.

# Eggs du Jour

Eggs for supper take center stage in this chapter. Poached, boiled, fried, scrambled, or souffléed, each recipe featuring eggs is quite different, but equally delicious.

Eggs got an undeserving bad rap some years back with all the hype about the cholesterol contained in the yolk. Luckily that negativity has relaxed, thanks to a bevy of alternative egg products, greater diet consciousness, and the realization that the egg is not such a bad guy after all.

Individuals are more aware than ever of where eggs fit into an overall diet abundant in "real foods" such as whole grains, fruits, vegetables, low-fat dairy, and lean meats, fish, and poultry. The egg is still an amazing food to turn to when you want something quick that is high in protein, low in calories, and full in taste.

The protein- and mineral-rich egg is perfect in its entirety and has been known as a convenient source of nutrition for as long as people have been eating it. The yolk and white are synergistic nutritionally, so a long-term diet of egg whites without yolks is discouraged. If you still love your egg white omelet, include one yolk per every two to three whites to prevent a nutritional imbalance.

I use only Grade AA brown or white free-range or cage-free eggs, because I find they taste better, and it works for my environmental commitment to fair treatment of farm animals. Of course, the eggs you buy are a personal choice. There is a marked difference between organic and conventional eggs; in the organic variety the chickens dine upon organic unsprayed vegetarian feed and are not treated with excessive antibiotics. If you live in an area where someone sells extra eggs from his or her own chickens, or if you like having your own flock, you will be assured really fresh eggs. The nutritional value of all eggs is the same, except for those with DHA omega-3 fatty acids on the label, which designates that the chickens were fed flax seeds and/or fish oils with their regular grain diet. If you cannot use fresh eggs, commercial egg substitutes abound (powdered, refrigerated, or frozen), so that even restricted diets can include egg dishes now and then. There are also low-cholesterol, low-sodium fresh eggs, created by hens given a special feed.

Buy refrigerated eggs. I was surprised to learn that eggs refrigerated for 1 week are fresher than eggs kept at room temperature for 1 day. The sell date stamped on the end of the carton is the store pull date; it does not indicate the date by which you must use the eggs. Store the eggs with the pointed ends facing down (the yolk will stay centered as well) and away from strong foods, because the porous shell can absorb refrigerator odors, resulting in an off taste. Discard cracked eggs.

A final bit of advice: The multitalented egg tends to cool quickly, so warm your serving plates (just warm to the touch, please, so you don't cook the eggs further) and head to the table ASAP to enjoy your creation.

# Pasta Frittata

T his typical Italian supper is usually made with leftover pasta, but I make this lovely from-the-pantry dish with freshly cooked De Cecco thin spaghetti. You can use any dry long or tube pasta shape, such as linguine or penne. When you cut the frittata, there will be different patterns due to the pasta. Pasta frittata is a premier inexpensive, satisfying meal. Serve with a mixed salad or sautéed bell peppers. ○ *Serves 4*

**COOKING METHOD:** Stovetop
**PREP TIME:** 10 minutes
**COOK TIME:** 5 to 8 minutes with fresh pasta or 10 minutes with leftover

5 ounces dry pasta of your choice
9 large or extra-large eggs, slightly beaten
1 cup grated Asiago or Romano cheese
¼ cup fresh basil leaves, chopped
2 whole canned plum tomatoes, crushed with your hands, or ¼ cup ground peeled tomatoes, such as Pomi
Salt and freshly ground black pepper
¼ cup olive oil

**1.** Cook the pasta according to package directions. Drain in a colander and let cool for 10 minutes.

**2.** In a medium-size mixing bowl, beat together the eggs and ¾ cup of the cheese. Add the basil, tomatoes, pasta, salt, and pepper. Mix together well with a large spatula.

**3.** Heat a deep 12-inch skillet over medium-high heat. Add the oil and let warm for 2 to 3 minutes to be very hot (otherwise the pasta will stick), tilting the pan to coat the entire surface. Carefully pour in the pasta-egg mixture and immediately reduce the heat to medium. Cook until set and golden brown, 3 to 4 minutes. With a spatula, turn the frittata over and cook the second side for 1 to 2 minutes, until firm but still a bit moist.

**4.** Remove from the heat and, over a large plate, invert the pan so the frittata comes out. Sprinkle with the remaining ¼ cup cheese and cut into wedges. Serve hot or at room temperature.

# Zucchini and Tomato Frittata

A frittata is a large baked omelet, Italian style, served in wedges. It has gained a great following in the past few decades. Frittatas are sublime in taste and really easy to make. They make a great dinner with green salad and old-fashioned garlic bread, or even with a baked potato or brown rice. This is probably one of my oldest recipes; I started making it in the 1970s. It takes an ovenproof skillet; I have a special skillet just for making frittatas. If you use some other type of skillet, be sure to cover the handle with aluminum foil to protect it. This version, my favorite, has zucchini and fresh tomato, but you have a blank canvas here to substitute other vegetables, such as potatoes, artichokes, mushrooms, green onions, and bell peppers. Just keep to the technique and you can be master of the frittata in your kitchen. ○ *Serves 4*

**COOKING METHOD:** Stovetop and oven
**PREP TIME:** 10 minutes
**COOK TIME:** About 35 minutes

1 tablespoon unsalted butter

2 tablespoons olive oil

¼ onion, thinly sliced

2 medium-size zucchini, sliced on the diagonal (2 to 2½ cups)

8 large or extra-large eggs

½ cup water

Pinch of salt

Few dashes of hot sauce, such as Tabasco, or 1 teaspoon tomato sauce

1 medium-size ripe tomato, halved, seeded, and diced (about 1 cup)

1 cup shredded cheddar or fontina cheese

2 tablespoons grated Parmesan cheese

**1.** Preheat the oven to 350°F.

**2.** In a 12-inch ovenproof skillet or sauté pan over medium heat, heat the butter and olive oil; tilt the skillet to coat the bottom and sides. Add the onion and cook until soft, 3 minutes. Add the zucchini and cook a few minutes until crisp-tender; spread the vegetables over the entire surface of the pan.

**3.** In a medium-size bowl, beat together the eggs, water, salt, and hot sauce; pour the mixture over the vegetables in the pan. Sprinkle with the tomato. Let cook, uncovered, for 3 to 5 minutes, to set the bottom of the eggs.

**4.** Place the skillet in the preheated oven and bake for 20 minutes, until set. Sprinkle the top with the cheeses and cook for 5 more minutes. Cut into quarters with a metal spatula and serve immediately out of the pan.

# Denver Omelet

When I was in college, my boyfriend and I spent every Sunday with his grandparents, Granny and Grampy Weick. Grampy's brunch specialty was a Denver omelet. I used to hang over his shoulder while he was cooking, and he would shoo me away while waving the Tabasco bottle, exclaiming, "This is my secret recipe, don't peek, get back to the table." This is still one of my favorite egg dishes any time of day, ripe with happy memories. You can use leftover ham of any type. Omelets come together so quickly, I just make two separate omelets one after another without wiping out the pan and cut each in half for a serving, just like Grampy used to do. Serve with salad and toast. ● *Serves 4*

**COOKING METHOD:** Stovetop
**PREP TIME:** 15 minutes
**COOK TIME:** About 35 minutes

2 tablespoons unsalted butter

1 tablespoon olive oil

1 large yellow or white onion, diced

1 green bell pepper, diced

¾ cup finely diced cooked ham

8 large or extra-large eggs

2 tablespoons milk or cream

Salt and freshly ground black pepper

Few dashes of hot sauce, such as Tabasco

1 cup shredded sharp cheddar cheese (4 ounces)

**1.** Melt the butter and oil in a medium-size skillet over medium-high heat. Add the onion and green pepper; cook until soft and a bit browned, about 10 minutes. Add the ham and cook 5 minutes more, stirring a few times. Remove half of the mixture to a bowl and set aside. Spread the remaining ham and vegetables in the skillet in an even layer over the bottom.

**2.** In a bowl with a fork or whisk, beat 4 of the eggs with 1 tablespoon of the milk, some salt and pepper, and a few splashes of Tabasco. Pour the eggs over the ham and vegetables in the pan. Let cook for 5 to 10 seconds to set the bottom. Using a spatula, lift the edges and tilt the pan so the uncooked eggs can run onto the bottom of the pan. Do not stir or shake the pan. Continue in this manner of letting the uncooked eggs run under and then leaving it alone to cook until the wet eggs are all a firm consistency, yet still soft and moist.

**3.** Sprinkle with half of the cheese. Use the spatula to lift the side of the omelet, and fold it in half to make a half-moon shape. Divide the omelet in half and serve pronto. Add the reserved ham and vegetables back to the pan and make the second omelet using the remaining eggs, milk, salt, pepper, hot sauce, and cheese.

# Sweet Potato Turkey Hash

**C**orned beef hash, move over. Sweet potatoes and turkey are a smashing taste combination in this one-dish meal. This recipe originally came from the North Carolina Sweet Potato Commission. You will need leftover cooked turkey or a rotisserie turkey breast. ● *Serves 4*

**COOKING METHOD:** Stovetop
**PREP TIME:** 15 minutes
**COOK TIME:** About 30 minutes

2 large sweet potatoes, peeled and cut into ¼-inch dice
1 tablespoon unsalted butter
2 tablespoons olive oil
1 small red onion, chopped
1 red bell pepper, diced
1 pound skinless cooked turkey breast, cut into ½-inch dice
Salt and freshly ground black or white pepper
4 large or extra-large eggs
1½ tablespoons chopped fresh chives
1½ tablespoons chopped fresh flat-leaf parsley

**1.** Place the sweet potatoes in a saucepan; add enough water to cover by 1 inch. Bring to a boil and cook for 3 to 4 minutes, until the potatoes are just barely tender. Drain well and set aside.

**2.** Heat the butter and 1 tablespoon of the oil in a large skillet over medium-high heat. Add the onion and bell pepper and cook for about 5 minutes, until lightly brown. Add the drained sweet potatoes. Cook, stirring with a spatula, for about 8 minutes, until the sweet potatoes are browned and crispy. Add the remaining 1 tablespoon oil and the cooked turkey; season with salt and pepper, and cook for about 2 minutes, to heat the turkey.

**3.** Make 4 depressions (3 inches in diameter each) into the hash and break 1 egg into each. Reduce the heat to low, cover, and cook for 4 to 5 minutes, until the eggs are firm and cooked to the desired degree of doneness. Sprinkle with the chives, parsley, and additional salt and pepper, if desired. Cut the hash into 4 portions and serve immediately.

# Joe's Special

**G**rowing up in the San Francisco Bay Area had its culinary perks. One of them was an occasional dinner at Joe's restaurant, which has been serving traditional Italian food for decades. I always ordered homemade ravioli. But the other dish that exemplified Joe's style was simply called Joe's Special, and it was ground beef with mushrooms, spinach, onions, and garlic, all scrambled with eggs. To eat Joe's Special, you sat at the counter and watched the chefs work right in front of you and felt the steam of the pasta pots. The Special is especially good piled onto big toasted sourdough bread slices spread with garlic butter, an idea I got from my food professional cohort, Lou Pappas, but it is just as good plain or with rice or pasta. Joe's Special is a great dish to make at home. ● *Serves 4*

**COOKING METHOD:** Stovetop
**PREP TIME:** 15 minutes
**COOK TIME:** About 15 minutes

GARLIC TOAST
¼ cup olive oil
1 to 2 medium-size cloves garlic, crushed
4 large (or 8 small) slices sourdough bread

1 tablespoon unsalted butter
1 tablespoon olive oil
2 shallots or ¼ white onion, finely chopped
6 ounces fresh white mushrooms, sliced
1 pound ground beef chuck or ground turkey
1 clove garlic, crushed
12 ounces frozen chopped spinach, thawed and squeezed dry
4 large or extra-large eggs, slightly beaten
½ cup grated Parmesan cheese
Salt and freshly ground black pepper

**1.** To make the toast, in a small saucepan or in the microwave, gently warm the olive oil and add the garlic. Remove from the heat and set aside to let cool until needed. Place the bread slices in a toaster, under a preheated broiler, or in a toaster oven and toast both sides until golden brown. Generously brush one side of each slice with the garlic oil and cover with aluminum foil to keep warm.

**2.** Melt the butter and oil together in a large, deep skillet over medium heat. Add the shallots and mushrooms; cook for 1 minute. Add the beef and break up the lumps; brown and cook until no pink remains. Add the garlic and cook for 1 minute, then add the spinach and stir to evenly combine; cook for 3 minutes.

**3.** Pour in the eggs and stir constantly until they are set, 2 minutes. Sprinkle in the Parmesan and add salt and pepper to taste. Serve immediately, piled onto the sourdough toast.

# Egg Foo Yung

E gg foo yung was the first Chinese dish I ever made at home. It is a practical dish, very fast to assemble and cook with vegetables in your fridge, varying seasonally. Eggs are never served alone in Chinese cuisine, but always in combination with meat and/or vegetables. This is basically vegetables and egg, similar to a moo shu stir-fry, but made into hearty, chunky pancakes with a little soy sauce–based sauce poured over for serving. If you like, you can add a bit of cooked shrimp, pork, or duck; in any event, I suggest serving this with rice or Chinese noodles. Look for the dried mushrooms in a bag near the Asian ingredients in your supermarket. ● *Serves 4*

**COOKING METHOD:** Stovetop
**PREP TIME:** 15 minutes
**COOK TIME:** About 25 minutes

4 dried Chinese mushrooms

SOY SERVING SAUCE
1 cup water
1 tablespoon dry sherry
1 tablespoon cornstarch
2 tablespoons reduced-sodium soy sauce
1 teaspoon sugar

1 to 1½ cups finely shredded napa cabbage
1 cup mung bean sprouts, chopped in half
2 stalks celery, thinly sliced on the diagonal
¼ cup chopped green onions (white part and some of the green)
¼ cup chopped water chestnuts
8 large or extra-large eggs
1½ tablespoons cornstarch

**1.** In a small bowl, cover the mushrooms with boiling water. Let soak for 15 minutes. Drain and thinly slice.

**2.** Meanwhile, make the serving sauce. In a small saucepan, combine the water, sherry, and 1 tablespoon cornstarch. Add the soy sauce and sugar and cook over medium heat, stirring constantly, until thickened. Do not boil. Keep warm.

**3.** In a medium-size mixing bowl, combine all the vegetables and the sliced mushrooms. Toss to mix. In a small bowl, whisk together the eggs and 1½ tablespoons cornstarch; pour into the bowl with the vegetables and stir to evenly coat all the vegetables.

**4.** Heat a large skillet over medium heat and spray with vegetable cooking spray. Using a ½-cup dry measuring cup, scoop the mixture into the pan. Spread out and cook until the top surface is almost set, 4 to 5 minutes. Turn the pancake with a spatula and cook the other side for 2 to 3 minutes. Remove to an ovenproof plate and cover; keep warm in a low oven while making the other pancakes. Serve with the soy serving sauce drizzled over the top.

# Lobster and Asparagus Benedict

Eggs Benedict was the "it" dish of the 1920s, invented at the Delmonico Hotel in New York City. It included the famous hollandaise sauce, a basic butter sauce that makes everything it graces a taste treat. Once you taste my version of hollandaise, you will never again be reluctant to make this luscious sauce. There is just a dash of sour cream, which stabilizes it, allowing the sauce to sit in a warm water bath for hours before serving. This luxurious version of eggs Benedict is best prepared on an evening when you are up for a few preparatory steps, as you need to cook the asparagus and lobster, toast the muffins, and make the sauce all right before assembly. Pick up a bag of baby lobster tails on your next warehouse shopping excursion and keep them in the freezer. Serve with a green salad and a dry Riesling wine, slightly chilled. ○ *Serves 4*

**COOKING METHOD:** Stovetop
**PREP TIME:** 25 minutes
**COOK TIME:** About 30 minutes

12 thick asparagus spears
2 tablespoons unsalted butter, melted
1 to 2 tablespoons fresh lemon juice

MY HOLLANDAISE SAUCE
4 large or extra-large egg yolks
1 tablespoon fresh lemon juice
Dash of salt and freshly ground white pepper
1 cup (2 sticks) unsalted butter, melted and hot
⅓ cup sour cream

2 tablespoons cider or white wine vinegar
8 large or extra-large eggs
4 English muffins
1 pound frozen baby lobster tails, thawed and cooked according to package directions
1 tablespoon unsalted butter

**1.** Cook the asparagus spears in boiling salted water or in the microwave until crisp-tender, about 3 minutes. Transfer to a shallow baking dish. Drizzle with the melted butter and the lemon juice. Cover and set aside to keep warm.

**2.** To make the sauce, place the yolks, lemon juice, salt, and pepper in a food processor; process to combine. With the motor running, add the hot melted butter in a slow, steady stream, drop by drop at first, until the sauce is creamy and emulsified. Add the sour cream with a few pulses. Pour into a thermos or deep container that can stand in a warm water bath until serving time.

**3.** To poach the eggs, in a wide saucepan, bring 3 inches of water almost to a boil. Add the vinegar. Bring a second saucepan of water to a simmer; check with a thermometer to make sure the temperature is 150°F. Break each egg into a small heatproof bowl or cup. Maintaining the water just below a simmer on low heat, slide the eggs into the vinegar water and cook until the whites are set but the yolks are still soft. Remove with a slotted spoon to the 150°F water. Cover and let stand for 10 to 15 minutes to finish cooking while you prepare and assemble the rest of the Benedict.

**4.** To assemble the Benedict, toast the English muffins and place 2 halves on each plate. Cut the steamed asparagus spears in half, and place 3 pieces on each muffin half. Quickly sauté the lobster tails in the butter until heated through, and portion on top of the asparagus. Remove the eggs from the water with a slotted spoon and press the bottom of the spoon against a clean dishtowel to absorb the extra water before placing the eggs on top of the lobster. Pour some hollandaise sauce over the eggs and serve immediately.

**VARIATION**

Substitute 1 pound of cooked salmon fillets for the lobster.

# French Scrambled Eggs
# with Smoked Salmon and Chives

**A** friend once told me about a great little bistro in San Francisco off Union Street, called the Balboa Cafe. One trip and I was hooked; they had the best hamburgers ever. On subsequent visits I tried many of their homey dishes, one being the double-boiler-cooked scrambled eggs with a layer of smoked salmon on top. It is a divine way to eat smoked salmon and makes the eggs an even more substantial meal. Do not substitute dried herbs here; you must have the fresh to infuse their sublime taste. The double-boiler technique assures you of the creamiest eggs. There is a secret—don't rush. Serve with little crusty French rolls or a fresh sliced thin baguette and a tossed green salad. ○ *Serves 4*

**COOKING METHOD:** Stovetop
**PREP TIME:** 5 minutes
**COOK TIME:** About 15 minutes

4 tablespoons cold unsalted butter
12 large or extra-large eggs
½ cup milk or half-and-half
¼ teaspoon salt
⅛ teaspoon freshly ground black or white pepper
2 tablespoons chopped fresh chives
4 to 8 ounces thinly sliced smoked salmon

**1.** Bring water to a boil in the bottom of a double boiler and melt 1 tablespoon of the butter in the top pan. Adjust the heat to keep the water at a simmer.

**2.** Beat the eggs, milk, salt, and pepper in a small bowl with a fork just to combine the yolks and whites. Cut the remaining 3 tablespoons cold butter into pieces and add to the eggs. Pour the mixture into the top of the hot double boiler and stir constantly, using a heatproof rubber spatula. Slowly push the eggs as they set, gently folding and stirring from the bottom of the pan to form delicate soft curds. The eggs will cook more slowly than if you make them in a skillet, so allow 10 to 15 minutes total cooking time, until creamy, set, and still moist (they will keep cooking on the way to the table). Be patient. As the curds are beginning to form, sprinkle in the chives.

**3.** Remove from the heat while still moist, transfer the eggs to 4 warmed plates, top with the slices of smoked salmon, and run to the table.

## •• Quiche Tales ••

One day many years ago in the restaurant bakery where I worked, my baking guru and mentor Barbara Hiken declared she was going to make some quiches—the scrumptious cream, cheese, and vegetable open-faced savory French tarts—to put on the lunch menu. I had never attempted to make one on my own, so I was all eyes and ears.

Out came *Mastering the Art of French Cooking* by Child, Bertholle, and Beck, and she proceeded to make not one, but three of the offered recipe variations. As she worked at cooking bacon and chopping fresh mushrooms, she punctuated the process with exclamations like, "Oh, how luscious," "Where are the 8-inch removable-bottom pans?" and "The Roquefort one will be the best!" Ah, I thought, that smelly blue cheese on the salad station!? I decided, without voicing my opinion, that the classical quiche Lorraine, "with no cheese, just like the recipe is written," and the mushroom with Swiss cheese would be my choices.

As Barbara's piping hot rounds came out of the oven, I inspected the deliberately rough and natural-looking puffed brown tops and uneven crusts. They weren't more than 1½ inches deep. First glorious bites aside, I was amazed that the Roquefort tart was the most delicate and sumptuous due to the combination of blue cheese and cream cheese. It became an instant favorite of mine for special dinner guests. I promptly marked the recipes in my copy of the cookbook, where they are still prominent reminders of Barbara's quiches.

When I traveled to France a few years later, quiche was a standard in the zinc bars for my late lunches, as they were for supper alongside a brothy goose liver soup at one of the homes I visited. By the time I returned to the States, quiche had found its way out of tiny bistros and onto mainstream restaurant menus.

While some may claim that the hearty quiche is too rich for today's palate, remember that this tasty tart is native to a fertile, agricultural region of France that is downright frigid in winter, where soul-warming fare is welcome. The homey, savory custard can be made with milk instead of cream, but the results are less harmonious with low-fat products and the custard consistency a bit more rubbery.

While making quiches, I experimented with all sorts of fillings: a layering of parcooked zucchini and a bit of basil, tomato and cheese, crab and chives, and lots of spinach and freshly grated nutmeg. I sometimes substitute a frozen pie crust or store-bought puff pastry when I'm short on time (great if you have trouble manipulating pastry dough); both are excellent alternatives to your own pastry crust. What is important is to balance the tender filling with some flaky crust, with the emphasis on the golden, creamy filling.

# Individual Cheese Quiches

I found this recipe on a flyer advertising cheese from Switzerland. The little cheese pies are a fantastic supper entrée with a tangy salad vinaigrette or marinated vegetables, a fresh French baguette, and a cool, fruity white wine. Go ahead and use a refrigerated pie crust, which saves a lot of time. If you are a whiz whipping up pie crust, then by all means feel free to do so. While a large quiche will take some time to bake, individual ones are done in less than 30 minutes. You can use a muffin tin, but this is a nice recipe for using those individual fluted quiche pans with removable bottoms that you might have tucked away in your equipment drawer. Any leftovers can be frozen and then quickly reheated for another meal. ○ *Serves 4*

**COOKING METHOD:** Oven
**PREP TIME:** About 10 minutes
**COOK TIME:** About 25 minutes

One 15-ounce package refrigerated pie crust or your recipe for
    pie crust using 2 cups of flour
1½ cups shredded Gruyère or Swiss cheese (6 ounces)
1 tablespoon all-purpose or whole wheat pastry flour
4 large eggs
2 cups half-and-half
¼ teaspoon freshly ground black or white pepper
Pinch of ground nutmeg

**1.** Preheat the oven to 350°F. Set out a standard muffin tin with 12 cups or eight 4-inch individual fluted quiche pans with removable bottoms.

**2.** Roll out the pie dough on a lightly floured surface. Cut into 12 portions and fit into the 12 muffin cups. With the back of a knife, score little vertical lines around the top portion of the pastry to adhere to the sides of the pan.

**3.** Combine the cheese and flour in a small bowl, and sprinkle the bottom of each quiche with the mixture. Place a layer of meat or vegetable, if using (see variations, page 222), on top, or leave plain.

**4.** Beat together the eggs, half-and-half, pepper, and nutmeg in a bowl. Divide the mixture among the 12 quiches (about 2 tablespoons each). Bake in the center of the oven for 20 to 25 minutes, until firm and the tip of a knife inserted into the center comes out clean.

**5.** Let cool for 10 minutes before removing from the pan with a small metal spatula. Serve hot, warm, or at room temperature.

### VARIATIONS

**Bacon:** Add 6 ounces crisp, crumbled cooked bacon.

**Mushroom:** Add 4 ounces mushrooms of your choice, sliced and sautéed in 2 tablespoons butter.

**Ham:** Add ¾ cup finely chopped Black Forest or other ham.

**Onion:** Add 1 large yellow onion, chopped and sautéed in 2 tablespoons butter until translucent.

**Tomato:** Add 2 to 3 large fresh plum tomatoes, seeded, drained, and diced.

**Spinach:** Add 1½ cups thawed frozen chopped spinach, squeezed dry.

# Wine, Bread, and Cheese Soufflé

**T**his rustic casserole is a cross between a soufflé and a quiche. I have been making it for years. It has a crust of garlic-scented bread slices and a filling made with a dry white wine (such as Sauvignon Blanc). Whatever type of wine you use will affect the character of the dish, so use something you like to drink. All you need is tossed greens topped with some chickpeas and sliced tomatoes to round out the meal. **○** *Serves 4*

**COOKING METHOD:** Oven
**PREP TIME:** 15 minutes
**COOK TIME:** 30 to 35 minutes

6 tablespoons (¾ stick) unsalted butter, softened

2 to 3 cloves garlic, crushed

8 slices (no more than ¾ inch thick) day-old baguette, cut in half on the diagonal

½ cup dry white wine

½ cup milk

3 large eggs

¼ teaspoon salt

¼ teaspoon freshly ground black pepper

¼ teaspoon paprika

1 teaspoon Dijon mustard

Dash of Worcestershire sauce

2 cups shredded Swiss cheese, such as Jarlsberg or Emmental (8 ounces)

**1.** Preheat the oven to 325°F.

**2.** Cream together the butter and garlic in a small bowl. Spread the bread slices on one side with the garlic butter. Arrange, butter side down, in a 1½-quart ceramic casserole or 7½-inch soufflé dish. It does not matter if there are some uneven spaces between the slices, but place as close together as possible, lining the bottom and sides.

**3.** Whisk together the wine, milk, eggs, salt, pepper, paprika, mustard, and Worcestershire sauce in a medium-size bowl until smooth, 1 minute. Add the cheese and stir to combine. Pour into the bread-lined casserole. Bake for 30 to 35 minutes, or until the bread is crunchy and golden brown and the filling is puffed and set. Serve immediately.

# Green Chile Tortilla Pie

**E**very so often while shopping I see the oversized 12-inch flour tortillas that are almost as big as a pizza pan, usually in a warehouse supermarket. The size is so intriguing that I am always looking for ways to use them. Pressed into a large pie pan, the tortilla makes a lovely shell for a cream and egg filling, creating a dish similar to a quiche. Here are the delightful flavors of a chile relleno, only a whole lot simpler. If you only have regular-size flour tortillas, you can slightly overlap them to fill the pan; just be sure to leave 2 inches of tortilla around the rim of the pan. If you have time, make the Fast Winter Salsa (right), which lives up to its name, to spoon over the top. Serve with sautéed corn.

**o** *Serves 4*

**COOKING METHOD:** Oven
**PREP TIME:** 20 minutes
**COOK TIME:** 40 to 45 minutes

1 to 2 tablespoons olive oil
One 12-inch flour tortilla
1 cup shredded Monterey Jack cheese (4 ounces)
1 cup shredded sharp cheddar cheese (4 ounces)
One 4-ounce can roasted chopped green chiles, drained
3 large eggs, beaten
1 cup sour cream
Pinch of salt
Pinch of ground cumin
3 ounces fresh goat's milk cheese, crumbled
1 recipe Fast Winter Salsa (recipe follows)

1. Preheat the oven to 350°F (325°F if using a Pyrex pan).

2. Grease a 10-inch deep-dish pie pan with the oil. Place the tortilla in the pan and press down so it adheres to the sides. Sprinkle the bottom with two-thirds of each of the cheeses. Sprinkle the chiles over the cheese.

3. Beat together the eggs, sour cream, salt, and cumin in a small bowl. Pour over the chiles and cheese. Sprinkle the top with the remaining one-third of each of the cheeses and dot the top with the goat cheese. Bake in the center of the oven for 40 to 45 minutes, until set.

4. Let cool for 10 minutes before slicing into wedges and serving with some salsa spooned over.

## Fast Winter Salsa

**○ *Makes 1½ cups***

1 clove garlic
4 green onions, cut into chunks
1 jalapeño chile, seeded, or 1 chipotle chile in adobo sauce
1 handful fresh cilantro leaves
One 14½-ounce can fancy stewed tomatoes, plum tomatoes, or fire-roasted tomatoes, drained
Juice of 1 lime

Put the garlic, green onions, chile, and cilantro in the bowl of a food processor fitted with the metal blade. Chop coarsely using short pulses. Add the tomatoes and chop until chunky; season with the lime juice. This will keep for up to 3 days in the refrigerator.

# *Fresh Produce:*
# Main-Dish Salads

Nothing is as glorious on a hot summer's day as cool Mediterranean Greek Salad and fresh bread, Cobb Salad with Buttermilk Herb Dressing, or Mexican Roast Beef Salad. Want something a bit different? Try Duck Breast Salad with Blueberries, Walnuts, and Currant Vinaigrette or Double Tomato Baby Lentil Salad with Olives. Got the winter blues? Mix up a bowl of Italian Greens with Genoa Salami, Chickpeas, and Black Olives or Curried Turkey and Couscous Salad. Salads for dinner work year-round.

A well-made salad is an irresistible delight. It is healthy eating at its best and appeals to all types of eaters. These self-contained meals can also be expanded or contracted to serve any number of people. A main-dish salad often combines the usual types of greens and other produce with exotic ingredients—artisanal cheeses, olives, tropical fruit, fresh lemons, first-press olive oil, and fun pasta shapes. A recipe is just the start; exercise the freedom to create your own signature everyday fare.

The type of oil used for a salad, which contributes greatly to its flavor, depends on the dish and/or the palate of the cook. Olive oil is the most common for its delicious taste, as well as its heart-healthy monounsaturated acids. Extra virgin is the strongest in flavor and is recommended especially for vinaigrettes, or just drizzled on its own to enjoy its assertive taste.

Other good salad oils are avocado oil, corn oil, toasted sesame oil, grapeseed oil, sunflower oil, and organic canola oil. Mix things up even more with the flavorful nut oils, especially walnut and macadamia, two of the healthiest oils around.

And don't forget all those leafy greens, each with its own special flavor. Many salads feature one type of lettuce, such as hearts of romaine in Caesar salad or a wedge of iceberg with bleu cheese dressing. There are also red and green leaf lettuces, butter lettuce, Belgian endive, and baby spinach. Mesclun, a popular bagged salad mix that has a combination of bitter greens, refers to a mix of seasonal greens that includes arugula, butter, frisée, limestone, mâche, radicchio, and mizuna; there are various mixtures from different growers, and they all make a nice bed for your main-dish salad.

# Mediterranean Greek Salad

I had a girlfriend whose favorite meal, almost every night of the week, was Greek salad and sautéed snapper. Need I say that this is one popular salad, both in restaurants and in the home kitchen? Hearty, robust, and soul-satisfying, Greek salad is rustic and simple, featuring fresh produce plus a few pantry items, such as olives, onion, and feta cheese. Feta is a brined medium-soft cheese made from sheep's milk that is frequently seen in Greek cuisine. Since it is brined, rinse it with cool water before crumbling it into your salad. Serve with pita bread.

**○ Serves 4**

**COOKING METHOD:** None
**PREP TIME:** 15 minutes

1 large cucumber, partially peeled if desired, seeded,
    and sliced into thick half-moons
1 large head romaine lettuce, torn into bite-sized pieces
3 large ripe tomatoes, diced
¼ medium-size red onion, thinly sliced
6 ounces feta cheese, crumbled (about 1½ cups)
1 cup pitted and sliced kalamata olives
Pinch of salt and freshly ground black pepper

**GREEK DRESSING**
⅓ cup olive oil
2 tablespoons red wine vinegar
2 tablespoons fresh lemon juice
Pinch of dried oregano or 1 teaspoon chopped fresh oregano

**1.** Combine the cucumbers, lettuce, tomatoes, onion, feta, and olives in a serving bowl. Sprinkle with salt and pepper.

**2.** To make the dressing, combine all of the dressing ingredients in a small jar with a tight-fitting lid; shake well.

**3.** Drizzle the salad with the dressing; toss to combine. Serve immediately, letting diners serve themselves.

# Fattoush-Toasted Pita Bread Salad with Falafel Balls

**B**read salads are not only filling but also tasty and economical. I always seem to have pita bread around, so this salad is a great way to use up day-old whole wheat pitas. It's strictly a summer and early fall salad because of its need for perfectly ripe fresh tomatoes, unless you luck out and find some perfect hothouse Romas. Don't skip the mint; it makes this salad special. This was originally introduced to me by chef and food writer Joyce Goldstein, who said: "This may well become your favorite summer salad." I love the falafel balls on top, made from readily available falafel mix, which is my own touch. **o** *Serves 4*

**COOKING METHOD:** Stovetop
**PREP TIME:** 20 minutes
**COOK TIME:** About 20 minutes

2 cups commercial falafel mix
½ cup fruity olive oil of your choice
3 tablespoons fresh lemon juice
Salt and freshly ground black pepper
4 whole rounds pita bread
4 to 6 ripe tomatoes, diced (about 2 cups)
2 medium-size cucumbers or 1 long English cucumber, peeled and diced
½ cup finely chopped red onion
4 green onions (white part and some of the green), finely chopped
3 tablespoons fresh flat-leaf parsley, minced
2 tablespoons fresh mint, minced
2 heads romaine lettuce, coarsely chopped
Canola or vegetable oil, for frying

1. Prepare the falafel mix according to the package directions and let stand for 15 minutes.

2. Meanwhile, in a small bowl, combine the olive oil and lemon juice. Add salt and pepper and set aside. Cut the pitas in half and toast in a toaster until crisp. Tear into 2-inch pieces and place in a mixing bowl. Add the tomatoes, cucumbers, red onion, green onions, parsley, and mint; add some dressing to coat and toss to combine. In another bowl, place the romaine and drizzle with the remaining dressing.

3. Pour the canola oil into a deep heavy skillet to a depth of ½ inch and heat over medium-high heat. Form the falafel mix into 16 balls with your hands, about 3 tablespoons each to make 2-inch balls. Set a plate covered with a double layer of paper towels next to the stove. Flatten the balls to a thickness of 1 inch. Place the balls in the hot oil and cook for 3 minutes per side, until browned and crisp. Cook in a single layer, in batches, because they won't cook properly if crowded. Cut one in half to make sure it is cooked all the way through. Transfer the cooked falafel balls to the plate to drain and continue until all the balls are cooked. Set aside.

4. Divide the lettuce into 4 portions on dinner plates. Mound the pita and vegetables and 4 falafel balls atop each pile of lettuce. Sprinkle with more salt and pepper, if desired, and serve.

# Double Tomato Baby Lentil Salad with Olives

More than once I have made a fantastic dinner comprised of this lentil salad, crusty peasant bread and butter, fresh fruit, and mineral water. The green le Puy lentils are very small in comparison to the larger brown lentils, and they cook in a fraction of the time. They also keep their shape nicely, so they look good in a salad. ● *Serves 4*

**COOKING METHOD:** Stovetop
**PREP TIME:** 20 minutes
**COOK TIME:** 25 minutes

1 pound (about 2 cups) French le Puy lentils, rinsed and picked over

5 cups water

2 cloves garlic

3 sprigs fresh flat-leaf parsley

2 stalks fresh basil leaves

4 stalks celery, finely chopped

½ pint cherry or grape tomatoes, halved or quartered

3 tablespoons drained, finely chopped, oil-packed sun-dried tomatoes

½ cup finely chopped pitted black olives of your choice

¼ cup olive oil

3 tablespoons fresh lemon juice

1 tablespoon red wine vinegar

Salt and freshly ground black pepper

6 ounces fresh goat's milk cheese, crumbled

**1.** Place the lentils in a saucepan with the water, garlic, parsley, and basil; bring to a slow boil. Reduce the heat to medium and simmer, uncovered, until almost tender, about 25 minutes; drain. Discard the garlic and herbs.

**2.** In a serving bowl, combine the warm lentils, celery, cherry tomatoes, sun-dried tomatoes, and olives. Drizzle with the olive oil, lemon juice, and vinegar, and mix to evenly combine; it is okay to add a bit more dressing if you like a moister salad. Season with salt and pepper, crumble the goat cheese on top, and serve.

# Tuscan Tuna and Beans

**N**eed a simple but substantial main-dish salad and time is of the essence? Here is one of the staples of Italy's scrumptious, economical *cucina povera*, tuna and white kidney beans, which should be among your staple pantry items. It's great with some crusty ciabatta bread to use as a scooper along with your fork.

○ *Serves 4*

**COOKING METHOD:** None
**PREP TIME:** 15 minutes

Three 15-ounce cans cannellini beans, rinsed and drained
Three 6-ounce cans tuna packed in olive oil, drained well and broken into rough chunks
⅔ cup finely chopped red onion
3 tablespoons minced fresh flat-leaf parsley
⅓ cup fresh lemon juice
1 small clove garlic, crushed
Pinch of salt
⅔ cup olive oil
1 to 2 heads butter lettuce, leaves separated

Combine the beans, tuna, onion, and parsley in a serving bowl. In a small bowl, whisk together the lemon juice, garlic, and salt; drizzle in the olive oil, whisking constantly. Pour the dressing over the beans and tuna; toss to combine. Place lettuce leaves on 4 plates and top with the salad. Serve immediately.

# Warm Garlic Salmon on Mixed Greens

One of the easiest main-dish salads is a big pile of mixed greens, whatever looks crisp and fresh at the produce market or what you have in the refrigerator, with a fish fillet, sea scallops, a thin-pounded poultry paillard, or a fried egg nestled right on top. Seek out the sherry vinegar for this recipe; it has one of the mellowest flavors in the world of vinegar and is quite addictive. You will have some extra dressing here for a second set of salads. This method for cooking the salmon in the microwave oven is from Victoria Wise and Susanna Hoffman, authors of *The Well-Filled Microwave Cookbook* (Workman, 1996). I also like this salad tossed with tomatoes and some Gaeta olives from the deli olive bar. ○ *Serves 4*

**COOKING METHOD:** Microwave
**PREP TIME:** 20 minutes
**COOK TIME:** 5 to 7 minutes

**SHERRY VINAIGRETTE**

¼ cup sherry vinegar

2 tablespoons fresh lemon juice

1 tablespoon coarse-grain mustard

1 tablespoon minced shallot

Salt and freshly ground black pepper

⅔ cup olive oil

1 to 2 tablespoons sour cream or crème fraîche (optional)

**GARLIC SALMON**

4 salmon fillets, ½ inch thick (1¾ pounds)

3 large cloves garlic, sliced

1 tablespoon fresh lemon juice

¼ teaspoon salt

1 tablespoon olive oil

10 ounces Italian salad green mix or baby lettuce mix or 8 cups mixed greens (such as red leaf lettuce, baby romaine or romaine hearts, mâche, mizuna, Belgian endive spears, arugula, and baby spinach)

¼ cup chopped green onions or fresh flat-leaf parsley (optional)

1. To make the dressing, in a small bowl, whisk together the vinegar, lemon juice, mustard, shallot, and salt and pepper. Whisk in the oil in a steady stream. If you like a creamy dressing, whisk in the sour cream. Set aside. You will not use all the dressing, so keep it in the refrigerator in a covered container for up to 2 days.

2. To make the salmon, put the fillets in a microwave dish that will fit the 4 pieces in a single layer. Sprinkle with the garlic, lemon juice, salt, and olive oil. Cover the dish with a lid or microwave-safe plastic wrap. Microwave on High for 5 to 7 minutes, or until white curds form on top of the fish and the edges are flaky but the center is still medium-rare. Let stand for 2 to 5 minutes.

3. To assemble, place the greens in a big bowl and toss lightly with ¼ cup of the dressing; add more if you like. Divide the lettuce among 4 dinner plates. Set 1 piece of salmon on top of each salad. Garnish with green onions, if desired. Have some dressing on the side, if desired, to drizzle over the salmon. Serve immediately.

**VARIATIONS**

# Warm Pan-Seared Sea Scallops on Mixed Greens

**⊙** *Serves 4*

**COOKING METHOD:** Stovetop
**PREP TIME:** 20 minutes
**COOK TIME:** 10 to 14 minutes

1½ pounds sea scallops (16 to 20 large), rinsed and patted dry
Salt and freshly ground black pepper
About 4 tablespoons canola or vegetable oil

Place the scallops on a plate and season with salt and pepper. Heat a nonstick skillet over medium-high heat with half of the oil. Arrange half of the scallops in the pan in a single layer and cook for 2 minutes on each side, until browned and cooked through; turn once and do not stir. When done, the scallops will be firm-springy to the touch and you will see on the sides that they have turned an opaque color; transfer to a plate and cover with foil. Wipe out the pan with paper towels, add the remaining oil, and sear the remaining scallops. (Cooking in 2 batches avoids crowding the pan, which will steam the scallops instead of browning them.) Immediately place 4 or 5 scallops on top of each salad and serve.

# Warm Chicken or Turkey Paillards on Mixed Greens

○ *Serves 4*

**COOKING METHOD:** Stovetop
**PREP TIME:** 20 minutes
**COOK TIME:** 8 minutes

4 boneless, skinless chicken breast halves or turkey breast slices
2 tablespoons olive oil
2 teaspoons chopped fresh thyme or basil
Salt and freshly ground black pepper

**1.** Place the chicken breasts in a gallon-size zipper-top plastic bag and gently pound with a flat mallet until ¼ inch thick (turkey breast slices are already thin). Place on a plate and toss with the oil, thyme, salt, and pepper.

**2.** Heat a grill pan or nonstick skillet over medium-high heat. Arrange the poultry pieces in the pan in a single layer and cook for 4 minutes on each side, until browned and cooked through. Immediately place on top of each salad and serve.

## ·· A Side of Greens ··

Elsewhere in this book, I often recommend serving a recipe with a simple green or mixed salad on the side. In this chapter, though, the recipes usually call for specific types of greens, and in these recipes the lettuce can be a star.

Think of lettuces in categories such as crunchy, tender, and bitter. The four categories of lettuce are crisphead, butterhead, leaf, and romaine, with each category having many selections and different lettuces appearing at different seasons. Many premixed bags of salad greens will combine these elements. Choosing your lettuce properly will help you put together a pile of greens that will complement your main dish. Remember to wash and blot dry, or spin, your lettuces, as they will wilt if left soggy.

Don't pass up iceberg lettuce just because it has been around forever and doesn't seem "gourmet." Think "universal" instead. There is nothing like an ice-cold wedge of crunchy iceberg lettuce drizzled with thick, creamy blue cheese or ranch dressing. Romaine lettuce is really popular, especially since some marketing genius invented packages of hearts only. Toss romaine leaves, either whole, torn, or chopped, with a Caesar, Thousand Island, or creamy French dressing, or a toasted sesame oil and rice wine vinaigrette.

Boston, or butterhead, lettuce is very tender and has large, rounded, soft leaves. It is rather sweet, so you can make a wine vinaigrette and drizzle it over the leaves. Another tender lettuce is red leaf. Mâche, also known as lamb's lettuce or corn salad, is a tender green with a tangy flavor and is good tossed with smooth fruit vinegar or sherry vinaigrettes.

Some of the new designer greens combinations are a big surprise: they are bitter. Contrast them with sweet additions, such as crumbled goat cheese, roasted vegetables, beets, canned beans, figs wrapped in bacon and broiled, strips of sun-dried tomato, or dried cranberries. Keep your vinaigrettes mild with these greens, instead of sharp and assertive.

Another favorite dinner salad green (especially in French cuisine) is curly endive, also known as frisée. People get addicted to its bitter flavor and sturdy texture. It is often topped with sautéed mushrooms, bacon or lardons, or even a poached egg, and a nice balsamic vinegar and olive oil dressing. Spinach salads, which are especially nice when made with baby spinach, are topped with a warm bacon and tart vinegar dressing, since the greens wilt under the warmth and taste really appealing. Many people love the peppery flavor of arugula and watercress so much that they make an entire salad out of the single green. For just a taste of their strong flavors, toss arugula or watercress with one of the leaf lettuces.

# Curried Turkey and Couscous Salad

Couscous makes a fantastic grain base for a meat and fruit salad, and poultry salads combining curry and mixed fruit have a perennial appeal. Mangoes are available almost year-round now. If you can't find any attractive ones, however, other fruits, such as pears, papayas, or cantaloupe, also work well. Use leftover roast turkey or deli turkey; chicken works well here, too. You will love this salad; it is refreshing and satisfying. ○ *Serves 4*

**COOKING METHOD:** Stovetop
**PREP TIME:** 25 minutes
**COOK TIME:** 5 minutes

### CURRIED COUSCOUS

1½ cups water
1 teaspoon curry powder
One 1-inch piece fresh ginger, grated
2 teaspoons olive oil
1 cup uncooked plain couscous

### CURRY YOGURT DRESSING

⅓ cup plain yogurt
¼ cup chopped fresh cilantro
3 tablespoons mayonnaise
2 tablespoons fruit chutney, such as mango or nectarine
½ teaspoon curry powder
¼ teaspoon ground ginger
2 tablespoons water

### SALAD

12 ounces cooked turkey breast, torn into thick shreds or cut into strips
1¼ cups halved red or green seedless grapes
1¼ cups diced fresh pineapple (use drained canned if you cannot find fresh)
1¼ cups diced fresh mango or papaya
1 cup chopped celery
2 heads Boston lettuce, leaves separated
¼ cup chopped green onions (white part and some of the green)

**1.** To make the couscous, bring the water, curry powder, ginger, and oil to a boil in a small saucepan. Add the couscous; remove from the heat and let stand, covered, until the water is absorbed and the couscous is tender, about 5 minutes. Transfer the couscous to a large bowl and fluff with a fork to separate the grains; place in the refrigerator for a few minutes to chill slightly.

**2.** To make the dressing, in a small bowl, whisk together the yogurt, cilantro, mayonnaise, chutney, curry powder, ginger, and water until blended. You can also make this in the food processor. Pour over the couscous; toss to evenly coat.

**3.** To assemble the salad, add the turkey, grapes, pineapple, mango, and celery to the couscous mixture; gently toss to mix and coat. To serve, line each of 4 plates with 3 lettuce leaves and divide the couscous mixture among the plates. Sprinkle each serving with 1 tablespoon green onions.

# Chinese Chicken Salad

C hicken salads on the whole are immensely popular, but this dish tops them all because it combines sweet, crunchy, spicy, cold, and sour all in one. One day when I was shopping in the produce department, a young man next to me was obviously struggling with indecision. I asked him what he was looking for and he replied cilantro; he was holding a bunch of watercress. I showed him the cilantro and then learned that he was a San Francisco fireman, and it was his night to cook. He told me about his recipe for Chinese chicken salad, and said that the firemen even published a cookbook to raise money to support surviving families of firefighters lost in the line of duty. This is a variation of the recipe he told me about. Serve with hot steamed rice or pot stickers, if you like.  ●  *Serves 4*

**COOKING METHOD:** Poaching
**PREP TIME:** 25 minutes
**COOK TIME:** 35 minutes

POACHED CHICKEN
1 pound boneless, skinless chicken breasts
3 tablespoons reduced-sodium tamari or soy sauce

CREAMY CILANTRO DRESSING
One 1-inch piece fresh ginger, cut into a few pieces
1 cup fresh cilantro leaves
1 cup mayonnaise
3 tablespoons rice vinegar
2 tablespoons Asian sesame oil
Juice of 1 small lime
2 teaspoons sugar
Hot sauce

1½ tablespoons sesame seeds

1 head iceberg lettuce, chopped

2 loose cups chopped napa cabbage

One 5-ounce can chow mein noodles

2 carrots, shredded

½ English cucumber, cut into 2-inch hunks and then into strips

3 green onions (white part and some of the green), chopped

**1.** To make the chicken, place the chicken, tamari, and enough water just to cover in a medium-size saucepan. Bring to a slow boil over medium-high heat. Cover and remove from the heat. Let stand for 30 minutes while you make the dressing and assemble the salad ingredients.

**2.** To make the dressing, in a food processor, chop the ginger. Add the cilantro and pulse to chop. Add the mayonnaise, vinegar, oil, lime juice, sugar, and hot sauce to taste. Process until smooth. Set aside in a small bowl.

**3.** Place the sesame seeds in a dry skillet and toast until golden, shaking the pan a few times to evenly toast them, about 2 minutes. Set aside.

**4.** In a shallow bowl, toss together the lettuce, cabbage, chow mein noodles, carrots, cucumber, green onions, and toasted sesame seeds. Remove the chicken from the poaching liquid and shred into bite-size pieces. Toss the chicken with the lettuce mixture. Either toss the salad with the dressing or place the dressing on the table and let people drizzle it over their own salads (this is the way I do it).

# Cobb Salad

**C**obb Salad was created at the legendary Brown Derby Restaurant in Los Angeles. One day the owner went into the kitchen and, at the request of a diner, tossed together a salad with what was on hand at the cold station. The salad was such a hit (it has all the ingredients for a club sandwich) that diners started asking for it, and it became a standard on the menu. I have had many Cobbs in my life, since it is an all-time favorite salad. Variables include applewood-smoked bacon, smoked chicken, French Roquefort or a domestic Wisconsin blue cheese, and even heirloom tomatoes. The combination of elements is perfectly satisfying and, if you think you can leave out one part, beware. It won't taste or feel quite the same with every bite. I use a buttermilk dressing for my Cobb, my contribution to the legacy. ◉ *Serves 4*

**COOKING METHOD:** Stovetop
**PREP TIME:** 25 minutes
**COOK TIME:** 7 minutes

BUTTERMILK HERB DRESSING
1 small clove garlic or 1 green onion
1 to 2 fresh basil leaves
1 sprig fresh flat-leaf parsley
½ cup buttermilk
½ cup mayonnaise
1 tablespoon cider vinegar
¼ teaspoon salt

SALAD
2 large eggs
2 cups finely chopped romaine lettuce
2 cups finely chopped Boston lettuce
2 cups finely chopped iceberg lettuce
¾ cup finely chopped watercress or ½ cup finely chopped flat-leaf parsley,
   coarse stems discarded
1 to 2 ripe avocados

3 cups finely diced cooked chicken breast (a rotisserie chicken from the
    grocery is a real time-saver) or cooked turkey breast
6 slices cooked bacon, finely chopped
½ cup crumbled Roquefort or other blue cheese of your choice
2 large tomatoes, 1 seeded and finely chopped and 1 cut into 8 wedges
2 tablespoons chopped fresh chives or green onion

**1.** To make the dressing, in a small food processor, chop the garlic. Add the basil and parsley; pulse to finely chop. Add the buttermilk, mayonnaise, vinegar, and salt; pulse a few times to combine. Store in a covered container in the refrigerator; the dressing will thicken as it sits.

**2.** To prepare the salad, place the eggs in a pot and cover with cold water by ½ inch or so. Bring to a gentle boil. Turn off the heat, cover, and let sit for exactly 7 minutes. Have a big bowl of ice water ready and, when the eggs are done cooking, place them in the ice bath for 3 minutes or so, long enough to stop the cooking. Crack and peel each egg. Set aside.

**3.** Toss together all of the lettuces and the watercress in a large salad bowl. Halve, pit, and peel the avocados and cut them into ½-inch chunks. Arrange the chicken, bacon, cheese, chopped tomatoes, and avocado decoratively over the greens and toss well.

**4.** Finely chop the hard-cooked eggs. Garnish the salad with the chopped egg, tomato wedges, and chives. Serve the dressing on the side.

# Duck Breast Salad with Blueberries, Walnuts, and Currant Vinaigrette

While duck once was reserved for special occasions, the availability of frozen duck breasts now makes it a delightful poultry alternative for weeknights. I was served this salad at a lunch party after one of my private cooking classes and it was really a hit. Because of the fresh blueberries, this is best served in the summer, but in the fall I have substituted fresh figs and in spring, sliced apricots. The vinaigrette is a unique combination of fruit jelly and dried currants; the currants will plump and soften as they sit in the dressing. The pan-seared duck breasts are done in minutes and taste really fantastic. You will feel like a master chef making this salad.  ● *Serves 4*

**COOKING METHOD:** Stovetop
**PREP TIME:** 25 minutes
**COOK TIME:** About 8 minutes

### CURRANT VINAIGRETTE

¼ cup cider vinegar

1 tablespoon Dijon mustard

2 tablespoons red currant, plum, or blackberry jelly

2 teaspoons chopped fresh thyme

½ cup extra virgin olive oil

Salt and freshly ground black pepper

¼ cup dried currants

### DUCK BREASTS

4 boned duck breast halves with skin on (about 6 ounces each)

Salt and freshly ground black pepper

1 tablespoon olive oil

1 tablespoon unsalted butter

**SALAD**

6 cups mesclun salad mix

4 cups baby spinach leaves

1½ cups fresh blueberries

¾ cup walnut pieces, toasted if desired

4 green onions (white part and some of the green), chopped

**1.** To make the dressing, put the vinegar, mustard, jelly, and thyme in a food processor and pulse a few times. With the machine running, drizzle in the olive oil until thickened. Add salt and pepper and the currants. Set aside or refrigerate until needed.

**2.** To prepare the duck breasts, sprinkle them with salt and pepper. Heat the olive oil and butter in a large sauté pan over medium heat. Add the duck breasts and sauté until browned, about 4 minutes per side for medium-rare. Do not overcook or they will be tough. Remove and cut each breast crosswise on the diagonal into strips, but keep the pieces together. Set aside.

**3.** To assemble the salad, combine the mesclun, spinach, blueberries, walnuts, and green onions in a bowl. Toss very lightly with some of the vinaigrette. Divide among 4 dinner plates. Top each with a duck breast and drizzle with more dressing. Serve immediately.

# Oriental Pork and Asparagus Salad

**M**ake this at the start of spring, when asparagus hits the produce bins. The marinade with fresh ginger, rice wine, and hoisin sauce is one of my favorites and will become one of yours; it makes a very popular flavoring for oven-roasted barbecued pork. ○ *Serves 4*

**COOKING METHOD:** Oven and stovetop or microwave
**PREP TIME:** 25 minutes
**COOK TIME:** 30 minutes

One 1- to 1½-pound pork tenderloin

PORK MARINADE

2 cloves garlic, crushed

1 tablespoon grated fresh ginger

½ cup Chinese rice wine or dry sherry

½ cup reduced-sodium soy sauce

3 tablespoons hoisin sauce

DRESSING

¼ cup reserved Pork Marinade

1½ tablespoons hoisin sauce

1½ tablespoons rice vinegar

1 tablespoon Asian sesame oil

1 teaspoon Asian chili-garlic paste

½ cup olive oil

SALAD

1 pound asparagus, ends trimmed and chopped into 3-inch pieces

½ pound fresh snow peas, cut in half lengthwise

2 red or yellow bell peppers (or 1 of each), quartered and
    cut into julienne slices

One 8-ounce can water chestnuts, drained and slivered

½ bunch green onions (white and green parts), cut into
    2-inch lengths and slivered

1. Place the pork tenderloin in a ceramic or glass baking dish.

2. To make the marinade, in a small bowl, whisk together the marinade ingredients and pour ¾ cup over the tenderloin (reserve the remaining ¼ cup for the dressing). Cover and refrigerate for 20 minutes, turning once to coat both sides.

3. Preheat the oven to 450°F. Pour half of the marinade out of the baking dish and discard.

4. Roast the tenderloin for 30 minutes. Remove from the pan and place on a cutting board; let stand for 10 minutes. Cut into ¼-inch-thick slices, stack, then cut into thin strips. Wrap and store in the refrigerator if not making the salad immediately.

5. While the pork is roasting, make the dressing. Place the ¼ cup reserved marinade, hoisin sauce, rice vinegar, sesame oil, and chili-garlic paste in the food processor. With the motor running, add the oil in a slow, steady stream to emulsify the dressing. Set aside.

6. To prepare the salad, steam the asparagus and snow peas for 2 to 3 minutes, until crisp-tender; do not overcook. Place in a salad bowl with the bell peppers, water chestnuts, green onions, and pork strips. Toss with the dressing, lightly coating the meat and vegetables. Serve immediately or refrigerate until serving.

Cornbread is a great accompaniment to salads, soups, and Southwestern-flavored chicken, beef, and pork dishes. Cornbreads have to be one of the easiest quick breads to whip up, since it's a breeze to stir everything together and pour it into a pan. I don't generally make muffins and cornsticks, especially on weeknights, since pouring the batter into one pan is easier.

I encourage you to get fresh cornmeal and keep it in the refrigerator. If you can get stone-ground, all the better. If you end up in a mad dash at dinnertime, go ahead and make cornbread from a box. Frankly, the box mix is delicious, and good to have on hand in the pantry. For an 8½-ounce package, instead of following the package instructions, blend the mix with ½ cup evaporated milk (which acts like cream in the batter), 1 large egg, and 1 tablespoon melted butter. I freshen up the batter with the grated zest of a lemon or an orange as well. Then just bake as directed on the box.

## Olive Oil Cornbread

○ Makes one 8- or 9-inch square cornbread

1 cup finely ground cornmeal
1 cup unbleached all-purpose flour
2 tablespoons granulated or light brown sugar
1 tablespoon baking powder
½ teaspoon salt
¼ cup olive oil
1 large egg
1 cup milk

**1.** Preheat the oven to 400°F (375°F if using a Pyrex pan). Grease an 8- or 9-inch square ceramic, metal, or Pyrex pan with nonstick cooking spray.

**2.** Combine the cornmeal, flour, sugar, baking powder, and salt in a large bowl.

**3.** In a small bowl, mix the oil, egg, and milk with a whisk. Make a well in the center of the dry ingredients and pour in the wet ingredients. Stir just until all the ingredients are moistened yet thoroughly blended, about 12 strokes. Take care not to overmix.

**4.** Pour the batter into the pan. Bake for 25 to 30 minutes, until golden around the edges and a skewer inserted into the center comes out clean. Serve warm.

# Sour Cream Cornbread
## with Cheddar and Corn Kernels

⊙ Makes one 9-inch square or round cornbread

1¼ cups finely ground cornmeal

¾ cup unbleached all-purpose flour

1 tablespoon baking powder

1 teaspoon ground coriander

½ teaspoon salt

¼ teaspoon chili powder or New Mexican ground chiles

1½ cups shredded sharp cheddar cheese (6 ounces)

One 7-ounce can corn kernels, drained, or 1 cup frozen corn, thawed

1 large egg

1 cup sour cream

⅓ cup buttermilk, milk, or half-and-half

¼ cup (½ stick) butter, melted

**1.** Preheat the oven to 425°F (400°F if using a Pyrex pan). Grease a 9-inch square or round ceramic, metal, or Pyrex pan with nonstick cooking spray.

**2.** Combine the cornmeal, flour, baking powder, coriander, salt, and chili powder in a large bowl. Add the cheese and corn and stir to combine.

**3.** In a small bowl, mix the egg, sour cream, and buttermilk with a whisk. Make a well in the center of the dry ingredients and pour in the wet ingredients. Pour in the butter over the top. Stir just until all ingredients are moistened yet thoroughly blended, about 12 strokes. Take care not to overmix.

**4.** Pour the batter into the pan. Bake for 20 to 25 minutes, until golden around the edges and a skewer inserted into the center comes out clean. Serve warm.

# Italian Greens with Genoa Salami, Chickpeas, and Black Olives

**N**othing is more satisfying than a cool salad that's a one-dish meal of meat, beans, and vegetables. I also like croutons with this salad, and I keep left-over baguettes in the freezer to make them if I don't happen to have any fresh bread in the kitchen. To make croutons, cut a thin baguette into twelve ½-inch-thick slices. Place on a clean baking sheet in a single layer and bake at 400°F for 5 minutes to dry them out. Remove from the oven and brush both sides with olive oil. Return to the oven and crisp until golden brown, about 3 minutes. ● *Serves 4*

**COOKING METHOD:** None
**PREP TIME:** 20 minutes

**BALSAMIC DRESSING**
⅓ cup olive oil
2½ tablespoons balsamic vinegar
2 tablespoons water
1 tablespoon grated Parmesan cheese
Pinch of salt
Pinch of sugar
Freshly ground black pepper

**SALAD**
10 ounces Italian salad green mix or red leaf lettuce
4 ounces sliced Genoa salami, cut into julienne strips
One 15½-ounce can chickpeas, drained
½ cup pitted ripe black olives
½ cup thinly sliced red onion
½ cup thinly sliced green bell pepper
Croutons (optional; see above)

**1.** To make the dressing, combine all of the ingredients in a jar with a tight-fitting lid and shake well. Refrigerate for up to 1 week. Shake well again before serving over greens.

**2.** To assemble the salad, in a large wooden or glass salad bowl, combine the greens, salami, chickpeas, olives, red onion, and bell pepper. Toss the salad with the dressing and toss in the croutons, if using. Serve immediately.

# Californio Taco Salad

**E**veryone I know loves a main-dish taco salad. It's even better than a taco, for some reason, perhaps because it is a knife-and-fork meal. This recipe has all the fixin's, but you can include only a few instead of all of them, if you wish. You can substitute guacamole slathered all over the top in place of the avocado slices. If you would rather serve the salad on top of a crisp corn tortilla instead of chips, preheat the oven to 400°F. Spray both sides of 8 tortillas with olive oil cooking spray (leave whole or cut into quarters) and place in a single layer on 2 baking sheets; bake for 5 minutes on each side, until crisp. For a vegetarian taco salad, just skip the meat, as there are plenty of beans. **o** *Serves 4*

**COOKING METHOD:** Stovetop
**PREP TIME:** 20 minutes
**COOK TIME:** About 5 minutes

TACO MEAT

12 ounces ground beef chuck or ground dark turkey

½ white or yellow onion, chopped

1 to 2 teaspoons olive oil (optional)

1 cup tomato salsa of your choice, preferably a chunky style

¼ to ½ teaspoon chili powder (optional)

1 to 2 chopped chipotle chiles in adobo sauce (optional)

SALAD

About 6 cups thickly shredded or chopped iceberg or romaine lettuce
    mixed with 1 head torn butter lettuce

3 cups corn chips

One 15½-ounce can pinto beans, kidney beans, or black beans, heated in
    a saucepan or microwave

2 large ripe tomatoes or 4 plum tomatoes, coarsely chopped

½ cup cold nonfat sour cream or thick plain yogurt (such as Greek yogurt)

1 to 2 firm-ripe avocados, sliced right before serving

¼ cup finely chopped red onion

One 4-ounce can sliced black olives or 8 whole black olives, left whole or halved

1½ cups shredded cheddar cheese or cheddar–Monterey Jack blend (6 ounces)

1 cup tomato salsa of your choice

**1.** To make the taco meat, heat a large skillet over medium-high heat and brown the meat and onion; break up the clumps of meat with a spoon. Add the olive oil if it is too dry. When the meat is no longer pink, stir in the salsa. Cook to evaporate most of the liquid, 1 minute. If you like your taco meat spicier, add the chili powder. If you like your taco meat smoky, add the chopped chipotles. Reduce the heat to low and keep warm while assembling the salad ingredients.

**2.** To serve, place all the salad components in separate containers and let diners prepare their own salad, or divide the ingredients into 4 equal portions and prep the plates beforehand in the kitchen. Prepare an individual plate with layers of lettuce, a handful of corn chips, hot meat, a quarter of the hot beans, some chopped tomatoes, sour cream, avocado, red onion, and olives. Top it all with some shredded cheese and salsa.

# Mexican Roast Beef Salad

**D**oes the roast beef at the deli counter look perfect today? Buy some, pick up some fresh produce, and whip up this fantastic salad. If you have leftover roast beef or grilled flank steak, all the better. I consider this a sort of Mexican chef's salad. Cook the potatoes on the stovetop or in the microwave and use lots of cilantro! ● *Serves 4*

**COOKING METHOD:** Stovetop or microwave
**PREP TIME:** 20 minutes
**COOK TIME:** About 20 minutes

### LIME AND CUMIN VINAIGRETTE

4 tablespoons fresh lime juice
¼ teaspoon ground cumin
¼ teaspoon chili powder
¼ teaspoon salt
⅓ cup olive oil

### SALAD

6 small red potatoes, halved or quartered, as desired
2 heads romaine lettuce, coarsely shredded
½ cup coarsely chopped fresh cilantro leaves
10 ounces deli-style roast beef or leftover roast beef, cut into thick strips
1 medium-size avocado, diced
2 large ripe tomatoes, diced
One 15-ounce can black beans, drained and rinsed
1 cup corn kernels
¼ medium-size red or white onion, sliced
4 whole wheat tortillas, warmed

**1.** To make the dressing, in a small bowl, whisk together the lime juice, cumin, chili powder, and salt. Whisk in the oil in a steady stream. Set aside.

**2.** To prepare the salad, place the potatoes in a medium-size saucepan and cover with cold water. Bring to a boil, and then lower the heat and simmer for 10 minutes, until just firm-tender. Drain and set aside.

**3.** Place the lettuce and cilantro on a serving platter and drizzle with some dressing. Put the roast beef, potatoes, avocado, tomatoes, beans, corn, and onion in a bowl; drizzle the remaining dressing over and toss to mix. Mound the beef mixture over the lettuce and serve with the tortillas.

## •• About Vinegars ••

When you discover the world of salads, the important ingredient (besides lettuce!) is vinegar. Using different vinegars will give a variety of delicious flavors to your freshly made dressings, and they will be healthy as well. Vinegar adds zest, a sour, tangy element of flavor that accents other ingredients, such as cabbage or meats. Even the most basic supermarket today has a selection of vinegars that includes raspberry and balsamic along with the cider and red wine vinegars. Here is a list of vinegars that are called for in this book.

**Cider Vinegar:** Don't pass up this vinegar because it seems so commonplace. Made from fermented unfiltered apple juice, this vinegar is now considered an artisan product and makes vegetables sing. Look for brands in health food stores with the natural "mother" starter floating at the bottom. Made in the same manner, pear vinegar, usually imported from France, is delicious; grab it if you see it.

**Wine Vinegar:** These are the all-purpose, yet elegant, salad-making vinegars, and a simple vinaigrette of wine vinegar, olive oil, salt, and pepper cannot be beat. Look for specialty wine vinegars, such as Merlot, Cabernet, or Champagne, next to the regular red and white wine vinegars. This vinegar can stand up to all manner of spices, herbs, citrus juices, and mustards.

**Sherry Vinegar:** Aged in wooden casks, sherry vinegar is strong and nutty flavored. Use it in a small percentage to the oil, or in combination with another vinegar.

**Balsamic Vinegar:** A viscous vinegar with a sweet-sour tang, this vinegar is prized in Italy and is now very popular in American cuisine. Made from the juice of the Trebbiano grape, it is aged in different types of wooden barrels to impart a complex flavor and a caramel-like color. Look for white balsamic, which is also excellent. Balsamic vinegars come in a wide range of prices, with some of the least expensive brands being very good.

**Rice Wine Vinegar:** Made from the liquid strained off of mashed rice mixed with sugar, rice vinegar has a sweet edge and is considered one of the gentlest of vinegars. It is perfect with Asian ingredients like ginger, citrus, toasted sesame oil, and hoisin sauce. I always have a bottle of unseasoned rice wine vinegar in the refrigerator. It also comes seasoned, which I don't recommend because it adds unnecessary elements to the dish; the seasoned variety should not be confused with the plain variety.

**Fruit Vinegars:** The beautiful people of the vinegar family, fruit vinegars are made from white wine vinegar infused with raspberries, blackberries, or cranberries, to name just a few. Inexpensive balsamic vinegars are also now blended with fruits, such as pomegranates, figs, and cherries, with delicious results. Fruit vinegars are lighter than aged wine vinegars or balsamic vinegar. Fruit vinegars are also good in pan sauces for meats and poultry.

**Herb Vinegar:** These are made by infusing herbs into white wine vinegar. Many varieties are available, but my favorite is tarragon vinegar.

**Malt Vinegar:** Made from the fermented liquid strained off of sprouted barley mash, malt vinegar is very distinctive and has some of the elements of flavor found in beer. It is traditionally sprinkled on fish and chips.

**Distilled White Vinegar:** White vinegar, made from grain alcohol, is clear and quite harsh. It is so acidic that it is used in pickling and as an all-purpose household cleaning agent (for such tasks as cleaning coffee machines and washing windows). It is also used to dye Easter eggs and is added to water used to poach eggs to keep the whites from running. I do not use white vinegar in my vinaigrettes.

# *Supper Out of Hand:* Sandwiches, Burgers, and Pizzas

Thick, thin, hot, cold, simple, piled high and served with lots of napkins. Let's talk about the original fast food—sandwiches, burgers, and pizzas. Sandwiches are often the most economical meal you can make, too.

A mainstay for quick meal making, sandwiches, burgers, and pizzas encompass a variety of flavor combinations that look like a cultural geography outline. Certainly the beloved grilled cheese on commercial white bread is as American as apple pie, but we have experienced some sort of sandwich revolution in the past decade, and the bread variables now are truly endless. There is pita bread, sourdough, tortillas, whole wheat bread, and a fabulous array of rolls from which to choose. Hot dog and hamburger buns are made from country bread dough and sprouted wheatberry bread for healthy alternatives to the soft white version. There are square ciabatta rolls, rectangular hoagie rolls, round onion rolls, sesame rolls, crusty little French rolls, kaiser rolls, toasted English muffins, split focaccia, brioche, and challah.

One of my favorite sandwiches from my childhood was cold roast beef on buttered flour-topped potato rolls from the bakery, eaten out of the back of the car with my family overlooking the ocean on Carmel's 17-Mile Drive. We had a hinged waffle iron that would grill both sides at the same time. There were many a "squished" grilled cheese sandwich made on that grill, a forerunner of today's panini grill and George Foreman grill. As an adult, I fell in love with a salami sandwich with paper-thin slices of lemon to cut the richness at a shoreside deli. In Europe I dined for lunch in a zinc bar and had Gruyère cheese and Normandy butter on an ultra-fresh baguette with a pot of tea. I went back every day for that sandwich while in Paris.

Burgers come under the sandwich moniker as well, and they aren't just beef anymore—how about a Lamb Gyro Burger (page 282)? Burgers can be made from tuna, chicken, turkey, salmon, pork, veggies—you name it. Mix and match to suit your taste and enjoy.

And then there is pizza. You can build a pizza on any number of quick-and-easy foundations, from English muffins and pita to Boboli prebaked crusts, tortillas, French bread, and store-bought frozen pizza dough. Don't pass up the refrigerated pizza dough, either. For the purist, I include a recipe for instant homemade pizza dough made in the food processor and ready to press into the pan within minutes. This is the place to create your own topping combinations. Be bold. Experiment. This is the fun part. You can cook or roast your own vegetables, or use precooked canned or frozen ones, such as artichoke hearts, olives, and sun-dried tomatoes. Or just revel in a plain tomato and cheese version, which has perennial appeal.

# Tofu Salad Sandwiches

I happen to be someone who does not like hard-boiled eggs, and that means no egg salad sandwiches, ever. But I got a great surprise when I tasted tofu prepared as egg salad and made into a thick sandwich with lettuce. Fabulous! This recipe uses silken tofu, which is ultra soft and has an uncanny similarity to the texture of boiled egg whites. The turmeric adds the yellow color provided by the egg yolks in egg salad. ○ *Serves 4*

**COOKING METHOD:** None
**PREP TIME:** About 10 minutes

12 ounces silken firm tofu
½ stalk celery, finely chopped
2 tablespoons finely chopped green or red onion
1 sprig fresh flat-leaf parsley, minced
2 teaspoons prepared mustard of your choice, such as yellow or Dijon
1 teaspoon fresh lemon juice
1 teaspoon honey
½ teaspoon ground turmeric
Pinch of paprika
Salt and freshly ground black pepper
8 slices whole wheat bread, toasted if desired

Place the tofu in a medium-size mixing bowl and mash with a fork until crumbly. Add all of the remaining ingredients, except the bread, and stir to combine. Spread on the bread and serve immediately. The tofu salad will keep in the refrigerator for up to 2 days.

# Eggplant Sandwiches

I used to make eggplant sandwiches for my boyfriend. We had an electric frying pan at his workshop, and it ended up being one of our favorite sandwiches. Fast forward many years, and now I see grilled eggplant sandwiches in delis and featured in magazines. What a thrill to see my old sandwich come back into vogue. You can prepare the eggplant in any sort of manner. Here I bake it, but you can pan-fry or grill it, if you like that better. ● *Serves 4*

**COOKING METHOD:** Oven
**PREP TIME:** 20 minutes
**COOK TIME:** 10 to 15 minutes

AIOLI
1 cup mayonnaise
2 to 3 cloves garlic, crushed

2 small purple or white eggplant
Salt
Olive oil cooking spray
3 tablespoons all-purpose flour
½ teaspoon salt
1 large egg
1 tablespoon milk
⅓ cup seasoned fine dry bread crumbs
⅓ cup grated Parmesan cheese
4 ounces whole-milk mozzarella cheese, thinly sliced
4 slices provolone cheese
4 focaccia rolls or 4 squares cut from large focaccia loaf, split and
    some soft insides pulled out if thicker than 2½ inches
2 Roma tomatoes, sliced
1 bunch arugula, tossed with 2 teaspoons red wine vinegar
    and 1 teaspoon olive oil

1. To make the aioli, in a small bowl, stir together the mayonnaise and garlic. Refrigerate until serving.

2. Trim both ends of the eggplant and slice crosswise into ¾-inch-thick slices. Sprinkle both sides with salt and layer between double layers of paper towels. Press firmly and let stand for 15 minutes.

3. Preheat the oven to 450°F. Line a large baking sheet with parchment paper and spray it with olive oil cooking spray.

4. On a plate, combine the flour and ½ teaspoon salt. In a shallow bowl, beat the egg with the milk. In a small shallow dish, combine the bread crumbs and Parmesan cheese. First lay the eggplant slices in the flour, then the egg, then the crumb coating. Arrange on the baking sheet.

5. Bake for 10 to 15 minutes, turning once with tongs, until browned. Place the mozzarella and provolone cheeses on top of each slice and bake for 1 minute more to begin melting.

6. Spread each side of the focaccia with the aioli and place the bottoms on the plates. Place eggplant slices on top of the bottoms, top with tomatoes and arugula, and close the sandwiches. Cut in half and serve immediately.

# Portobello Mushroom Sandwiches with Cranberry Dijon Mustard

I had my first portobello at a dinner hosted by students of the Culinary Institute in San Francisco. They served a single oversized grilled mushroom drizzled with olive oil for a first course; it was superb in its simplicity. Portobellos are the same as the small brown cremini mushrooms, just grown longer and larger. Portobellos have very little moisture, so they work well grilled or broiled, holding their shape perfectly and shrinking very little. To store, wrap them in paper towels and place on a plate in the refrigerator. Serve this sandwich hot, juicy, and crispy, with a little salad or a bowl of soup. **o** *Serves 4*

**COOKING METHOD:** Oven broiler (or charcoal or gas grill)
**PREP TIME:** 25 minutes
**COOK TIME:** 10 to 15 minutes

CRANBERRY DIJON MUSTARD
1 tablespoon olive oil
1 medium-size shallot, minced
¼ cup Dijon mustard
¼ cup whole berry cranberry sauce
2 tablespoons balsamic vinegar

¼ cup olive oil
2 tablespoons balsamic or red wine vinegar
1 teaspoon dried marjoram or basil
1 clove garlic, crushed
Pinch of sugar
4 large portobello mushrooms, stems and gills removed
4 fresh round sandwich rolls of your choice
Sea salt and freshly ground black pepper

**1.** To make the mustard, heat the oil in a small skillet and sauté the shallot until soft, about 3 minutes. Combine the mustard, cranberry sauce, cooked shallots, and vinegar in a food processor; pulse until pureed. Use immediately or store in the refrigerator for up to 1 week.

**2.** To marinate the mushrooms, whisk together the oil, vinegar, marjoram, garlic, and sugar in a bowl. Set the clean mushrooms, stem side down, in a glass baking dish. Pour the marinade over the mushrooms. Cover with plastic wrap and refrigerate for 15 minutes.

**3.** Preheat the broiler or prepare a hot fire in a charcoal or gas grill.

**4.** Arrange the drained mushrooms on a broiler pan and broil 6 inches from the heat, or place on the grill. Cook for 3 to 5 minutes on each side, depending on the size of the mushrooms. Set aside to cool slightly.

**5.** Lightly toast the cut sides of the split rolls. Place each on an individual serving plate and spread with the cranberry mustard. Place a grilled mushroom on each roll bottom. Sprinkle with salt and a few grinds of black pepper. Top with the other half of the roll and serve immediately.

## •• Weeknight Supper Baked Beans ••

I adore baked beans, and often that is what I want on the side with a burger or sandwich. Here is one of the fastest and easiest recipes I know. Pop this into the oven before you do anything else and by the time the burgers are ready, your beans will be ready, too.

**⊙ Serves 4 to 6**

Olive oil cooking spray
One 15-ounce can black beans, rinsed and drained
One 16-ounce can vegetarian baked beans
½ cup finely chopped white onion
2 tablespoons molasses
2 tablespoons ketchup
1 tablespoon brown sugar
1 tablespoon Dijon mustard
1 tablespoon cider vinegar
Few shakes of garlic powder

**1.** Preheat the oven to 375°F. Spray a 2-quart casserole dish or an 8-inch square pan with nonstick olive oil spray.

**2.** Place the beans in the dish, then scatter the onion on top. Add the molasses, then the ketchup, brown sugar, mustard, vinegar, and garlic powder. Stir gently with a spatula to evenly combine.

**3.** Bake for 40 minutes, uncovered, until hot and bubbly. Serve immediately.

# Mozzarella in Carrozza with Sun-Dried Tomatoes

**N**ow this is what I call a grilled cheese sandwich, a cross between grilled cheese and French toast. Mozzarella "in a carriage" is as famous in Italy as pizza is here. Seek out fresh whole-milk mozzarella; it is spectacular and mild enough for young diners to appreciate. I also like the mozzarella in combination with a bit of Bel Paese or smoked cheddar cheese, though that's certainly non-traditional. Anchovies or chopped olives can be substituted for the sun-dried tomatoes. ○ *Serves 4*

**COOKING METHOD:** Stovetop
**PREP TIME:** 20 minutes
**COOK TIME:** About 10 minutes

1 oblong loaf French or Italian bread, cut into sixteen ¼- to ½-inch-thick slices
1 pound fresh mozzarella cheese, cut into ¼-inch-thick slices, then cut in half
8 oil-packed sun-dried tomatoes, well drained and patted dry, cut in half
3 large eggs
3 tablespoons milk
½ to ¾ cup olive oil, or as needed

**1.** Make 8 small sandwiches, each using 2 slices of bread, 1 slice of cheese arranged to fit the bread so it does not overhang, and 2 pieces of sun-dried tomato.

**2.** In a shallow bowl, beat together the eggs and milk until foamy. Place the sandwiches in the egg mixture. Let stand for about 2 minutes on each side to let the sandwiches absorb some of the egg mixture.

**3.** In a large skillet over medium-high heat, pour in enough olive oil to just cover the surface with a film. When the hot oil ripples on the surface, remove the sandwiches from the egg and let the excess drip off. Arrange as many of the sandwiches as will fit in the pan at one time without touching and sauté, turning once, until golden on both sides, 2 to 4 minutes total. As they cook, press down on them with a spatula so that the cheese is enclosed. Drain on paper towels and keep warm until all the sandwiches are cooked (add more olive oil for each batch). Serve immediately.

# Potato-Crusted Tilapia Sandwiches

**H**ere is a basic preparation with one of my secret kitchen weapons—dehydrated potato flakes. Tired of cornmeal, panko, potato chips, cracker crumbs, crushed pretzels, or bread crumbs coating your fillets? Try flavorful potato flakes. Tilapia cooks in a flash, so have your sandwich accompaniments ready as you put the fillets in the pan. This is also good with halibut or catfish and can be served in tortillas instead of the toasted bread. ● *Serves 4*

**COOKING METHOD:** Stovetop
**PREP TIME:** 25 minutes
**COOK TIME:** 8 to 12 minutes

CILANTRO COLESLAW
4 cups finely shredded green and red cabbage
1 jalapeño chile, finely chopped
1 bunch fresh cilantro, chopped
2 green onions (white part and some of the green), chopped
¼ to ⅓ cup mayonnaise
Juice of 1 lime
1 teaspoon brown sugar
1 teaspoon hot sauce, such as Cholula or Tabasco
Pinch of ground cumin
Pinch of garlic powder
Pinch of salt

1¼ cups dehydrated potato flakes
Salt and freshly ground white pepper
Pinch of thyme, chili powder, or curry powder (optional)
3 large eggs
1 tablespoon buttermilk, milk, or plain yogurt
4 tilapia fillets (4 to 6 ounces each)
2 to 3 tablespoons olive oil
8 slices whole-grain bread, toasted
2 to 3 tablespoons grated Parmesan cheese

1. To make the coleslaw, combine the cabbages, chile, cilantro, and green onions in a medium-size bowl. In a small bowl, stir together the ¼ cup mayonnaise, the lime juice, brown sugar, hot sauce, cumin, garlic powder, and salt until evenly combined. Add to the vegetables and stir to evenly coat; add a bit more mayonnaise if you like. Cover and refrigerate until serving.

2. On a shallow plate, combine the potato flakes, salt, pepper, and thyme, if using. In a bowl, beat the eggs with the buttermilk until foamy. Dip the fillets in the egg mixture, then dredge both sides in the potato coating mixture.

3. Heat the olive oil in a large skillet over medium-high heat. Cook the fillets for 2 to 3 minutes per side, turning once, until firm and crispy. Cook in two batches, if necessary.

4. Remove from the pan with a spatula and place each fillet on one slice of the toasted bread; sprinkle with some Parmesan. Place 1 cup of the coleslaw on top of each fillet and top with another bread slice. Cut in half and serve immediately.

# Chicken Fajita Pitas

**T**he fast food realm cannot even touch the homemade version of this tasty sandwich, composed just like the Mexican restaurant favorite. ● *Serves 4*

**COOKING METHOD:** Stovetop and oven
**PREP TIME:** 20 minutes
**COOK TIME:** 10 to 15 minutes

Four 6-inch white or whole wheat pita bread rounds, cut in half
One 15-ounce can refried beans
1 tablespoon olive oil
1 medium-size white onion, sliced and then cut into half-moons
1 green or red bell pepper, cut into strips
1 pound boneless, skinless chicken breasts, cut into ½-inch strips
1 tablespoon fajita seasoning or chili powder
1 tomato, sliced and then cut into half-moons
1 cup shredded cheddar cheese (4 ounces)
2 cups shredded iceberg lettuce
1 cup cold sour cream

1. Preheat the oven to 350°F.

2. Open each pita half and spread with a layer of refried beans, using up all of the beans. Place on a baking sheet in a single layer and cover with aluminum foil. Place in the oven to warm for 10 to 15 minutes, while preparing the fajitas.

3. In a large skillet, heat the oil over medium-high heat. Add the onion and pepper strips; cook for 5 minutes. Push to the side of the pan, add the chicken, and toss with the seasoning. Cook for 5 minutes, stirring a few times, until the chicken is cooked through. Combine the onion, peppers, and chicken.

4. Spoon the mixture into the warmed bean-filled pitas. Tuck in 2 slices of tomato and sprinkle in some cheese. Serve immediately, with the lettuce and sour cream on the side.

Rotisserie chickens from supermarket delis have found their place in mainstream American kitchens. They are delicious, hassle free, and extremely versatile.

## Pulled Chicken Sandwiches

This is messy and fantastic. It has the moist chicken, onion rings, and coleslaw layered up in a perfect pile. Do the shredding while the chicken is still warm, if possible.  ❍ Serves 4

**COOKING METHOD:** Oven
**PREP TIME:** 25 minutes
**COOK TIME:** About 12 minutes

**16 frozen onion rings**

**CITRUS COLESLAW**
**1 very small head green cabbage or ½ large head (1¼ pounds), finely chopped**
**1 medium-size carrot, grated**
**⅔ cup mayonnaise**
**¼ cup frozen orange juice concentrate, thawed**
**1½ teaspoons sugar**
**¼ teaspoon salt**
**Few grinds of freshly ground black or white pepper**

**4 cups shredded rotisserie chicken (usually the whole chicken)**
**½ cup plain barbecue sauce of your choice**
**3 tablespoons cider vinegar**
**2 tablespoons adobo sauce from a can of chipotle chiles in adobo**
**4 split kaiser rolls, toasted if desired**

**1**. Place the onion rings on a baking sheet in a single layer and bake in a preheated oven according to package directions.

**2.** To make the coleslaw, combine the cabbage and carrot in a medium-size bowl. In a small bowl, stir together the mayonnaise, orange juice concentrate, sugar, salt, and pepper until evenly combined. Add to the vegetables and stir to evenly coat; add a bit more mayonnaise if you like a wetter slaw, but keep in mind that the cabbage will give off moisture and get wetter. Cover and refrigerate until serving.

**3.** Place the chicken in a medium-size bowl and mix with the barbecue sauce, vinegar, and adobo sauce until evenly coated. Place the bottoms of the rolls on individual dinner plates. Pile the chicken on the rolls, then top with the slaw, then 4 warm onion rings, and then the tops of the rolls. Serve immediately.

# Open-Faced Hot Turkey Sandwiches with Tarragon Gravy

One of the great things about the Thanksgiving holiday weekend is the left-over bonanza that fosters casseroles, soups, enchiladas, and at least one open-faced hot turkey sandwich. But I like turkey all year round. Inspired by a recipe from Brooke Dojny's *The New England Cookbook* (The Harvard Common Press, 1999), this is one of the best ways I've ever found to use those packaged presliced boneless turkey breast cutlets. I am a proponent of packaged turkey gravy, which is way faster and easier than a pan sauce from scratch, and I boost the flavor with herbs and wine. Definitely serve this with cranberry sauce, and grab a knife and fork. ● *Serves 4*

**COOKING METHOD:** Stovetop
**PREP TIME:** 20 minutes
**COOK TIME:** 20 minutes

TARRAGON GRAVY
One 1.2-ounce package turkey gravy mix
1¼ cups water
2 tablespoons dry red or white wine
1 teaspoon finely chopped fresh tarragon

4 thick slices white, whole wheat, or country bread
1 pound thinly sliced turkey breast cutlets
Sea salt and freshly ground black pepper
2 teaspoons poultry seasoning
2 tablespoons olive oil
2 tablespoons unsalted butter

**1.** Prepare the gravy by combining the mix, water, wine, and tarragon in a small saucepan. Blend with a whisk and cook over medium-high heat, stirring constantly and bringing to a boil. Reduce the heat to a simmer and cook for 2 minutes, until thickened. Set aside, keeping warm.

**2.** Toast the bread in a toaster or under the broiler. Set 1 slice each on individual dinner plates.

**3.** Season the cutlets on both sides first with salt and pepper, then with the poultry seasoning. In a large skillet, melt the olive oil and butter over medium-high heat. Place the cutlets in the pan in a single layer (cook in 2 batches) and sauté until lightly browned, 2 minutes per side. Divide the cutlets into 4 portions and arrange over the toast. Ladle the gravy over the top. Serve immediately.

# Turkey Ciabatta Sandwiches with Caramelized Onions, Cranberry, and Provolone

**P**robably one of the most fantastic new sandwich rolls to join the ranks of the hamburger bun is the flour-dusted ciabatta roll, a simple square roll with a thinner crust than a baguette. Once in the realm of artisan bakeries, they are now so popular that my local supermarket stocks a bin of them. This sandwich can be made with leftover turkey breast or deli turkey. Little baskets of fresh boiling onions, especially the red ones, are a winter produce specialty, so that's a perfect time to make this sandwich. ○ *Serves 4*

**COOKING METHOD:** Stovetop
**PREP TIME:** 25 minutes
**COOK TIME:** 20 minutes

3 tablespoons olive oil
12 small boiling onions (red, yellow, or white), sliced
½ teaspoon salt
4 crusty white sandwich rolls, such as ciabatta, sliced in half and toasted
½ cup mayonnaise
¾ cup whole berry or jellied cranberry sauce
12 good-sized slices cooked turkey breast
4 thin slices provolone cheese
Arugula or butter lettuce leaves

**1.** In a small sauté pan, heat the oil over medium heat. Add the onions. Cook for 5 minutes, then reduce the heat to medium-low. Cover and cook for about 15 minutes, until soft and slightly browned. Add the salt.

**2.** Spread the top of each sandwich roll with mayonnaise and the bottom with cranberry sauce. Layer 3 slices of turkey and 1 slice of cheese on the bottom rolls, then divide the caramelized onions among the 4 sandwiches. Top with a layer of arugula, close the sandwiches, cut in half, and serve.

# Vegetable and Tofu Quesadillas

**I** went to a buffet at my friend Mary Cantori's house right after she returned from her first visit to Rancho La Puerta spa, right over the border from San Diego in Baja, California. She served these quesadillas, cut into quarters, on a small platter. She had brought the recipe back from La Puerta, and I got her to recite the directions. Good thing I did, for not long ago I reminded her about the recipe, and since she had never written down the proportions, she'd forgotten them. Well, here they are for everyone. ● *Serves 4*

**COOKING METHOD:** Stovetop and oven
**PREP TIME:** 20 minutes
**COOK TIME:** 15 to 20 minutes

5 tablespoons olive oil

½ medium-size white onion, diced

2 cloves garlic, crushed

3 medium-size zucchini, diced

2 plum tomatoes, seeded and diced

1½ teaspoons reduced-sodium soy sauce or tamari

1 teaspoon dried oregano

Freshly ground black pepper

12 ounces firm tofu, drained and diced

8 fresh whole wheat tortillas

2 to 3 cups shredded part-skim mozzarella cheese (8 to 12 ounces)

1. Preheat the oven to 400°F. Line a large baking sheet with aluminum foil.

2. In a large skillet, heat 2 tablespoons of the olive oil over medium-high heat. Add the onion and cook until soft, 3 minutes. Add the garlic and cook for 30 seconds. Add the zucchini, tomatoes, soy sauce, oregano, and pepper. Cook for 5 minutes to soften and brown the vegetables slightly, stirring a few times. Add the tofu; gently stir to combine and warm. Remove from the heat.

3. Lay the tortillas on a clean work surface and divide the filling equally among them, spreading in an even layer on the lower half of the tortilla. Sprinkle the cheese on top of the filling and fold each tortilla over to make a half-moon shape. Place on the baking sheet. Lightly brush both sides of the quesadillas with the remaining 3 tablespoons olive oil.

4. Bake until hot and crisped and the cheese is melted, about 8 minutes. Serve immediately.

# Chile Relleno Sandwiches with Two Salsas

**T**hese savory sandwiches, a California version of that venerable French grilled cheese, the *croque monsieur*, are constructed just like French toast, and mimicking the individual rellenos so popular in Mexican cuisine. They are topped with two easy, delicious sauces—one red and one green. These are positively addicting. ● *Serves 4*

**COOKING METHOD:** Stovetop
**PREP TIME:** 25 minutes
**COOK TIME:** About 10 minutes

8 thick slices sourdough bread
About 12 ounces Monterey Jack cheese, thinly sliced
Two 4-ounce cans whole fire-roasted green chiles, patted dry

**GREEN SALSA**
One 18-ounce can whole tomatillos, drained
1 small bunch fresh cilantro, leaves only
1 to 2 jalapeño chiles
Pinch of sugar

**RED SALSA**
2 cucumbers, peeled, seeded, and cut into chunks
1 cup cherry tomatoes
1 cup bottled tomato salsa of your choice

4 large eggs
½ cup milk
Butter-flavored cooking spray or olive oil

**1.** Lay out 4 slices of the bread and top with the cheese, cut to fit. Split the canned chiles on the side, remove the seeds, and layer the chiles over the cheese. Top with another slice of bread.

**2.** To make the green salsa, in a food processor, combine the tomatillos, cilantro, jalapeños, and sugar. Process until smooth. Remove to a bowl or refrigerate, covered, until serving. For the red salsa, in a food processor, pulse the cucumbers and tomatoes until chunky. Remove to a bowl and stir in the salsa. Use immediately or refrigerate, covered, until serving.

**3.** In a shallow medium-size bowl, beat together the eggs and milk with a whisk. Spray a large skillet with cooking spray and heat to medium-high. Dip both sides of the sandwiches into the batter, allow the excess to drip off, and arrange in the hot skillet without touching. Cook in 2 batches, if necessary. Cook on the first side for about 2 minutes, until golden brown and the cheese is melted. Spray the top of the bread with some more cooking spray, and turn over with a spatula. Cook the other side until golden, 1 to 2 minutes. Remove to a plate, cut in half, and serve with the cold salsas spooned on top.

# Creamy Cheese Enchiladas

O kay, this isn't technically a sandwich, but this enchilada recipe is so fast and so tasty that it would be a crime not to share it with you. I usually combine two cheeses for plain enchiladas, and here it's Muenster mixed with some fresh goat cheese. Serve with a side of refried beans, some guacamole, lots of shredded iceberg lettuce, and even some chunky tomato salsa. Pray for leftovers.

**◦ *Serves 4***

**COOKING METHOD:** Stovetop and oven
**PREP TIME:** 25 minutes
**COOK TIME:** 35 to 40 minutes

ENCHILADA SAUCE

4 cups plain tomato sauce (I use Muir Glen)

2 teaspoons chili powder

1 teaspoon dried oregano

½ teaspoon dried basil

½ teaspoon ground cumin

½ teaspoon garlic powder or 1 clove garlic, crushed

Salt and freshly ground black pepper

⅓ cup olive oil

12 yellow or white corn tortillas

3 cups shredded Muenster cheese (12 ounces)

One 4¼-ounce can roasted whole green chiles, drained
    and cut into 12 long strips

5 ounces soft fresh goat cheese, crumbled

1 cup sour cream

**1.** Preheat the oven to 350°F.

**2.** To make the enchilada sauce, in a saucepan, combine the sauce ingredients. Warm to a high simmer over medium-high heat, about 5 minutes.

**3.** In a small deep sauté pan, heat the oil to hot (not splattering).

**4.** Using tongs, dip each tortilla into the hot oil, then into the sauce, lifting up to let the sauce drip off, and transfer to a clean plate or piece of waxed paper. Fill each tortilla with ¼ cup of the Muenster cheese, then top with a chile strip and some crumbled goat cheese. Roll up and place seam-side down in a 9 × 13-inch baking dish. Repeat to fill all the tortillas and lay side by side in the baking dish (it is okay for them to be touching). Whisk the sour cream into the remaining sauce and pour the sauce over the tortillas. Bake for 30 to 35 minutes, until bubbling and hot. Serve immediately.

# Gold Beef Burgers with Cold Pea Salad

I once picked up a little recipe pamphlet at the supermarket near the liquor section advertising specific brands of liquor for holiday entertaining. I found this recipe there, using Jose Cuervo Gold Tequila, and I adapted it. Tequila is a moist, flavorful addition. Mexican gold tequila, also known as *añejo*, is aged for more than a year in wooden casks so the flavor is mellowed and the color becomes amber. Don't use expensive tequilas, advises my friend Magdalene, who owns a local Mexican restaurant, as they are too sweet for cooking; the cheap stuff is better. Here sliced avocado is called for, but if you have some guacamole around, slather that on top. ○ *Serves 4*

**COOKING METHOD:** Stovetop
**PREP TIME:** 25 minutes
**COOK TIME:** About 10 minutes

COLD PEA SALAD
¼ to ⅓ cup reduced-fat sour cream
¼ to ⅓ cup plain yogurt
¼ teaspoon dried dillweed
2 green onions, minced
½ teaspoon curry powder
One 10-ounce package frozen petite peas, thawed
Squeeze of fresh lemon juice
Pinch of salt

GOLD BURGERS
1 pound ground round
1 small shallot, minced
1 teaspoon Dijon mustard
2 teaspoons coarse kosher or sea salt
4 hamburger buns
2 tablespoons unsalted butter
¼ cup gold tequila

Green or red hot sauce
4 slices white American cheese
4 slices Bermuda onion
Sliced avocado and lettuce for topping

**1.** To make the pea salad, put the sour cream, yogurt, dillweed, green onions, and curry powder in a medium-size bowl; stir to combine. Add the peas, lemon juice, and salt and stir to combine. Cover and refrigerate until serving.

**2.** To make the burgers, place the ground round in a medium-size bowl and add the shallot and mustard; shape into 4 equal-size patties and press some of the coarse salt onto one side of each. Split and toast the buns; set aside.

**3.** Preheat a large sauté pan over high heat and add the butter. Let the butter melt and become golden brown. Place the patties in the pan, salt side down, and brown quickly, 3 to 4 minutes. Turn over with a spatula and brown the second side. Add the tequila to the pan and bring the tequila to a boil. If you feel adventurous, you can carefully ignite the tequila and let it burn off. Otherwise, let it boil in the butter, spooning the sauce over the patties a few times. Cook the burgers a total of 4 to 6 minutes for medium-rare.

**4.** Remove the burgers from the pan and place on the toasted buns, spooning a bit of the tequila sauce over each. Splash with hot sauce. Place 1 slice of cheese and 1 onion slice on each burger. Top with the avocado, lettuce, and top of the bun. Serve the pea salad on the side.

# Lamb Gyro Burgers with Cilantro Yogurt Sauce

Souvlaki is seasoned grilled lamb kabobs that, when served in a pita, are a traditional Greek hot sandwich. This is a food of the street, but small restaurant eateries always offer it. Here, ground lamb makes a fabulous burger with all the flavors of that more complicated spit-grilled meat. When you see very fresh ground lamb in the market, this is what to make with it. The yogurt sauce and the pita are essential to this sandwich. ○ *Serves 4*

**COOKING METHOD:** Stovetop
**PREP TIME:** 25 minutes
**COOK TIME:** About 10 minutes

**CILANTRO YOGURT SAUCE**
2 green onions (white part and some of the green), thinly sliced
Handful of fresh cilantro leaves
3 mint leaves
1 cup thick low-fat plain yogurt or plain Greek yogurt
1 tablespoon fresh lemon juice
¼ teaspoon garlic powder or 1 small clove garlic, crushed
Pinch of salt

1¼ pounds ground lamb
½ teaspoon dried oregano
¼ teaspoon freshly ground black or white pepper
¼ teaspoon garlic powder
¼ teaspoon onion powder
⅛ teaspoon ground cumin
Salt
1 tablespoon olive oil
Four 6-inch white or whole wheat pita bread rounds
4 leaves romaine lettuce, chopped
1 large ripe tomato, sliced

**1.** To make the sauce, in a food processor, pulse the green onions, cilantro, and mint to finely chop. Add the yogurt, lemon juice, garlic powder, and salt; process until well mixed. Refrigerate for up to 4 hours.

**2.** In a large bowl, mix together the ground lamb, oregano, pepper, garlic powder, onion powder, cumin, and salt; mix well. Form into 4 patties, each about ¾ inch thick, and coat lightly with the olive oil.

**3.** Heat a large sauté pan or grill pan over medium-high heat and cook the patties for 3 to 4 minutes per side. Remove from the pan, wipe out the pan, and heat the pitas for about 1 minute on each side.

**4.** Cut about a 3-inch strip off the top of each pita; open up the pita to make a pocket. Drop the pita strip into the pocket, along with a burger, one-quarter of the chopped lettuce and sliced tomato, and a generous few spoonfuls of the yogurt sauce. Serve immediately.

# Tuna Burgers with Wasabi Mayo

This burger is one of the finest ways to prepare rich, high-quality tuna. You can mince everything by hand, like the French apprentice chefs of old, or quickly pulse in your food processor, like us post–Julia Child cooks, just not too much or it will get slushy. The burger is given the Asian flavor treatment with ginger, soy sauce, and toasted sesame oil and topped with a mellow wasabi mayo, made from the same green paste that sits next to your sushi. You can buy wasabi powder in a small can at Asian markets. ○ *Serves 4*

**COOKING METHOD:** Stovetop
**PREP TIME:** 25 minutes
**COOK TIME:** About 10 minutes

**WASABI MAYO**
3 green onions (white part and some of the green), cut into chunks
One 1½-inch chunk fresh ginger
2 teaspoons soy sauce
2 teaspoons wasabi powder
½ cup mayonnaise

3 green onions (white part and some of the green)
One 1½-inch chunk fresh ginger
1 to 1¼ pounds tuna steaks, dark spots trimmed away
¼ cup (½ stick) cold unsalted butter, cut into chunks
2 tablespoons soy sauce
2 teaspoons toasted sesame oil
Few grinds of freshly ground black pepper
4 round sesame seed–topped buns
Butter lettuce leaves for serving

**1.** To make the mayo, in a food processor, add the green onions and ginger; pulse to finely chop. Add the soy sauce, wasabi powder, and mayonnaise. Process until smooth. Remove to a small bowl, cover, and refrigerate until serving.

**2.** In the food processor, toss in the green onions and ginger; pulse to chop. Cut one-quarter of the tuna into ¼-inch dice and place the rest in the food processor with the butter; pulse to combine the butter and tuna; do not overprocess. Place in a bowl and add the diced tuna, soy sauce, sesame oil, and pepper. Shape into 4 equal-size patties.

**3.** Split and toast the buns; set aside.

**4.** Preheat a large sauté pan over medium-high heat. Place the patties in the pan and brown quickly on one side, about 3 minutes. Turn over with a spatula and brown the second side to the desired degree of doneness, 3 to 4 minutes, leaving the center moist and reddish for medium-rare.

**5.** Slather the toasted buns on both sides with the wasabi mayo and top with butter lettuce leaves. Place the burgers on the buns and serve immediately.

Here are two homemade pizza sauces that can be used interchangeably in the following recipes.

## 15-Minute Pizza Sauce

This is an excellent all-purpose tomato sauce, a salsa pizzaiola, for any style of homemade pizza, from a friend whose family has been making it for decades. It takes only 15 minutes of cooking before it is ready to slather on your pizza dough (or to pour over spaghetti). There is enough for two 12-inch pizzas. A favorite!  ❍  **Makes 2 cups**

**2 tablespoons olive oil**
**¼ cup finely chopped yellow onion**
**Two 8-ounce cans tomato sauce or ground peeled tomatoes**
**1 clove garlic, crushed, or ¼ teaspoon garlic powder**
**½ teaspoon dried oregano or marjoram**
**Salt and freshly ground black pepper**

**1.** In a large skillet over medium heat, add the oil and sauté the onion until soft and the edges begin to brown. Add the tomato sauce, garlic, oregano, salt, and pepper. Bring to a low boil and then adjust the heat to low. Simmer, uncovered, for 15 minutes.

**2.** Remove from the heat and let cool. Leave chunky, or use an immersion blender to puree. The sauce will keep in the refrigerator for up to 3 days or in the freezer for up to 1 month.

## Jiffy No-Cook Pizza Sauce

This version is a no-cook sauce and is even faster than the 15-Minute Pizza Sauce (above). It is a good sauce in which to use organic canned tomato products with a bright flavor, such as Muir Glen. It makes enough for two 12-inch pizzas.  ❍  **Makes 1¾ cups**

**One 8-ounce can tomato sauce**
**One 6-ounce can tomato paste**
**1 tablespoon olive oil**
**1 teaspoon dried mixed Italian herbs**
**Few shakes of garlic powder**
**Pinch of red pepper flakes**
**Salt**

In a medium-size bowl, combine the tomato sauce, tomato paste, olive oil, herbs, garlic powder, red pepper flakes, and salt. Whisk to combine. Set aside until ready to use. Refrigerate any leftovers for up to 5 days.

Not in the mood to wrangle regular pizza dough? Well, the good news is that pizza can be made on a number of different crust shells, all different and all perfectly delicious. So when you want a fast pizza, consider using a ciabatta loaf, oversized flour tortillas, or a pita bread round. And don't forget the prebaked shells called Boboli. Fast and fantastic!

## Vegetable and Prosciutto Ciabatta Pizza

Muir Glen tomato products have gotten a reputation as a premier brand, from fire-roasted stewed tomatoes to tomato sauce and paste. Here is an adaptation of one of the recipes from the 2006 Muir Glen Organic Tomato Recipe Contest—ciabatta bread pizza. You can be creative with your own toppings, of course. Since this is pizza, anything goes. This recipe uses roasted red onion, prosciutto, and broccoli raab. Get ciabatta bread at your supermarket bakery or at your favorite artisan bakery.  o  Serves 4

**COOKING METHOD:** Microwave and oven broiler
**PREP TIME:** 30 minutes
**COOK TIME:** 10 to 15 minutes

1 small red onion, halved and thinly sliced
1 tablespoon extra virgin olive oil
Pinch of salt and freshly ground black pepper
1 bunch broccoli raab, stems trimmed and chopped (2 cups)
2 tablespoons water
One 1- to 1½-pound loaf ciabatta bread, split horizontally
1 recipe 15-Minute Pizza Sauce or Jiffy No-Cook Pizza Sauce (left) or
    1¾ to 2 cups store-bought pizza sauce
8 ounces fresh whole-milk mozzarella, thinly sliced
3 ounces paper-thin prosciutto slices
½ cup grated Parmesan cheese
Red pepper flakes (optional)

1.  Preheat the broiler. Line 2 large baking sheets with aluminum foil.

2.  In a small bowl, combine the onion with the olive oil, salt, and pepper. Place in a single layer on 1 baking sheet and broil 6 inches from the heat until soft and browned, 10 minutes, stirring once with a spatula. Set aside.

3.  Place the broccoli raab and water in a microwavable bowl. Partially cover with a lid or microwavable plastic wrap. Microwave on High for 4 minutes, until tender. Drain and cool.

**4.** Place the 2 bread halves on the other lined baking sheet, cut side up. Broil for 1 minute, until toasted. Spread 1 cup of the pizza sauce on each half, then layer each with half of the mozzarella and the prosciutto, then top with the broccoli raab and onion. Sprinkle with the Parmesan cheese.

**5.** Broil for 2 to 3 minutes, until hot and the cheeses are melted. Sprinkle with some red pepper flakes, if using, and cut the pizza into big pieces. Serve immediately.

## Ratatouille Tortilla Pizzas

This is a very fun recipe from master chef and TV personality Jacques Pépin. I get a kick out of casual recipes from notable chefs. This recipe was developed for use on the Oceania Cruise Line. The flour tortilla makes a surprisingly delicate and pastry-like thin crust. This recipe calls for 10-inch tortillas, the ones used for burrito making, not the smaller ones designed for tacos. Once in a while, like in a Mexican or warehouse market, you will find oversized flour tortillas that are 12 inches plus in diameter, and you can use them as well. Use a food processor slicing blade to make fast work of the slicing, especially if you plan to double this recipe.  **o  Serves 4**

**COOKING METHOD:** Oven
**PREP TIME:** 20 minutes
**COOK TIME:** 15 minutes

2 tablespoons olive oil
2 Chinese eggplants, sliced
1 medium-size onion, halved and sliced
2 medium-size zucchini, sliced
1 large green bell pepper, sliced
1½ tablespoons chopped fresh basil or oregano
Salt and freshly ground black pepper
4 large flour tortillas
1 recipe 15-Minute Pizza Sauce or Jiffy No-Cook Pizza Sauce (page 286) or 1¾ to 2 cups store-
   bought pizza sauce
8 to 12 ounces whole-milk or part-skim mozzarella cheese, thinly sliced or shredded

**1.** Preheat the oven to 400°F and adjust the rack to the lower- and upper-third positions. Line 2 large baking sheets with aluminum foil; place in the oven to heat up while assembling the pizzas.

**2.** In a large skillet over medium heat, warm the olive oil. Add the vegetables, sprinkle with the basil, and season lightly with salt and pepper. Sauté for 5 minutes, stirring occasionally, to parcook.

**3.** Remove the hot baking sheets from the oven and place the tortillas on them in a single layer. Bake for 1 to 2 minutes, until beginning to crisp (don't overbake or the tortilla will be too hard). Remove from the oven and immediately spread with the pizza sauce, leaving a ½- to 1-inch border. Divide the vegetables among the 4 tortillas to make an even layer, covering the sauce. Top with the cheese. Return the pans to the oven and bake for 5 to 6 minutes, until hot and the cheese is melted, switching the position of the pans halfway through baking. You can also bake 1 pan at a time.

**4.** Cut into quarters and serve hot.

## Stuffed Pita Pizzas

These pizzas are the busy mom's calzone. They are made in a plain style with simply cheese and basil, but you can spoon in leftover cooked vegetables, sautéed mushrooms, or olives if you like. Use plain or whole wheat pitas interchangeably. These are great with soup or salad. ○ **Serves 4**

**COOKING METHOD:** Oven
**PREP TIME:** 15 minutes
**COOK TIME:** 8 to 12 minutes

4 pita bread rounds, cut in half (to make 8 half-moons with pockets)
½ cup olive oil
About 2¼ cups thick tomato marinara sauce or 1 recipe 15-Minute Pizza Sauce or Jiffy No-Cook
    Pizza Sauce (page 286)
12 ounces whole-milk mozzarella cheese, thinly sliced or shredded
2 tablespoons chopped fresh basil

**1.** Preheat the oven to 375°F and adjust the rack to the lower-third position. Line 2 baking sheets with parchment paper.

**2.** Lay the pita on the sheets and brush both sides with olive oil. Open the pockets and, using a spoon, place some sauce inside and spread it all around (¼ to ⅓ cup each). Tuck in some cheese and sprinkle with basil; press the top side of the pita down onto the filling.

**3.** Bake until crispy, 8 to 12 minutes. Serve hot and eat with your hands, like a sandwich.

# The Great White Vegetable and Garlic Pizza

**T**his recipe features a fast homemade pizza dough made in the food processor and ready to roll out in 15 minutes. The cake flour makes a more tender dough that has less stretchiness, making it easy to roll, and the bit of olive oil keeps the dough silky. This dough recipe makes enough for one rectangular homestyle pizza, as made here, or two 12- to 14-inch round pizzas. If you would like to skip making the dough, use refrigerated pizza crust or thawed frozen bread dough. Believe me, you will never miss the red sauce here. The cheese trio is a combination of mozzarella, Gorgonzola, and Parmesan. ○ *Makes one 9 × 14-inch pizza*

**COOKING METHOD:** Oven
**PREP TIME:** 40 minutes if making dough, 15 to 20 minutes if using store-bought
**COOK TIME:** 18 to 25 minutes

NOT YOUR MOTHER'S FASTEST PIZZA DOUGH

2 cups unbleached all-purpose flour, plus a few tablespoons for kneading

1 cup cake flour (not self-rising)

1 package (2½ teaspoons) fast-rising yeast

1 teaspoon sugar or honey

1¼ teaspoons salt

1 cup hot water (125° to 130°F)

1 large egg, warmed by running under warm tap water

2 tablespoons olive oil

Olive oil cooking spray

TOPPING

4 tablespoons extra virgin olive oil, plus more for drizzling

1 head garlic, finely chopped (can be pulsed a few times in a food processor, but do not let it get mushy)

1 pound mozzarella cheese, thinly sliced and cut into strips

1 red bell pepper, sliced into thin rings

8 ounces fresh white mushrooms, sliced

¼ cup sliced black olives

1 cup crumbled Gorgonzola or domestic blue cheese

1 cup grated Parmesan cheese

2 tablespoons crumbled dried basil, marjoram, or oregano

**1.** To make the dough, place ½ cup of the all-purpose flour, the cake flour, yeast, sugar, and salt in the work bowl of a food processor fitted with the metal blade. Pulse once or twice to mix. Add the hot water, then the egg and olive oil through the feed tube. Process for 10 to 15 seconds. Open the bowl and add the remaining 1 ½ cups of all-purpose flour at once. Close and process until the dough comes away from the sides of the work bowl to form a moist ball, 1 minute. Remove from the work bowl by pulling out the blade and remove the dough ball with a spatula; place on a floured work surface. Gently knead by hand about 10 times to make a moist, springy ball; add a bit more flour if sticky, but keep very soft. Spray a gallon-size zipper-top plastic bag with olive oil spray. Place the dough ball inside and close the bag. Let stand for 15 to 20 minutes.

**2.** Preheat the oven to 475°F, using a baking stone if desired on the lower rack of the oven. Spray or oil a 9 × 14 × 1-inch rimmed baking sheet.

**3.** Place the dough ball in the center of the pan and flatten with your fist. With your fingers and knuckles, stretch and flatten out the dough to fill the pan, lifting and gently pulling the dough to press into the pan and toward the edges in an even layer. Shape a ½-inch rim around the crust edge. If the dough sticks to your fingers, flour them lightly.

**4.** To assemble the topping, rub the olive oil over the surface of the dough with your fingers or the back of a spoon. Sprinkle the dough with the garlic.

**5.** Layer the ingredients in the order listed: first scatter the mozzarella over the garlic, then arrange the pepper rings, mushrooms, and olives, then the Gorgonzola and Parmesan. Sprinkle the top with the basil and drizzle with a bit more olive oil, if you like.

**6.** Bake until the cheeses melt and the crust is crispy brown, 18 to 25 minutes. Remove from the oven and slide the pizza off the pan onto a cutting board. Wait 5 minutes before slicing and serving, to allow the cheeses to set slightly. Cut into portions and serve (it's worth it to buy a pizza wheel if you are a serious pizza maker, since it cuts so efficiently).

## A Few Tips for Great Pizza

- Use the best ingredients you can: olive oil, fresh or premium dried herbs that have not been stored for more than a year, fresh vegetables, and freshly grated or sliced cheeses that have been stored properly.

- A very hot oven is the key to producing a crisp crust with a chewy inside. If the oven is too low, you will get a tough crust.

- Always use precooked sausage, seafood, etc. on your pizzas; never use raw meats.

- Cheeses that melt well, such as mozzarella, Gorgonzola, fontina, Brie, feta, and goat cheese, are best for pizza.

- Invest in a ceramic pizza stone. Preheat it in the oven for 15 minutes before baking your pizza. It helps distribute even, strong heat in the home oven. I preheat before rolling out the dough and assembling the toppings, since once it is assembled, you want to pop the pizza directly into the oven.

- Layer the sauce, the meat and/or vegetables, the herbs or spices, and the cheese. You want a bit of each flavor in every bite, so distribute evenly.

- Pizzas can be partially baked, cooled to room temperature, and then frozen. Bake for half the required time, cool on a wire rack, then slide the pizza onto a baking sheet. Place in the freezer, uncovered, for 30 minutes. Remove from the freezer and wrap in plastic wrap, then aluminum foil. To serve, remove the pizza from the freezer and preheat your pizza stone for 15 minutes at 425°F. Unwrap and slide directly onto the hot stone or a baking sheet. Bake until hot and the cheese is bubbling.

# Classic Cheese Pizza

**J**ust like with vanilla ice cream, there are hard-core proponents of the plain cheese pizza, literally dripping with delectable whole-milk mozzarella, the premier melting cheese. This is the pizza to top with one item, if desired, such as 2 ounces of pepperoni or a crumbled cooked Italian sausage.

o *Makes one 12- or 14-inch pizza*

**COOKING METHOD:** Oven
**PREP TIME:** 40 minutes if making dough, 15 minutes if using store-bought
**COOK TIME:** 10 to 12 minutes

½ recipe Not Your Mother's Fastest Pizza Dough (page 290) or store-bought pizza dough
1 tablespoon extra virgin olive oil, plus more for the pan and drizzling
½ recipe 15-Minute Pizza Sauce or Jiffy No-Cook Pizza Sauce (page 286) or
    1 cup store-bought pizza sauce
8 ounces mozzarella cheese, thinly sliced
½ cup freshly grated Parmesan cheese

**1.** Preheat the oven to 475°F, using a baking stone if desired on the lower rack of the oven. Oil a 12- or 14-inch round pizza pan (I like the power pans with holes or a screen).

**2.** Place the ball of dough in the center of the pan and flatten with your fist. With your fingers and knuckles, stretch and flatten out the dough to fill the pan, lifting and gently pulling the dough to press into the pan and toward the edges in an even layer. If the dough sticks to your fingers, flour them lightly.

**3.** Rub the olive oil over the surface of the dough with your fingers or the back of a spoon, then spread the sauce over the dough in an even layer, leaving a ¼-inch border. Top with the mozzarella, then the Parmesan.

**4.** Bake until the cheeses melt and the crust is crispy brown, 10 to 12 minutes. Remove from the oven with heavy oven mitts and slide the pizza off the pan onto a cutting board. Wait 5 minutes before slicing and serving, to allow the cheeses to set slightly. Cut into portions and serve hot.

# Measurement Equivalents

Please note that all conversions are approximate.

## Liquid Conversions

| U.S. | Metric |
|---|---|
| 1 tsp | 5 ml |
| 1 tbs | 15 ml |
| 2 tbs | 30 ml |
| 3 tbs | 45 ml |
| ¼ cup | 60 ml |
| ⅓ cup | 75 ml |
| ⅓ cup + 1 tbs | 90 ml |
| ⅓ cup + 2 tbs | 100 ml |
| ½ cup | 120 ml |
| ⅔ cup | 150 ml |
| ¾ cup | 180 ml |
| ¾ cup + 2 tbs | 200 ml |

| U.S. | Metric |
|---|---|
| 1 cup | 240 ml |
| 1 cup + 2 tbs | 275 ml |
| 1¼ cups | 300 ml |
| 1⅓ cups | 325 ml |
| 1½ cups | 350 ml |
| 1⅔ cups | 375 ml |
| 1¾ cups | 400 ml |
| 1¾ cups + 2 tbs | 450 ml |
| 2 cups (1 pint) | 475 ml |
| 2½ cups | 600 ml |
| 3 cups | 720 ml |
| 4 cups (1 quart) | 945 ml |
| (1,000 ml is 1 liter) | |

# Weight Conversions

| U.S. / U.K. | Metric | U.S. / U.K. | Metric |
|---|---|---|---|
| ½ oz | 14 g | 7 oz | 200 g |
| 1 oz | 28 g | 8 oz | 227 g |
| 1½ oz | 43 g | 9 oz | 255 g |
| 2 oz | 57 g | 10 oz | 284 g |
| 2½ oz | 71 g | 11 oz | 312 g |
| 3 oz | 85 g | 12 oz | 340 g |
| 3½ oz | 100 g | 13 oz | 368 g |
| 4 oz | 113 g | 14 oz | 400 g |
| 5 oz | 142 g | 15 oz | 425 g |
| 6 oz | 170 g | 1 lb | 454 g |

# Oven Temperature Conversions

| °F | Gas Mark | °C |
|---|---|---|
| 250 | ½ | 120 |
| 275 | 1 | 140 |
| 300 | 2 | 150 |
| 325 | 3 | 165 |
| 350 | 4 | 180 |
| 375 | 5 | 190 |
| 400 | 6 | 200 |
| 425 | 7 | 220 |
| 450 | 8 | 230 |
| 475 | 9 | 240 |
| 500 | 10 | 260 |
| 550 | Broil | 290 |

# Index

# With the Not Your Mother's® Cookbooks, Dinner Is Served!

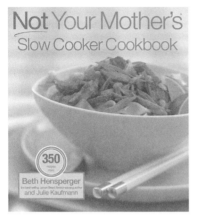

### Not Your Mother's Slow Cooker Cookbook

"From meatloaf to soups to desserts, this book might make your oven a storage space . . . The perfect companion to a Crock-Pot."
—*Boston Herald*

"With detailed explanations of everything from product choice to food safety . . . [there is] a wide range of sound recipes and advice for every meal, even snacks." —*San Francisco Chronicle*

"One of the best . . . a compilation of recipes that is thoroughly modern, covering a wide flavor spectrum." —*Times Union*

". . . gives slow cooking a hip new twist."
—*Slow Cooking* (*Woman's Day* special publication)

### Not Your Mother's Slow Cooker Recipes for Two

"Great gift for singles and small families who want the convenience of a small slow-cooker-made meal without sacrificing wholesomeness and flavor."—*Orlando Sentinel*

"The recipes are fresh and sophisticated." —*Ann Arbor News*

"Recipes are for homey, hearty fare; there is also a short chapter of quick and easy accompaniments prepared separately along with a good, basic introduction to slow cooking." —*Library Journal*

"Recipes call for fresh ingredients and cater to modern tastes and nutrition concerns . . . [Gives] the single diner or a hungry twosome reason to forget takeout and really enjoy a home-cooked dinner without unwelcome after-work hassle."—*San Francisco Chronicle*

### Not Your Mother's Slow Cooker Recipes for Entertaining

". . . fabulous, from mushroom-gorgonzola risotto in radicchio wraps with balsamic syrup to Mexican pork roast with tomatillo sauce."
—*Beaumont Enterprise*

". . . Can help you serve a great meal, even if you're an occasional cook."
—*Los Angeles Daily News*

". . . [coaxes] more ambitious food from the Rodney Dangerfield of appliances . . . Entrees rise above the usual chilis and stews, with non–slow cooker recipes for complementary side dishes and salads."
—*Washington Post*